TERMS OF RESPONSE

Robert L. Montgomery

TERMS OF RESPONSE

Language and Audience in
Seventeenth- and Eighteenth-Century
Theory

The Pennsylvania State University Press
University Park, Pennsylvania

Library of Congress Cataloging-in-Publication Data

Montgomery, Robert Langford.
  Terms of response : language and audience in seventeenth- and eighteenth-century theory / Robert L. Montgomery.
      p.   cm.
  Includes bibliographical references and index.
  ISBN 0-271-00764-8
  1. Literature, Modern—17th century—History and criticism—Theory, etc. 2. Literature, Modern—18th century—History and criticism—Theory, etc. 3. Criticism—History—17th century. 4. Criticism—History—18th century. 5. Reader-response criticism. I. Title.
  PN741.M66 1991
  801'.95'09032—dc20   90-22296
                                                                     CIP

Copyright © 1992 The Pennsylvania State University
All rights reserved
Printed in the United States of America

It is the policy of The Pennsylvania State University Press to use acid-free paper for the first printing of all clothbound books. Publications on uncoated stock satisfy the minimum requirements of American National Standard for Information Sciences—Permanence of Paper for Printed Library Materials, ANSI Z39.48–1984.

Contents

Acknowledgments　vii
Introduction　1

1　Baroque Surprise:
　The Pleasures of Metaphoric Form　11

2　"Contre le Baroque":
　Bouhours and Boileau　49

3　Addison and the
　"Helps and Ornaments of Art"　69

4　"The Irregular Fancy of the World"　89

5　"An Unaccountable Pleasure":
　The Attractions of Tragedy　127

6　Connections and Discontinuities:
　Du Bos, Condillac, and Diderot　159

Index　207

Acknowledgments

I am grateful to Harold Toliver, James Engell, and the late O. B. Hardison, Jr., for sympathetic readings and helpful advice on the later stages of my manuscript. Steven Varni, Susanne Shumway, and Joseph Chaney provided very useful research assistance. A Senior Research Fellowship from the National Endowment for the Humanities made possible the composition of the major portion of the manuscript, and a grant from the School of Humanities at the University of California, Irvine, helped with travel to various libraries, chiefly the British Library. Chapter 3, with slight changes, is reprinted from "Addison and the 'Helps and Ornaments of Art,'"; *Criticism* 25:4 (1983), 329–46, by Robert L. Montgomery, by permission of the Wayne State University Press. Copyright © 1984, Wayne State University Press, Detroit, Michigan 48202.

Introduction

René Rapin, in his *Reflections on Aristotle's Treatise* (1674), summed up his instructions to the poet by saying that he "must above all know what eloquence has of art and method for the use of figures, for it is only by figures that he gives force to the passions, luster to the discourses, weight to the reasons, and makes delightful all he speaks. . . . Nature must be the only guide that can be proposed in the use of these figures and metaphors . . . for no portraits can be drawn that have resemblance without it, and all the images that poetry employs in expressing itself are false unless they be natural."[1] The certainty that traditional rhetorical

1. *The Continental Model: Selected French Critical Essays of the Seventeenth Century in*

artifice will generate portraits of emotion and that that emotion will be both the source of pleasure and our access to nature is conventional and seems to belong as much to the Renaissance as to the later seventeenth century, but in fact it endures with some modifications through the eighteenth century.

George Campbell remarks on "what manner passion to an absent object may be excited by eloquence, which, by enlivening and invigorating the ideas of imagination, makes them resemble the impressions of sense and the traces of memory."[2] The effect is like that of using a telescope, "things remote are brought near, things obscure rendered conspicuous." Likeness is seconded by intensity and proximity in the cause of arousal, whether it is aesthetic pleasure or sympathetic feeling. The connections between nature or authentic object, language, and the feelings of the audience are a central interest of this book, as they were a central interest of literary and aesthetic theories from the baroque rhetoricians of the mid-seventeenth century to the Enlightenment philosophers of the mid-eighteenth century. Though the distinction is not always noticed, it was understood that passion can be mirrored by art, as well as stimulated. At the same time the connections of mind to nature supplied by language and perception were variously and differently understood. For example, the neoclassical tolerance of figured discourse evident in Rapin was carefully restricted to tragedy and epic. Under other circumstances, one notices a distaste for ornament, influenced in part by the efforts of scientists to encourage a language accurately descriptive of the objects and processes of nature and more conducive to civil tranquillity, a language virtually exempt from human interference.

Here is Thomas Sprat on the subject: "[The ornaments of speech] make the *Fancy* disgust the best things, if they come sound and unadorn'd; they are in open defiance against *Reason*, professing not to hold much correspondence with that, but with its Slaves, *the Passions;* they give the mind a motion too changeable and bewitching to consist with *right practice*. Who can behold without indignation how many mists and uncertainties these specious *Tropes* and *Figures* have brought on our knowledge?"[3] Normally,

---

English Translation, ed. Scott Elledge and Donald Schier, rev. ed. (Ithaca: Cornell University Press, 1970), 292.

2. George Campbell, *The Philosophy of Rhetoric* (1776), ed. Lloyd F. Bitzer (Carbondale and Edwardsville: Southern Illinois University Press, 1963), 94.

3. Thomas Sprat, *The History of the Royal Society*, in J. E. Spingarn, ed., *Critical Essays of the Seventeenth Century*, 3 vols. (Bloomington: Indiana University Press, 1957), 1:116–17.

however, the literary critics treated the passions more positively, seeking instead a manner of expression that would accommodate the natural and the emotional. The natural, whether of expression or feeling was something that had to be recovered, an intuition noticeable in the reactions against the baroque in the seventeenth and early eighteenth century and still compelling well beyond the chronological limits of my study. Paul De Man calls it "the act of naming . . . as implying a return to the source, to the pure motion of experience at its beginning."[4] In the same piece De Man remarks that where post-Romantic critics might begin to investigate literature as a whole by looking at metaphor, that would have been "inconceivable for Boileau, for Pope, even for Diderot" (p. 2).

This is only partially correct. Boileau's contemporary, Bouhours, is vitally interested in metaphor, as are the baroque theorists he contends with. Language, and in particular whatever renders it opaque, becomes for neoclassical theory the agency that threatens to draw us away from "experience at its beginning," and almost simultaneously in certain guises the medium by which a return might be managed. Addison, whose approval of Virgil's *Georgics* depends on their use of a refined and ennobling style, nevertheless, in reaction against the artificialities of Martial and Cowley, says, "an ordinary song or ballad that is the delight of the common people cannot fail to please all such readers as are not unqualified for their entertainment by their affectation or ignorance; and the reason is plain—because the same paintings of nature which recommend it to the most ordinary reader will appear beautiful to the most refined."[5] But such an apparently simple taste is already qualified by ambivalences about metaphor and by Addison's own fumbling efforts to imagine that the spontaneous and the natural are somehow compatible with the cultivation of an urban and ordered society.[6]

Readers will find that in each chapter I deal with different theories of the affective power of language—language at large and, of course, the language of the poet—and the related topics they pull into their net. Chapter 1

4. Paul De Man, *The Rhetoric of Romanticism* (New York: Columbia University Press, 1984), 3.
5. *Spectator* 70 [1711], *Critical Essays from* The Spectator *by Joseph Addison*, ed. Donald F. Bond (Oxford: Clarendon Press, 1970).
6. The social and political implications of the theories I deal with are in part taken up in Ronald W. Paulson's recent study, *Breaking and Remaking: Aesthetic Practice in England, 1700–1820* (New Brunswick: Rutgers University Press, 1989). Paulson deals with the ways in which poets and artists work and places them and the aesthetic assumptions they entertain in a broad context of change and revolution, as well as the forces resisting them.

centers on the arguments for wit as entertainment, examining three Italian baroque theorists, Emmanuele Tesauro, Matteo Peregrini, and Sforza Pallavicino, whose enthusiasms for verbal play (explicitly derived from Aristotle's *Rhetoric*) reflect the interests of the Renaissance concentrated into the details of metaphoric style and innocent of the larger formal and didactic motives of the generation of theorists just before them. In this critical universe an emotional or fully affective response is quite secondary to the pleasures of diversion. That priority, which translates into the preference for wit, wordplay, and other forms of verbal display, is exactly what prompted or gave the excuse for French and, later, English neoclassicism.

The neoclassical reaction is epitomized in chapter 2 in the theories of Bouhours and Boileau: dealing explicitly or silently with what they considered baroque excesses, or in the case of Boileau with the fondness for detail of the Moderns, they concentrate on style. The neoclassical argument in general favors restraint in ornament, a matching of language to subject that seeks a bond between the laws of nature and audience expectation mediated by conventional genre and the word as transparent sign. This neat system is complicated by the intrusion of the sublime which first appears, through the agency of Longinus, as a discrepancy between the level of word and level of idea. Chapter 3, on Addison, explores the increasingly contradictory imperatives of neoclassical aesthetics and measures Addison's significant and insistent emphasis on audience psychology. Here the clash between the desire for the natural and the figurative as a source of affect begins to emerge.

Chapter 4 takes up a number of problems of affect that gather under the broad heading of taste. I have organized them by looking at the ways in which taste is identified as emotive or cognitive or both, with its character as a matter of intuited and more or less unanalyzed preference, as rationalized imaginative response (as the German Enlightenment proposed), or as the cultivation of a critical standard (Hume's position). Chapter 5 moves forward from Aristotle's *Poetics* and once again to Hume, this time to his theories of tragedy and tragic pleasure, in order to examine the ways in which concepts of audience reaction interact with concepts of form.

Finally, Chapter 6, on Du Bos, Condillac, and Diderot, traces a movement of thought that begins in an affirmation of the coherence of the links between nature, the work of art, and audience and concludes with Diderot's virtual dismantling of this affirmation. The dominant intellectual effort of neoclassical and Enlightenment critical theory was to imagine an integrated system of the arts that preserved intention, judgment, and feeling in a valid whole.

A major part of that effort was the close study of psychologies of perception and responsive feeling in order to ground aesthetic theory in what could be reasoned about general human experience. This is the program that Diderot challenges in his personas of the viewer of paintings who turns them into dramatic narratives and of the spectator in the theater totally dominated by emotions he believes real and spontaneous but which are in reality the product of a detached artistic calculation and, finally, due to language alone.

Most of the texts I deal with are commonly understood as historically crucial, providing stages in the movement of literary and aesthetic theory that their successors recognized and responded to, for example, Addison's use of Bouhours and Boileau to authorize his own remarks. One might also cite the ways in which German aesthetic thinking answered Addison, Burke, and Hume or in which Diderot treated the insights of Du Bos and Condillac. But I have thought it more important to look at works that offer detailed studies of questions of artistic and literary affect, studies that uncover the ways in which the larger concerns of this period become problematical.

The champions of baroque wit, Tesauro, Peregrini, and Pallavicino, accepted and promoted the theatrical properties of language as the object of attention. They proposed a basic contrast between the strange and the familiar, a contrast mediated and also emphasized by metaphor, with the delight of the audience a function of the skill with which the interplay is managed. In this narrow system the reader or listener must fix his attention on the ornamental, exalting the artist as virtuoso, as showman. The intricacies and dynamics of verbal wit, however carefully justified as serious intellectual play, were still "rhetorical" and susceptible to the charge that they offer no reality beyond themselves or the vanity of the poet. It is not surprising that a strong reaction set in. A classical purist such as Bouhours exhibits a sharp distaste for such a display of the author's skills and for what he considered the obscurity, excess, and lack of rational discipline found in such poets as Ronsard and Tasso.

However, a widespread distaste for styles of verbal wit is not sufficient to describe the profound changes in aesthetic thinking that occurred in the seventeenth and early eighteenth centuries. Just as influential were developments in thinking about epistemology and therefore about the philosophical use of language by Francis Bacon. Bacon's *Advancement of Learning* (1605) sought to reform and sanitize the language of learning and science: "For as knowledges are now delivered, there is a kind of contract of error between the deliverer and the receiver: for he that delivereth knowledge desireth to deliver it in such form as may best be believed, and not as may best be examined; and he that receiveth knowledge desireth rather present satisfaction than expectant inquiry."[7] Bacon proposed to reduce the influence of traditional rhetoric, to remove it from the area of natural inquiry. The effect on later generations was pervasive and at a certain level permanent: the ornamental in language was now assigned to poetry and rhetoric alone, to the expressions of the fancy and of wish.[8] A purer, more exact and denotative language was required to satisfy the claims of reason and science. But, as I trust my text shows, this attitude toward ornament—one might almost say an attitude toward metaphor—colors and influences the thinking of literary theorists who are not scientists at all but who exhibit a persistent worry about language and who are concerned that in certain forms it gets in the way of feeling and imagination. In this case, it is not the objective interest of scientific knowledge and unbiased description that dictate verbal restraint but the subjective appetite for the natural or the emotionally authentic. These are to some extent concerns about the nature of language and perception themselves, as witnessed by Descartes's pointing out that objects and our ideas about them do not resemble each other.[9] This question and the way it involves thinking about language influences eighteenth-century discussions about the differences between painting and poetry. The questions raised about the relationship of concepts in the mind to language go deeper than pronouncements about what are proper styles.

These questions address and perhaps help exacerbate the concern that language and art seem in some modes to distance themselves and us from nature. If we look, as Jean Hagstrum has done, at Addison's critical doctrine, we notice how powerful is the expectation that the language of literature will

---

7. Quoted in Charles Whitney, *Francis Bacon and Modernity* (New Haven: Yale University Press, 1986), 137. See 55–75 for an account of Bacon's fairly complex attitude toward eloquence in general. For a discussion of Bacon's own style, see John C. Briggs, *Francis Bacon and the Rhetoric of Nature* (Cambridge, Mass.: Harvard University Press, 1989), ix–xi; see 150–74 for a treatment of what Briggs calls Bacon's "natural rhetoric of reversal, surprise, and contradiction" (163).

8. Brian Vickers has argued vigorously against the notion that rhetoric ceased to be influential at the end of the seventeenth century. See his *In Defence of Rhetoric* (Oxford: Clarendon Press, 1988), 299–305. The consequence of Bacon's and later Locke's, attitude was more effectively to concentrate the association of rhetorical and poetic theory, to draw rhetoric closer to aesthetic interests, and to remove it, at least putatively, from those modes of discourse that belonged to science.

9. René Descartes, *Optics*, in *The Philosophical Writings of Descartes*, trans. John Cottingham, Robert Stoothoff, and Dugald Murdoch, 2 vols. (Cambridge: Cambridge University Press, 1985), 1:153.

compensate for its apparent distance from nature, that is, from the nature that is seen. "Addison's aesthetic system," writes Hagstrum, "retains the old association of literary *enargeia* with the rendition of particular, visible nature." But Addison provides another dimension: "Under impulses from the new psychology *enargeia* now arises from the process of seeing and no longer resides primarily in the thing seen."[10] Among other things, this shift is symptomatic of a broader development in European critical interests. It is tempting to characterize this as a change from an emphasis on mimetic formalism to predominantly affective theories, from an interest in the nature of the poem to theories that explore the nature of the audience and its responses. But as a previous book of mine sought to demonstrate, the Renaissance paid vigorous and sustained attention to the audience.[11]

Whatever capacity language has to recover and represent the visual is valued not only because it returns us to nature; it also, as Addison argues in *Spectator* 416, allows us a more complete "seeing" of objects. Here, for example, is a statement of the conventional position. Alexander Gerard is remarking in 1759 on "the main excellence of poetical or eloquent descriptions; the characteristical perfection of which arises from the author's judiciously selecting the most essential and striking qualities of his subject, and combining them into such a picture as quickly revives in the reader, and strongly impresses on his mind a lively idea of the original."[12] Just two years earlier, the publication of Edmund Burke's *Philosophical Enquiry* (1757) had offered the complicating view that words do not produce pictures in our minds without extraordinary efforts on our part and that in any case the affective power of language is due to repeated use, not a consequence of pictures raised in our minds.[13] Usage or repetition becomes an issue in the transaction between the form of the object, its linguistic representation, and its affective consequences.

Burke's effort to divorce mental seeing and verbal affect is a minority view, but an important one. Imagination for him works in the darkness of obscurity and depends on inference, not clarity as with Addison. Men-

10. Jean Hagstrum, *The Sister Arts: The Tradition of Literary Pictorialism and English Poetry from Dryden to Gray* (Chicago: University of Chicago Press, 1958), 137–38.
11. Robert L. Montgomery, *The Reader's Eye: Studies in Didactic Literary Theory from Dante to Tasso* (Berkeley and Los Angeles: University of California Press, 1979).
12. Alexander Gerard, *An Essay on Taste* (1759) (London: Scolar Press, 1971), 50.
13. Edmund Burke, *A Philosophical Enquiry into the Origin of Our Ideas of the Sublime and the Beautiful*, ed. James T. Boulton (Notre Dame: University of Notre Dame Press, 1968), 166–67. See W. J. T. Mitchell's analysis of Burke's argument in *Iconology: Image, Text, Ideology* (Chicago: University of Chicago Press, 1986), 124–25.

delssohn and Lessing, who were aware of Burke's views, established partly similar theories of aesthetic perception, but theirs are based in a different psychology and argue for a more cognitive mode of response. For the most part the eighteenth century held to linguistic pictorialism and tended to link visual proximity or presence to the spectator's or reader's responsive emotions. What Burke does is to demonstrate that what words allow us to "see" is a function of our individual experience, a view possibly in conflict with his argument earlier in the *Enquiry* that there is an objective standard of taste. Kames, as I argue in chapter 4, is similarly ambivalent. The discrepancy between the assumption that everyone visualizes in essentially the same way and the implications of association psychology (which Kames embraced wholeheartedly) for highly subjective and disparate kinds of taste remained unresolved in England and France. And apart from Burke's shrewd comments just noted, it is never really explained why being able to visualize something, even a fictional character in the throes of emotion, should necessarily raise emotions in the spectators. These matters are central to my last three chapters, those on taste, on tragedy, and on Du Bos, Condillac, and Diderot.

One way of handling the problems of beauty and taste and the awkward puzzle of subjective reaction is the German tradition, stemming from Wolff and Baumgarten; continuing in Mendelssohn, Lessing, and others; and culminating in Kant's *Critique of Judgment* (1790). I have already mentioned its cognitive bias. The general thrust is to isolate specific types of object that are understood to be coordinate with specific types of perception and controlled, even rationalized, emotional response. The intention is not all that distant from the purposes of Hutcheson and Kames and their efforts to establish either a sense of beauty or a standard of beauty, though they are less successful than the Germans in preserving a theory of such experience somehow uncontaminated from the pressures of culture, mood, education, and individual disposition. Diderot, finally, in effect discards this direction of inquiry, at least in *Paradoxe sur le comédien* where he asserts that the supposed fraternity between artist, actor, and spectator is an illusion. According to this unsettling view, the spectator attends, without the least awareness of their real status, to words and gestures that have no origin in nature or direct human experience. He thus establishes a theory of almost pure formality so distanced from nature that it is not recognized at all as form. Affect depends entirely on the audience's belief in the referentiality of a set of gestures and words that are almost totally nonreferential, that extend only to the performance of which they are a part. By dwelling obsessively on the illusive complexities of a naturalistic theater, Diderot abolishes the mimetic system of the Enlightenment.

If at this point we recall that one feature of the baroque theory of linguistic form is that it assumes on the part of readers or listeners an overriding interest in the play of language itself, almost to the exclusion of its capacity to refer and represent, then we might be tempted to see Diderot's conclusions as an odd kind of return to an earlier point of view. If language is all there is, or at least all that is important for the spectator, if there is no feeling, no authentic experience behind theatrical presentation, then he can respond only to the surface of words or to what he subjectively believes to be their nature. But of course there is a substantial difference between the baroque interest in trope and Diderot's concept of illusion, even though each in its own way is a kind of theatricality. Diderot's audience is blind to the brilliance and wit of the playwright, absorbed as it is, not so much in the words, but in its own emotions. It believes in what it sees and hears precisely because of the dramatist's and the actor's artifice; its emotion, however, is ironically balanced by their cold lack of emotion, but that indifference is hidden. The art conceals, just as much as it fashions. Tesauro's audience seeks and enjoys the spectacle of artifice, whereas Diderot's acts out perhaps the furthest and most baffling reach of the doctrine that art, especially verbal art, is the occasion for subjective emotional response and so should remain respectfully invisible.

A note on procedure: in almost every instance I have used English translations of Italian, French, and German texts, either those available in print, or where I have been unable to locate them, my own. Where they are reasonably accurate, I favor eighteenth-century translations.

1

Baroque Surprise

The Pleasures of Metaphoric Form

> *But it is not only the difficulty and labour which men take in finding out of truth, nor again when it is found that it imposeth upon men's thoughts, that doth bring lies in favour, but a natural though corrupt love of the lie itself. One of the later school of Grecians examineth the matter, and is at a stand to think what should be in it, that men should love lies, where neither they make for pleasure, as with poets, nor for advantage, as with the merchant, but for the lie's sake. But I cannot tell: this same truth is a naked and open daylight, that doth not show the masks and mummeries and triumphs of the world, half so stately and daintily as candlelights. Truth may perhaps come to the price of a pearl, that showeth best by day; but it will not rise to the price of a diamond or carbuncle, that showeth best in varied lights. A mixture of a lie doth ever add pleasure. Doth any man doubt, that if there were taken out of men's minds vain opinions, flattering hopes, false valuations, imaginations as one would, and the like, but it would leave the minds of a number of men poor shrunken things, full of melancholy and indisposition, and unpleasing to themselves?*
> —Francis Bacon, "Of Truth"

In Italian literary theory the seventeenth-century successors to the abundance of theorists in the previous generation are three Italian rhetoricians, Emmanuele Tesauro, Matteo Peregrini, and Sforza Pallavicino. If we include the Spaniard Balthazar Gracian, together with him they produced the significant whole of baroque literary theory, though taken at face value their work seems limited in scope and narrow in objective. Their interests centered in the conceit and forms of verbal wit, features that Tesauro grandly claimed could produce a "whole theater of marvels." These interests stretched well beyond the borders of poetry, fiction, or drama to include all the forms of artificial discourse. Yet with the possible exception of Tesauro's attempt to propose Aristotle as the supreme authority on style, their work adds little to the history of rhetoric. What they bring to the history of literature, explaining and in part justifying the eccentricities of Marinism and Metaphysical style, is more important and more interesting,[1] but their significance in this study involves their place in the history of affective theory.

Although they extend the sixteenth-century interest in the affinities between rhetoric and poetic and keep alive the long-standing reference to Aristotelian faculty psychology to describe audience reaction, their work effects substantial changes in emphasis. Style is proposed as the object of audience attention. The audience in turn is more to be entertained than moved or instructed. For Tesauro, and only slightly less drastically for Peregrini and Pallavicino, form is equivalent to style, and style is resolved into witty and conceited language. Wit and conceitedness cross generic boundaries and inform all types of discourse, and Tesauro, in his own effusion of wit, finds these qualities in the natural and the supernatural.

At the same time the baroque theorists say nothing whatever about plot or character. Verisimilitude was one of the more urgently debated topics in Renaissance literary theory. It survived and flourished as a central value in neoclassical doctrine. But for the apologists of wit it is not simply a secondary concern, its worth is implicitly denied in the deliberate and conscious elevation of verbal artifice, and the traditional view that delight was an instrumental, not a terminal value, is called in question, though not entirely abandoned.[2] They exploit the tendency emerging in the later sixteenth century to divide poetry and truth, ornament and doctrine, image and reality, all at the expense of content or "matter" as a major value in artistic discourse, though modern students of baroque aesthetics have tended to state the development rather too categorically and simply. For the baroque thinkers what distinguishes poets is neither their wisdom nor capacity to render nature; they are no longer the dutiful servants of the verisimilar or the unities. Instead, their talent for surprise, for cleverness, and for verbal fireworks is the mark to know them by, and these are called

1. See J. A. Mazzeo, *Renaissance and Seventeenth-Century Studies* (New York: Columbia University Press, 1964), 29–59. As an addendum it is worth remarking that throughout the later seventeenth century Italian critics, however susceptible in theory to the general movement away from baroque aesthetics, nevertheless defended the Italian Renaissance poets. This situation ended with Gravina's *Ragion della poetica* (1708). See chapter 2 below.

2. See G. Morpurgo-Tagliabuie, "La retorica umanistica e Aristotele," *Retorica barocca*, in *Atti del III congresso internazionale di studi umanistici*, ed. E. Castelli (Venice, 1954), 143–45, and Giuseppe Conte, *La metafora barocca* (Milan: University of Mursia, 1972), 98.

into being by the audience's desire for marvels.³ By mid-seventeenth century Pallavicino can state flatly that the intrinsic and proximate ends of poetry are not to be found in utility but in delighting the common intellect, though poetry should not make use of "whatever delights them, obviously, but that which they derive from conversations or writings composed where marvelous things are discovered by the author."⁴ The authority for such a view derives, perhaps surprisingly, from Aristotle.⁵

Aristotle and Metaphor

The text to which the baroque theorists—Tesauro being the most prominent in this respect—turned was the *Rhetoric*, and for them its crucial element was the analysis of metaphor in Book III. Aristotle thought of metaphor as fundamentally artificial, and his notion of artifice can be gathered from the earlier definition in the *Poetics*: "Metaphor is the application of a strange term either transferred from the genus and applied to the species or from the species and applied to the genus, or from one species to another or else by analogy."⁶ The key term is "strange." Golden's translation reads "the transference of a name from the object to which it has a *natural* application" (emphasis added),⁷ but Aristotle's discussion of nouns at the beginning of chapter 21 seems to indicate that he is thinking of usage as either familiar and ordinary or strange and unfamiliar: "Every noun is either 'ordinary' or 'rare' or 'metaphorical' or 'ornamental' or 'invented' or 'lengthened' or 'curtailed' or 'altered.' An 'ordinary' word is used by everybody, a 'rare' word one used by some; so that a word may obviously be both 'ordinary' and 'rare,' but not in relation to the same people" (Loeb

---

3. In the later sixteenth century, Italian criticism divided over what Baxter Hathaway has labeled "marvels and commonplaces," and the division was often expressed as a preference either for the motive of instruction instead of delight or the requirement of sound doctrine as opposed to the claims of ornament. The impulse behind most critical efforts, as Hathaway emphasizes, was to find ways to reconcile these apparent incompatibilities. See *Marvels and Commonplaces: Renaissance Literary Criticism* (New York: Random House, 1968).
4. Sforza Pallavicino, *Trattato dello stile e del dialogo* (Rome, 1662), chap. 30, par. 15.
5. Cf. Morpurgo-Tagliabuie, *Retorica barocca*, 139.
6. *Poetics* 21, Loeb trans.
7. *Aristotle's Poetics: A Translation and Commentary for Students of Literature*, trans. Leon Golden, commentary by O. B. Hardison, Jr. (Tallahassee: Florida State University Press, 1981).

trans.).[8] Only if "natural" is understood to refer to familiar usage, that which seems natural because it is habitual to those who use and hear language, is Aristotle's concept of metaphor as felt artifice fully clear. The terms, therefore, are not absolute but are instead relative to user and audience. To make a metaphor is a more conscious, deliberate manipulation of language than simply using a term already familiar to identify an object. Metaphor thus carries with it what Aristotle calls a "foreign air" (*Rhetoric* III.ii), a sense of strangeness, of something calculated and special, a work of art, perhaps, in miniature. There is also the hint that metaphor is a kind of deliberate misnaming, or catachresis, as Foucault believes.[9] Ricouer also calls attention to catachresis, but explains it as a movement from "literal incongruence to metaphorical congruence between two semantic fields."[10] In treating metaphor as an art Aristotle dwells first on propriety (*Rhetoric* III.ii), giving examples of "inappropriate" metaphor and suggesting that the distance between the two "objects" involved in metaphoric compounding must not be too great: there must be some likeness, though not so much that it is too readily evident to anyone. The maker of metaphor is considered gifted—many of Aristotle's examples are drawn from the poets—and what we notice first of all is skill or cleverness. "And generally speaking," Aristotle says, "clever enigmas furnish good metaphors; for metaphor is a kind of enigma, so that it is clear that the transference is clever."[11] He thus lifts metaphor beyond the utilitarian and involves our thinking about it in the character of the maker and the response of the audience.

What metaphor does for the audience is to put "'the matter before the eyes,' for we ought to see what is being done rather than what is going to be done" (III.x.6). Considered in this way, it approaches the neoclassical requirement of perspicuity, but in that case it has to be so discreetly managed that it would seem natural and spontaneous, rather than noticeably contrived. For Aristotle something more than visual presence is involved;

---

8. Paul Ricoeur analyzes Aristotle's "alien" (*allotrios*) into four contingent concepts: deviation, borrowing, "proper" versus figurative meaning, and substitution; *The Rule of Metaphor: Multi-disciplinary Studies of the Creation of Meaning in Language*, trans. Robert Czerny (London: Routledge and Kegan Paul, 1978), 18–19.

9. Michel Foucault, *The Order of Things* (New York: Vintage, 1973), 114. Foucault is emphasizing the "tropical" nature of language as a freedom to alight wherever the user wishes.

10. Raul Ricoeur, "The Metaphorical Process as Cognition, Imagination, and Feeling," *On Metaphor*, ed. Sheldon Sacks (Chicago: University of Chicago Press, 1979), 145. Ricoeur's account avoids simply designating metaphor as static catachresis and emphasizes complexity of process.

11. Loeb trans., here and throughout the discussion.

there is also an aesthetic consideration: "Metaphors should therefore be derived from what is beautiful either in sound, or in signification. . . . For it does make a difference, for instance, whether one says 'rosy-fingered morn,' rather than 'purple-fingered,' or, what is still worse, 'red-fingered'" (III.ii.13). The emphasis here is on the need to strike just the right balance in the form of the metaphor, for if the listeners or readers cannot accept its cleverness as well as its propriety, then they have no pleasure in it and any further purpose is lost. Aristotle thus views metaphor as a close and delicate transaction between author, form, and audience.

The pleasure we take in metaphor is also ascribed to what Aristotle terms "easy learning" (III.x.2), and ease has to do with how quickly we get the point. Once again, however, there is a correct or appropriate moment between the too easy and the too difficult. Since what everyone knows is boring, a metaphor whose terms are too obvious makes no impact; at the same time no one takes delight in an enigma so obscure it can't be understood. We can now grasp why in both the *Poetics* and the *Rhetoric* Aristotle insists on what he calls the "strangeness" of metaphor, for what he is really talking about is a combination of strangeness and familiarity. The listeners or readers cannot be totally passive: they must work, however lightly and briefly, to grasp the point and must appreciate as well the way in which something is identified and qualified by the alien term, that is, by what that something is not. Thus, it is not what we learn but the manner in which we learn it that gives force to metaphor and, to a lesser extent, to simile. The speed with which we move from ignorance to knowledge is crucial. And, although Aristotle does not mention it, there is also implied in the concept of strangeness a form of mortality. Repeated too often, metaphor becomes familiar and stale. Like slang, its surprise and the impression of its novelty (qualities the baroque rhetoricians emphasized) have a brief power, and this mortality guarantees that metaphor is especially dependent upon an audience.

One aspect of this dependence is the author's attempt to deceive the audience. In addition to having to learn something, listeners must be aware suddenly and almost in spite of themselves that they *have* learned something. Listeners thus not only undergo a change from ignorance to knowledge but also reach a conclusion that is contrary to their expectation. Versions of this process are central to baroque concepts of wittiness and the motives these concepts discover for its appeal.

Finally, Aristotle talks about concreteness. We have already noticed that he has said that metaphor "places things before the eyes." In III.xi this is one of the powers attributed to "smart sayings." "I mean," he explains, "that things are set before the eyes by words that suggest actuality." "Actuality" indicates that Aristotle relies on a concept of words representing things in such a way that more than reference is involved, that the word is capable of making us picture the thing imaginatively. Metaphors are thus predicates in which picturing is part of the relationship established by transference. What we learn, presumably, is something about an object we did not know or perceive before, and we do so by being able to see it as if it were some other object. Therefore, two events are taking place, learning and the manner in which learning is brought about. Aristotle does not lay the weight of his discussion on manner as much as his baroque followers do, and if they can be said to modify Aristotle in any profound way, it is in their shifting attention from the issue of learning to that of manner, in the sense that manner is celebrated as a play of mind and the creation of new and marvelous fictions.

Tesauro

The peculiarity of Emmanuele Tesauro's *Cannocchiale aristotelico* (1654) is its effort to concentrate all that is interesting in artifice into what he calls *argutezza*, a term that translates with some awkwardness into English but means, roughly, keenness, sharpness of wit.[12] For Tesauro *argutezza* is the heart of wit, and the figure that surpasses all others in witty expression is metaphor. This sequence of priorities surrounds and controls Tesauro's discussion of style, which opens with a flamboyant set of assertions making "argutezza" and hence metaphor virtually coextensive with poetry or discourse itself:

> A divine part of the mind, better known through its appearance than through its birth, has been in every country and by virtually all men held in such great admiration that, when read or listened to by those who do not know it, like a beautiful miracle it is received with the highest rejoicing and applause. This is KEENNESS, the great mother

---

12. An excellent translation and explanation of this and related terms is available in James V. Mirollo, *Poet of the Marvelous: Giambattista Marino* (New York: Columbia University Press, 1963), 116–17.

of every ingenious conceit, the clearest light of oratory and poetic elocution, the vital spirit of dead pages, the most pleasant sauce [seasoning?] in civil conversation, ultimate power of the intellect, vestige of divinity in the human soul.[13]

In its turn metaphor is "the most witty and acute, the most strange and marvelous, the most pleasant and useful, the most eloquent and fecund part of the human intellect" (66). There is, he suggests, something divine in metaphor, life teased from the inert, the strange and exotic bursting through the familiar, the element without which all formal discourse is flat: "In sum, everything is dead that does not taste of the wine of sharpness" (2). Exaggerations aside, Tesauro thinks of metaphor as much more than a figure, more even than the most central of figures. In miniature it stands for verbal artistry at large, so that when one talks about the several issues involved in rhetoric and poetic in Tesaurian terms, one is talking about metaphor.[14]

What some of these issues are is already evident from our review of Aristotle. Tesauro points constantly to the cleverness of the maker of conceits and justifies cleverness as the source of our pleasure and hence our willingness to listen. He proceeds then to examine "argutezza" in all the arts, even in the lapidary, though it is predominantly a verbal quality. In an effort to define it, he says (7) that it is first of all characterized by vivacity and then by words being well put together, striking, and graceful (from Cicero's "sententiis non tam gravibus et severis quam concinnis et venustis"[15]). Another feature is Aristotle's *asteia* (urbanity), which is more than suavity of style: urbane discourse is the mark of civilization. The writer capable of managing these qualities is the object of admiration, though beyond repeating this kind of generality, Tesauro really says very little about the rhetor or poet. The ethos of the writer or speaker is thus effectively absorbed into the nature of the task; it is, in other words, almost identical

---

13. Emmanuele Tesauro, *Il Cannocchiale aristotelico*, 1. This and subsequent quotations are from the facsimile of the 1670 edition, ed. August Buck (Bad Homburg: Gehlen, 1968).

14. Tesauro's categories of metaphor are: (1) simple metaphor; (2) metaphorical propositions (i.e., allegory); and (3) metaphorical argument. He calls these, respectively, the first, second, and third operations of the intellect, and they are ranked hierarchically. Within simple metaphor and metaphorical argument are eight subtypes: likeness (*simiglianza*), unity (genus to species and vice versa), punning (*equivoco*), hypotyposis (*ipotiposi*), hyperbole (*iperboli*), laconism (*laconismo*), opposition or antithesis (*oppositione*), and deception (*decettione*). Cf. 298.

15. *Brutus* 95.325 (Loeb ed., 282–83). Cicero describes a style "less characterized by weight of thought than by the charm of balance and symmetry."

with the formal properties of wit. A kind of magician, the verbal artist is a stager of theatrical events who can make us see in a single word "a full theater of marvels" (267). As a maker of metaphor the poet is endowed with "a most agile wit," but it is only the activity of wit that we attend to. In all other respects the poet is anonymous and without depth or individuality.

Tesauro's theatrical analogy underscores the power of metaphor to condense, to collapse almost spatially a variety of ideas into a single word or phrase. The example he uses is interesting: "If you say, 'The fields are pleasant,' you represent to me nothing more than the greenness of the fields. But if you say, 'The fields are smiling,' you make me see, so to speak, the earth as animated human being. The field is his face, the pleasantness is his glad laughter, so that in one small word appear all these notions of different genres, earth, field, amenity, human being, laughter, gladness" (267). The reader's "performance" is thus the reverse of the author's: he notices and no doubt marvels at the skill involved in the compression of the many into the one, but he also experiences the unraveling of the one back into the many from which it seems to have derived. However, such a line of thought is followed no further. Instead, Tesauro's attention to the formal properties of metaphor centers in two qualities familiar to modern critics of baroque and Metaphysical poetry, the discovery of likeness in apparently different things and *energeia* or liveliness.

As to the first of these, he draws on Aristotle's observation in the *Poetics* that metaphor involves a transference from genus to species, species to genus, species to species, or genus to genus. It is the most ingenious figure of all, says Tesauro, "because if wit consists (as we have said) in binding together remote and separate notions of the proposed object, this is exactly the office of metaphor, and of no other figure, thus drawing the mind, no less than the word, from one genus to another, it expresses one concept by means of another quite diverse, finding similarity in dissimilar things" (266). It is evident from this statement and from his later discussion of types of metaphor, as well as of extended metaphorical argument, that he has in mind a whole central category of language and thought conceived on very broad terms and including particular figures that we ordinarily assign separate and different names. And what is central is the concept of similarity in difference, the feature Dr. Johnson described as "heterogeneous ideas yoked by violence together." For Tesauro there is no violence, but there are surprise and novelty.

Novelty, *pellegrina*, is the term he uses to translate Aristotle's "strange" or "alien" (though we should not assume too great a bending of Aristotle's meaning: Tesauro uses a Latin version of Aristotle, and in the margin quotes from *Rhetoric* III.2, "peregrinum affert Translatio . . ."). "Novelty" is a generously inclusive term already familiar in literary theory to account for some of the appeal of poetry. Tesauro claims it derives from compression ("Della *Brevita* nasce la NOVITA . . ."), and illustrates brevity by elaborating Aristotle's example of the pleasure to be derived from easy learning (*Rhetoric* X.iii): "for when Homer calls old age stubble, he teaches and informs us through the genus." Tesauro begins with a full statement of the logic of the example: just as stubble is the stalk of the grain which was once green and vigorous and now is dry and withered, so old age is a lack of vigor in a body that was once robust and healthy." Metaphors squeeze everything into a single word, and "in an almost miraculous way they make you see the one in the other." What one learns is not a new fact, at least insofar as this example is concerned, but a new perspective, a way of seeing. "Hence," he continues, "the greater is your delight in the sense that it is more curious and pleasant to view many objects through the penetration of perspective, than if the same originals came to you by passing successively before your eyes" (301).

Novelty, then, is to be found in manner of expression. The combination of two words whose usage is familiar when apart results in fresh expression because it is unanticipated: "For although the word 'stubble' is ordinary and familiar among the people, even so, standing for old age it is a fresh word insofar as this meaning is concerned" (301). Novelty is also involved in the deception practiced on the audience, which Tesauro classifies as his eighth type of metaphor (294). But for his concept of metaphor to work, novelty understood as a departure from the ordinary or commonplace is the most essential feature, and it appears to sum up or contain almost all the other elements described by Aristotle and Tesauro both: similarity in difference, compression, displacement, or transference. All these must result in expression that is fresh, different, and unexpected. The upshot of removing metaphor from the realm of familiarity, of insisting on its capacity to display, is to give weight to what the listener or reader *sees*. This in turn amounts to bringing the remote into proximity, making both knowledge and delight obedient to spatial distance.

The observation that metaphor is a way of bringing things before our eyes amounts, as I have suggested, to a transition from unfamiliarity to familiarity. Novelty is a temporary state of affairs, therefore, and hence a moral value attaching to the form of the trope, but Aristotle, as well as the later rhetoricians we are examining, is essentially concerned with liveliness.

Aristotle's phrase, "to set things before the eyes," is not quite the same as liveliness, but the two are near neighbors and are usually discussed as if they were identical. The first refers to the concreteness of metaphor, its capacity to turn concepts into objects or to fuse concept and object so that we see the one in the other. Liveliness, or *energeia*, is the attributing of human or animal qualities to inert things (insofar as acts only, not feelings, are invoked, the technical term is *hypotyposis*, but Tesauro considers that a separate class of metaphor). One of Aristotle's examples is "one 'calls upon dangers to help against dangers'" (*Rhetoric* III.x.7); Tesauro goes much further, citing what he terms "sensible qualities," such as in the phrase "Virtutum fragrantia: Vitiorum foetor," as conferring vividness on discourse and classifying these qualities with metaphors employing the "natural faculties of men, transported to incorporeal or insensate things" (315). In his chapter on *hypotyposis* he traces it through the usual topoi of substance, quantity, quality, and so on. The same procedure is repeated for *hypotyposis* as a mode of argument.

What is gained by liveliness? Aristotle seems to connect it to the process of easy learning. The principle is "actuality": "we ought to see what is being done rather than what is going to be done" (*Rhetoric* III.x.6). Whether this is a temporal or spatial concept or both, it obviously involves a concept of presence and also, perhaps, of presence as accessibility to the senses. Cicero repeats this observation in *De Oratore*, noting that the brilliant style takes us beyond understanding and "makes us feel that we actually see [the thing] before our eyes,"[16] and *Ad Herrenium* informs us that "It is ocular demonstration when an event is so described in words that the business seems to be enacted and the subject to pass virtually before our eyes."[17] The subsequent illustration is a detailed narrative description of the assassination of Gracchus, but rhetorically it is amplification not metaphor.

Tesauro is far less summary. He remarks that *energeia* comes from metaphors of proportion that use terms of movement and adds that these give "force and nerve to an oration" (332). *Hypotyposis* is a particularly explicit form of ocular demonstration: "likewise, material instruments, bring actions in lively and individual fashion before the eyes" (402), and more extensively he says that "its formal difference consists in representing the word with such liveliness that the mind views the object almost as if with bodily eyes" (286). To some extent all metaphor partakes of this materiality

16. Loeb trans., 326–27.
17. Loeb trans., 408–9.

in motion, so *hypotyposis* is simply the most lively type of a generally lively mode of figuration. Furthermore, Tesauro, for all his reputation as an innovator, still belongs to the ancient tradition of visual epistemology, which tends to equate certain words with objects and links the capacity to visualize the object imaginatively through the word with knowledge of the object.

The cognitive work of metaphor is a topic he gives detailed attention. The word as bridge between the object and the mind is central, and the following remarks will indicate that he holds firmly to the ancient belief that words can be accurate mimetic vehicles: "the word passing through the ear no less than the picture through the eye, impress[es] a lively image of things in the mind. Then the mind, like Vertumnus, is transformed by all your words successively in their represented form. And then the mind is joyful if the things are pleasant, frightened if they are horrible, admiring if they are great, belittling if they are despicable; these alterations, in altering the eye and the appearance of the listener, as in the natural mirror of the soul, if you are cunning you will see openly shown" (155). One difficulty here is that in metaphor its material image is not what one is meant to gain knowledge of; what is being described is instead a process of drawing the object closer or clothing it in the presence of something it is not. Finally, it is not clear whether he means that the object itself has emotional properties or whether these are conferred by the rhetorical qualities of the management of trope.

He does, however, pair concreteness and wit. In his chapter entitled "Argutie Humane" he notes that wit functions in two ways: it is perspicacious, peering into the heart of things, and it is "versabile," that is, versatile. In Tesauro's terms it seems to be close to imagination, according to general Renaissance concepts of that faculty: "Versability quickly collates all circumstances among themselves or according to a subject: it adds or divides, it enlarges or diminishes, it deduces one thing from another, it indicates one thing by another, and with marvelous skill, it puts one thing in place of another. And this last is metaphor, the mother of poetry, of symbols, and imprese" (82).

Wit is also to be distinguished from prudence or common sense. Prudence is judicious and steady, and considers what is true. Wit is perspicacious and quick and considers appearances. Prudence has usefulness or practicality as an end, but wit aspires to popular admiration and applause. "Hence, not without some reason have witty men been called divine, for just as God produces that which is from that which is not, so wit makes being from not being and makes a lion become a man or an eagle a city. It grafts a woman upon a fish and produces a siren as a symbol of adulation," and so on through several more instances of Horatian improprieties (82–83). Wit is thus by definition involved in the manipulation of material images. As Gracian remarks, "Each perceptive faculty of the soul—I mean those that perceive objects—enjoys some artifice in them. With things seen, the proportion between the parts is beauty; among sounds, it is harmony: so that even the common taste finds some relation between seasoning and blandness, between sweet and sour. The understanding, then, as the first and foremost faculty of the soul, carries off the bounty of cunningness, the consummation of beauty, in all dissimilarities of subject matter."[18] So also for Tesauro wit adjusts and readjusts particulars and sensible appearances. More especially, he emphasizes the illusion of movement as well as proximity.

What I have been reviewing I take to be the gist of Tesauro's understanding of metaphoric form and its relationship to the mental habits that produce it. It is time now to look more deliberately at what he has to say about its impact on the audience, and to see whether he produces any substantial theory of affect.

Although Tesauro's effort to absorb all witty discourse into metaphor can be seen as changing the direction of literary theory, his concept of language is conventional for its time. For him language is subordinate to the human will and intention and is capable of directly representing the objects it signifies. "All the power of each signifying word consists in representing the thing signified to the human mind. But this representation can be effected either with a plain and proper word [*nudo e proprio*] which requires no work from the wit, or with some ingenious signification which at the same time represents and delights" (235). Delight generally speaking is caused by such departures from ordinary [*cotidiano*] speech, "whence there is instruction joined to novelty, and the listener at the same time learns by enjoying, and enjoys by learning" (124). As it is meant to, this reminds us of Aristotle's matter-of-fact remark that "easy learning is naturally pleasant to all . . . [and] all words which make us learn something are most pleasant" (*Rhetoric* III.x.3). We should also keep in mind Aristotle's list in *Rhetoric* I.xi.19–25, of things that are pleasant, among them change or variation and learning.

Tesauro's tactic is to turn Aristotle's comments on their head and come up with a theory of human boredom and vanity as the cause of ornament. Nature, he says, has given men, in contrast to beasts and angels, "a certain nausea for ordinary things, however useful." This, he continues, is reflected in a craving for ornament:

18. *The Mind's Wit and Art*, trans. Leland H. Chambers (University of Michigan diss., 1962), Discourse 2, p. 95.

Now pride is greater than virtue. He disdains to take shelter unless lured there by ornament. He thinks it unworthy to keep off the falling rain unless the roof pierces the clouds with figured cornices. He does not enjoy delicate drinks unless he drinks them in figured crystal, which slakes the thirst of the eyes as well. Nor will he sleep in other than purple and jewels. . . . Now the same satiety obtains in discourse. In fact, so much more here than in the above does he look for such delights that it is quite easy to satisfy the sense of hearing. For human discourse is not presented all at once; it is infused bit by bit. Therefore there is nothing man loathes more than learning, so that he listens to elevated and useful doctrines with yawning and daydreaming. Unless keenness and novelty of style pierce his wit, he cannot stay awake. For that reason therefore all the ornaments that usually give variety to the hulls of ships, to walls, to vases, are in Greek called SCIMATA and in Latin FIGURAE. Thus all that, which to relieve the boredom of the listener, differentiates words, aphorisms, and enthymemes from the plain, unadorned, daily style, is called rhetorical schemes and figures. Whence comes delight and the listener's applause for words that are new and perspicacious, not to mention whatever sets before the eyes a strange and foreign appearance. (122)

I have troubled to quote at such length because the passage shows how Tesauro's mind works. Aristotle says nothing of boredom, remarking only that ease of learning is more pleasant than hard mental work and that a certain strangeness in diction is attractive. It is likely that the motive for Tesauro's remarks also has something to do with Aristotle's comment that rhetoric is necessary, though unfortunate, "for, as a matter of right, one should aim at nothing more in a speech than how to avoid exciting pain or pleasure." Cases should be decided on "facts alone," but style is "of great importance owing to the corruption of the hearer" (*Rhetoric* III.i.5). Novelty for Tesauro, if his comment derives from this passage, seems to be less something unexpected than a departure from the utilitarian and functional, almost an aesthetic in which form is not allowed to follow function.

Remarks of this nature, as well as Tesauro's frequent reference to the audience, are no doubt responsible for the modern classification of his theory as "hedonistic," a choice of adjective involving some condescension. But it is a mistake to take the deprecatory tone of the passage on ornament at face value: the human need for decoration is after all what calls forth *argutezza* and occasions ingenious figures, "the most noble flowers of the intellect" (234). Such hyperboles are scattered through the treatise and suggest that Tesauro's emphasis on an order of language outside nature or the ordinary round of compelled human activities amounts to a theory that relieves human beings of their relatively inert dependence upon the natural, that is, the given. Language as ornament liberates them from the need to accept what is set before them and reminds them that they can fashion and admire an arrangement of the world of objects arbitrarily conceived and skillfully executed. For a moment Tesauro also offers us a glimpse of artifice independent of the usual requirements of decorum, and the drift of his entire treatise, as many have noted, is away from the prevalent Renaissance belief that art is a form of sweetness masking the bitter pill of truth.[19] In separating the appetite for ornament from any further purpose except distraction, he implies that our enjoyment of artifice comes from our perception of the difference between it and the ordinary purpose of the object to which it is attached.

After such attention to human frailty, if that is what it is, we might expect Tesauro to embark on a systematic investigation of appetite and artistic affect, and he does move a certain distance in this direction. He recognizes three general classes of figured language, each responsive to a level of human perception or apprehension. The first level is harmonic (or, we might say, rhythmic), the second pathetic (or emotional), and the third ingenious or witty. These correspond and appeal to sense, feeling, and intellect, respectively. Figures of sense are illustrated by the periodic sentence, which he brilliantly analyzes for the manner in which it plays upon expectation and creates the impression that the speaker is himself controlled by the movement of the sound: "and when, after long circling, he comes to the point at last, [the listener] applauds the orator not for what he has said, but for keeping silent" (124–25).

Pathetic figures are the category of language most appropriate to the study of affect. According to Tesauro they have great power, especially in the mouth of a skilled speaker, but he is wary of them. They can, he notes, be used to make the false appear true, because we are in the habit of inferring a state of emotion from outward expression. The clever depiction of a face with a mournful expression will strike a note of sympathy in the beholder as if one were looking at an actually suffering human being. In a parody of Horace, he remarks that response of this kind is automatic and

---

19. On this topic, see Giuseppe Conte, *La metafora barocca*, 97–99.

unreflective because of "that knot of sympathy by which human souls are bound together. . . . If you yawn, I yawn" (207).

But, as he says in a slightly different context, "the passions of the soul can whet the edge of human wit, and as our Author says, perturbation adds to the force of persuasion. And the reason is that sentiment inflames the spirits that are the torch of the intellect, and the imagination concentrates on a single object" (90).[20] Allowed full rein, the imagination, necessary both to passion and to the exercise of wit, alters, magnifies, or duplicates what it has seen, and according to the authority of Aristotle the orator may "inflame his listeners with anger, pity, love, or hatred" because "the passions rouse the wit but put the judgment to sleep" (91). Tesauro also seems to expect an audience at times to respond in an almost literally mimetic fashion. We have already seen that he believes that lively images are "stamped" on the mind and that the mind responds in mirror fashion to the affective nature of the image: it "rejoices if the object is pleasant" and so on (155). This notion of affect has several limitations. It depends upon the belief that words are able to transmit objects to the mind in the same fashion as the mind perceives the object itself. And it seems to suggest naively that objects have intrinsic affective properties that are also coordinate with our knowledge of the object. But we have to remember that Tesauro is not talking about the "transparency" of language, even though he may acknowledge its existence. Rather, he insists, as we have seen, that the human audience requires artifice and ornament if it is to be attentive, and these are qualities primarily conferred on objects by language used in certain deliberate ways. Moreover, he holds to a distinction between the emotive and the conceited.

The term Tesauro most often applies to the effects of artifice is "pleasure," and as is the habit of most Renaissance critics, he is usually content to allow us to simply understand pleasure by whatever element in a work of art is assumed to produce it. In another work, *La filosofia morale* (1670), he discusses pleasure in some detail. Sensitive pleasures "derived from passions are momentary vehemences founded in appetite, not in reason, when the vehemence ceases, so does the delight" (54).[21] Variety,

---

20. In the margin Tesauro refers both to *Rhetoric* II.1-17 and to *Poetics* 14, but his point is underscored by *Rhetoric* II.1-17, which lists the topoi of emotion. Tesauro's intention is not to encourage unrestrained emotionalism in discourse. The reference to *Poetics* 14 is inapt, for in this chapter Aristotle argues that "the poet must by 'representation' produce the pleasure which comes from feeling pity and fear," rather than rely too much on emotive language. Aristotle does not, however, explain the difference between such language and emotion generated by the action.

21. To some extent Tesauro is simply echoing standard Scholastic psychology in making

he adds, is naturally pleasing, and both the senses and the intellect are eager for new experience and new knowledge. Emotional images, such as those in tragedy, move us powerfully because there is a "sensible sympathy between affect and object, and when the senses are moved, the imagination works more vividly" (455). If we put these comments together with his discussions of the passions and "pathetic" figures just reviewed in *Il Cannocchiale aristotelico*, we might be tempted to think that he holds to a theory in which the appeal of art lies in the intensity of its sensible and emotive images, in which the representations of passion in the text stimulate a responsive passion in the reader, listener, or viewer.

But from his point of view such a process, however powerful, is secondary to the formal artifice he understands as *argutezza*, which in its highest manifestation, metaphor, gives pleasure not because it rouses the feelings but because we are drawn to the freshness and cleverness of the form itself, to a mode of arranging the representation of objects. Moreover, if pleasure is to be derived from manner and if one of its major sources is the *peregrine*, the unexpected, the strange, the new, then the kind of response that interests Tesauro most cannot be one of emotional sympathy. Indeed, there is a moment in *La filosofia morale* where he indicates an important difference. Objects of emotion, he remarks, can be experienced repeatedly and still continue to please precisely because they touch the imagination more vividly and thus move our passions to a kind of sympathy with them. The sensitive appetite is never sated, but "intellectual discourses please only once, because the mind is satisfied" (455). Metaphoric form, the product of wit, is precisely an appeal to intellect and it has to involve, as Tesauro describes it, rational understanding, as well as an appreciation of the manner in which it is presented. Representation "can be effected either with a plain and proper word, which requires no effort of the wit, or with some ingenious signification, which at the same time represents and delights" (235). Delight in this mode therefore supersedes that produced by passion and is distinct from it in the same way that emotion differs from reason. Affective language is thus carefully circumscribed and kept subservient. This hierarchy of linguistic values implies that while material or sensory images may indeed stir the passions, the metaphorical construct controls such a response or subordinates it to the effects produced by the

---

sensory pleasure brief and without enduring satisfaction, whereas spiritual or intellectual pleasures, because they fasten on worthier objects, are seen as more conducive to enduring joy.

processes of transference and condensation. If this is what Tesauro has in mind, he nevertheless neglects to explain it. And at one moment he seems to concede something quite different, noting that "figures of pathos" can at times surpass the impact of a more ingenious figure that is "weakly launched."

This limitation is one of the consequences of the way in which Tesauro's thinking allows affective questions to be absorbed by and perhaps confused with those of linguistic form, and no one who takes the trouble to examine *Il cannocchiale aristotelico* can doubt that his paramount interest is not just form at large but metaphoric form, which in its grandest, most impressive manifestation amounts to a kind of argument. Some idea of why Tesauro thinks this form compelling can be derived from an example quite early in the work, where he notes that a simple metaphor imitating nature is joined to another derived entirely from the wit, "signifying a figurative proposition, as Alexander painted by Apelles hurling lightning seems to say, 'The earth has no other Jove but me'" (12). Taken literally the proposition is patently false, but as a stroke of wit it displays the triumph of artifice over nature, and of metaphor over denotation.

This much remarked tendency to widen the distance between artificial discourse and the natural, to value the ornamental over the useful, and the rare or unusual over the familiar is nevertheless ambiguous. On the one hand, it would seem that Tesauro has abandoned a mimetic theory of art, as Raimondi, for example, claims.[22] A somewhat different but also antimimetic reading is that of Eugenio Donato who has argued that Tesauro's celebration of metaphor amounts to a treatise on the failure of language to represent and thus makes him in certain respects our contemporary.[23] But Tesauro's theory is fundamentally dependent upon the mimetic views he is supposed

---

22. Ezio Raimondi, *Letteratura barocca* (Florence: Olschki, 1961; repr. 1982), 8. Raimondi believes that Tesauro's concept of metaphor amounts to a theory of "creative associationism" which is not mimetic but expressive.

23. Eugenio Donato, "Tesauro's *Cannocchiale aristotelico*," ed. Eileen Reeves and Elizabeth Statmore, *Stanford Italian Review* 5 (1985), 101–14. The essay is stimulating and useful in pointing up important issues in Tesauro's theory. Donato argues that the privileging of metaphor is in effect an effort to reduce all discourse to metaphor and a subversion of "the Aristotelian definitions of the production of meaning to dramatize the ultimately material and metaphorical nature of all signs, all semiological systems, and all signification" (109). But at base Tesauro seems to be arguing not that interpretation of a semiologically direct and accurate nature is impossible, but that it would be dull. The ornamental, according to Tesauro, is psychologically necessary. Hence, in Tesauro's work we have the outline of an aesthetics of discourse that can be seen in broad terms to anticipate some aspects of Enlightenment aesthetics whatever other differences emerged.

to have deserted, and this dependence comes straight from his interest in audience perception. As he sees it, for the metaphorical process to work the audience must not simply be stupefied with *argutezza*, with variety or surprise or urbanity, but in order to perceive and appreciate these qualities in discourse they must also be able to measure fairly exactly the difference between the familiar and unfamiliar, between the quotidian and the rare, in other words between two modes of language as well as between the object and its metaphorical representation. Tesauro does distance himself from a naive concept of artistic imitation, and he is at the opposite end of the critical spectrum from those who held that representation should be fundamentally verisimilar, but metaphoric form from his point of view would have no significance unless perceived as such, unless a kind of negative mimetic connection is acknowledged at the moment of audience reception. And that acknowledgment implies an awareness that another more positively analogical (and less entertaining) mode of representation is possible. The conviction that metaphorical discourse is a matter of choice, not necessity, is evident in Tesauro's discussion of the difference between rhetoric and dialectic—the rhetorician is concerned with fine phrasing and an order of language to please the listener, while the dialectician seeks only clear logic—which leads him to a fairly extreme illustration, punning.

Innocent of any deception, a pun jokingly imitates the truth without suppressing it and "imitates the false in such a way that the truth shines through to you as through a veil. When I say to you, *Prata rident*, I don't intend you to believe that the fields grin like a man but that they are pleasant; thus the metaphorical enthymeme implies one thing so that you may understand another" (494). Pleasure, in Tesauro's universe of artifice, takes precedence by some distance over stark truth, and this precedence can be seen as part of a more widespread tendency in the seventeenth century to separate discourse into two opposed camps: the attractions of *argutezza* are not by any means a sign that another order of discourse does not exist. In fact, for Tesauro they are important precisely because they are superfluous to strict logic, to denotative meaning, indeed to the whole universe of language as a system oriented to significance. Tesauro looks both backward and forward, backward to the notion that words may directly relate to and precisely convey the observable properties of objects and forward to a view already alive in his time that divides language in two, separating its imaginative, affective, and metaphoric functions from those that were thought scientific and logical with what was hoped by others, such as the followers of Bacon, would be a permanent divorce.

Peregrini

Matteo Peregrini's *Delle acutezze* precedes Tesauro's *Cannocchiale* by fifteen years and is usually thought of as a piece of "moderate" baroque theorizing because it is critical of some of Marino's metaphorical extravagances.[24] The establishment of rules governing the exercise of wit was no doubt his central motive, but such an aim now seems quaint, whereas his interest in the question of beauty and the nature of the audience's appreciation gives him a place in the history of aesthetics. And that interest also allows him to focus more directly and coherently on affect than Tesauro was inclined to do.

Peregrini begins with some important distinctions. First of all, he separates wit clearly and irrevocably from what we would call rational thought, and hence from logic. *Acutezza*, a variant of Tesauro's *argutezza*, similarly means cleverness, keenness, sharpness. But it is for Peregrini only an element in style and "consists not in reasoning but in speech." This is the first of five "truths," or basic propositions, the others being, second, that "such speech . . . will necessarily belong to the genus of the beautiful and the delightful"; third, that in eloquence beauty and delight extend all the way across what he calls the interval between more and less; fourth, that the beauty and delight appropriate to *acutezza* tend not to be associated with the lesser range of eloquence, nor with the mediocre or commonplace; and fifth, that *acutezza* is not a property of the subject matter or the signified object but "by the artifice and form of utterance."[25] The first and the fifth are the more crucial items.

These propositions are about as plain as one could ask, and they form the basis for the view that the reader's or listener's attention is almost entirely attracted by manner of utterance, in other words, by artifice. Peregrini concedes that there are different categories of plausibility (that which teaches, moves, or delights) so that the subject matter with practically no artifice can be persuasive—or that words can be persuasive largely by virtue of the material—but he is chiefly concerned with the sort of plausibility that results from evident artifice and especially that sort in which the wit of the speaker—his virtuosity, skill, or brilliance—is on display (24–31). As with Tesauro, so with Peregrini: this skill does not consist in imitating nature or

---

24. Franco Croce, *Tre momenti del barocco letteraria italiano* (Florence: Sansoni, 1966), 95–96, 154–60.
25. Matteo Peregrini, *Della acutezze* (Genoa, 1639), 4.

in discovering its laws but in violating them. For example, he says that in making comparisons, "When the means of joining and the things joined remain in their natural condition, they cannot form anything rare, and lacking absolutely any other artifice of value they can only give off a good and clear syllogistic connection, and so they are quite satisfying to the intellect but not to the wit" (43).

Here Peregrini touches on a distinction that Tesauro did not make and would in all likelihood deny. Wit and reasoning are both concerned with the linkages between things, in other words, with complex structures. Tesauro separates the syllogism from the enthymeme by pointing out that the former is a property of dialectic and is thus an instrument of the mind's inquiry into truth, but rhetoric and dialectic to some extent mirror each other, and their forms appeal to the same rational faculty (*Cannocchiale*, 495–97). Peregrini quite differently sees the enthymemic structure as artificial, "created" not discovered; the wit of the listener or spectator then is touched only when some element in an argument or chain of reasoning is "artificial," that is, not evidently or necessarily true. And there is no art unless speech is figured in such a way that a graceful reciprocity is achieved between the elements being joined. When this occurs, the "power of the fashioning wit is itself the principal object of admiration" (42–43). Style, Peregrini implies, is the diversion of interest from one faculty to another, and of course, it is equally the product of one faculty, not the other.

Keenness of wit—Peregrini keeps nervously redefining it—is a "happy discovery of the means to join figuratively diverse things with wonderful fitness in one word" (46), a statement that might easily at this period define the imagination or fancy. Such a divorce of "rational," scientific discourse from the rhetorical or figurative, is symptomatic of seventeenth-century thinking about language from Bacon forward, but we should remember that Tesauro, Peregrini, and Pallavicino all base their distinctions in Aristotle's contrast of the syllogism with the enthymeme.[26] Peregrini's differences from Tesauro are worth noting because Peregrini wants to associate cleverness with what he calls beauty and, furthermore, proposes that its appreciation is the task of a special faculty in the mind.

If this faculty, common to both artificer and audience, resembles the imagination, it is also something more than simply a power of finding and responding to resemblances. It must also startle and surprise the audience with the rarity or novelty of its creations, and because the aptitude of the

26. Cf. *Rhetoric* I.ii.8–9; see also the *Prior Analytics* II.23, and the *Posterior Analytics* I.1.

audience leans to admiring the skill of the artificer, that skill will exert itself in producing appearances: "It follows, then, that this admired cleverness is governed much more by appearances than by reality: for its function is to delight and to make itself admired in the presence of the listeners. But to be graceful and wonderful, it has no need necessarily of reality; indeed the wonderful is so much more the wonderful as it has more of appearance and less of substance" (46).

This is not an easy passage. Is Peregrini saying that the witty speaker is a fashioner of illusions, employing the Platonic concept of appearance as a deceptive surface that we take for reality? Or is appearance simply a term including surfaces deliberately and transparently fictive, appealing primarily to vision and pleasing by the quality of their arrangement? In his remarks immediately following those just quoted, he insists that the apparent has to have the support of reality; otherwise, it will lack rarity of arrangement: the openly "sophistic" will be "affected, childish, base, but never ingenious" (46), an admission that the consciousness of the audience is as much a force in determining *acutezza* as the cleverness of the author.

The audience's awareness is a consciousness of the difference between the "communale" and the rare and unusual. As Peregrini remarks, "And even if arrangement by itself is a great deal, it will often also have a rarity . . . , for the rare to our way of thinking is not only perfect, but also at a distance from the common phantasy" (45). Though such distancing is not required for clarity or coherence, its importance is to declare what he calls the "generating wit of clever speech." It is this that concentrates and governs the pleasure of the listeners. Just as our bodily eyes see nothing that is not put before them, so our inward wit, "the eye of the soul," is dependent for its experience of beauty on the powers of arrangement of the speaker, and the more uncommon those powers, the greater the listener's admiration (49). What pleases us is not just a harmonious whole, but the subtlety of the structuring power of the speaker, of his or her management of complex arrangements. Not only do we measure the gap between the arbitrary figurative reasoning of the enthymeme and the unalterable and necessary order of the syllogism, we also are able to distinguish the quality of urbane utterance from the casual, commonplace, or simply denotative. It is as if the power of fashioning things that are not expresses our independence of forces that might otherwise manage us.

Like Tesauro, Peregrini locates the "excess" of delight in novelty, but not just novelty in general or in diction; rather, it is a rarity of formal arrangement. This he distinguishes quite explicitly from the effects of sensory images. "When speech is very sensate and strong, the movement [it produces] leaves no room for wonder" (51). For both speaker and listener the faculty involved is not just the sensory imagination, although it seems plain that in calling wit the eye of the soul he has moved no very great distance from the concept of the imagination commonly held in the Renaissance—a power of inward reproduction of sensory, and primarily visual, images and a power also of combining them into new wholes. For baroque rhetoricians that faculty has as its main work the piecing together of complex verbal statements perceptibly different, "alienated" even, from an understood norm of common everyday speech. The listener's or reader's wit, then, is not a capacity for emotional response, but for perception, and if he is persuaded, we might add, it is unlikely that he is persuaded to some form of action or moral judgment but instead brought to appreciate the appropriateness and pleasantness and cleverness of an arrangement of words.

In this respect Peregrini is careful to insist on a very precise understanding of his meaning. "We know," he says, "that the power of the mean term in making a brilliant arrangement depends not only upon its own quality but also upon that of the extreme terms or things which it joins together." But the effect comes from the joining, not from the objects themselves. Furthermore, this is not simply a matter of verbal dexterity, but an arrangement involving both things and words, an enthymemic structuring. Peregrini's example shows the degree of complexity he has in mind. He repeats Martial's quip about a modest matron who went to the baths of Baia and returned a changed woman: "Penelope venerat, abiit Helene."[27] Here is his comment:

> The joining of the words Penelope and Helen, because it is applied to things alien to their native significance, is artificial. Nor is it only of words and things, but of things and things, because he links Penelope and Helen to the woman in question. . . . It is an enthymeme because it joins two things by means of a third. In addition the enthymeme is double. One is in saying she arrived Penelope, and in this she is linked to Penelope and the mean term is their common modesty. The other is in the statement that Helen left, and the mean term is their common immodesty. From this I consider that to produce an admirable cleverness one of the above connections is not

27. Martial, *Epigrams* I.62.6: "Penelope when she left, Helen when she returned."

enough, for in each one considered in itself the mean term as well as the extremes are such as would occur to anyone of average knowledge. But the addition of the second [enthymeme] is what makes the rarity and, separating it from what might occur to many people, makes evident that particular adroitness of wit, and as a result produces admirable cleverness. (55–56)

The reason we admire such things is all too simple: "our nature is friendly to novelty" (57). Like Tesauro, Peregrini has little more to add in explanation of audience pleasure. He explains the appeal of jokes as follows: though laughter requires a certain detachment from objects of novelty or beauty, it does not always depend upon our sense of superiority, "for at other times we see that laughter occurs through something like a gentle touching of the mind by an object that is agreeable and, so to speak, tickling" (86). Such effects are partly a matter of degree, for great misfortunes produce compassion. Rather than describe affect more precisely, he introduces the issue of intensity of response to the marvelous, but his language is more suggestive than descriptive. The power of wit "shows itself of such a quality that the effect of the marvelous can be quite weighty, and the mind will be, so to speak, not tickled but profoundly surprised and, it might also be said, softly deafened. At that point the mind is not open to laughter but sweetly loses itself in delight at the marvelous" (93). All these remarks suggest that the habit of accounting for affect almost totally by the nature of its object is extremely difficult to get beyond. Form completely dictates response, and the audience brings little more than general, normative faculties to the aesthetic system.

The final item of interest in Peregrini's theory is his discussion of the poetic lie. Although the lie is not quite a synonym for rarity, almost all the five forms he lists might be so construed. All exhibit some departure from natural meaning or arrangement. They are (1) *l'inopinato* (the incredible), (2) *l'ingannevole* (the false), (3) *il concerto* ("the rare enthymemic linking of two or more things mutually in series"), (4) *imitatione* (*prosopopeia*, or personification), and (5) *l'entimemo* (the express or tacit enthymeme) (102–4). The figures Peregrini groups in the first two categories depend for their effect on not being literally believed. The anonymous epigram, "Sed tamen Nymphe cavete quia Cupido pulcher est, / Totus est in armis idem, quando nudus amor est" ["But yet be on your guard, young lady, for Cupid is beautiful, / And love is totally armed when naked"] (107) illustrates this point, and figures of falsehood "are speech in which the speaker uses an artificial form of talking so that he seems to be signifying one thing, but in reality signifies another" (109–10). Such figures depend for their effect on a strong sense of the real or verisimilar in the audience, and it is this dimension of his thought that has caused Peregrini to be called moderate. His sense of a mimetic norm from which figured discourse departs is more explicit than Tesauro's.

The figure *imitatione* "forms an image of a true thing which is, then, true as an image but false as a thing. This occurs in speech that contains a verisimilar untruth, but figured in such a way that the shrewd wit is not deceived" (122). Such figures have what Peregrini calls "an artificial image of the true, but they are not true. When they are true, poetry is written easily quite without the lightning flash of cleverness." Therefore, the most graceful figures are those in which artifice links the imitative with the natural. They are most pleasant "because they join the imitative figure with the natural possibility and achieve a more lively depiction of the object, while the naturalness retains a strong likeness" (124).

Liveliness also characterizes the figure he calls *fintione* (a form of *prosopopeia*). It is an open lie "but is so suited to the truth that it is gazed at with delight. It is thus different from irony, which means the opposite of what it says, from the concealed lie, which intends to deceive, and from the sophistic syllogism, whose end is to confuse the intellect. It is quite like painting which does not intend to give the understanding an appearance as reality, but only to form it in such excellence as to make you marvel. The artificial open fiction does the same. It does not seek to be believed as having contained a truth; it pretends only to be praised for having depicted a very lively semblance" (141). If Peregrini seems here to revert to an earlier mode of criticism and to prefer verisimilitude, he nevertheless has his eye fixed on that quality for reasons of his own. The appeal is to aesthetic judgment, to a kind of connoisseurship in the audience separate both from a taste for truth or fact and from an appetite for emotive satisfaction.

Pallavicino

Sforza Pallavicino, though less ambitious than Tesauro in his treatment of figurative utterance, is more comprehensive in his attention to style, more prone to acknowledge generic contexts for types of discourse, and more steadily alert to questions of affective impact. More obviously than his companions he enlarges his account of reception into something approaching a system. His interest in affect and its attendant psychology is especially evident in his earliest work, a large treatise on moral philosophy entitled *Del bene* (1644), and it is continued in his work on rhetorical theory, *Considerazioni sopra l'arte dello stile e del dialogo* (1644).[28] Although there is in the latter a modification of what one modern critic thinks of as his hedonistic poetic theory,[29] we can accept both works as offering a substantial account of the interplay of certain modes of style and the affective psychology of the audience. Where Tesauro and Peregrini neglect the emotional in favor of the witty, Pallavicino's supposes something approaching a narrative of reception, a theory of special responses determined both by formal properties and particular psychological disposition. This aspect of his theory makes him perhaps the most interesting of the three.

Del bene, a dialogue in which Pallavicino's mouthpiece is named "Querengo" and his interlocutor the "Saracen," openly classifies poetry and fine arts as forms of recreation, rather than as modes of knowledge. The classification is significant, first of all because Pallavicino identifies the recreative as independent of any other type of response. The recreative response he labels *prima apprensione,* the initial experience of the senses and imagination. First apprehension is spontaneous, immediate, unreflective, and involuntary. It is the earliest stage of perception and does not seem to involve any contextual decision about the object; that is, we do not at this level of awareness decide that the object is true or false, good or bad, useful or vain. Here is Pallavicino's definition: "The first . . . of these three modes is called 'first apprehension,' because it takes, as it were, the object in its hands without even certifying it as true or condemning it as false, as when we read the narratives of Virgil or Homer uncertain whether they deal with history or are created by invention and so we render no judgment of truth or falsehood" (*Del bene* III.49). The second apprehension is judgment, and the third is what he calls "discourse," a mode of cognition in which knowledge of a distant object is mediated by something closer to hand.

---

28. The revised edition, published in 1662, is called *Trattato dello stile, e del dialogo*. The usual abbreviation, which I shall use, is *Dello stile*. My quotations are from the revised edition but the references are to chapter and numbered paragraph, which are common to all editions. My quotations of *Del bene* are from the 1644 edition, and here also I refer to book and chapter.

29. Franco Croce, *Tre momenti*, 180–83. According to Croce *Dello stile* gives some attention to the instructive end of poetry, with the result that Pallavicino has rather awkwardly to acknowledge two modes of art, one recreative and the other didactic.

Second apprehension establishes the nature of an object on the basis of its appearance in the mind or on the basis of previous experience. The simple judgments of second apprehension, somewhat distant cousins to Locke's "simple ideas," are few in number but fertile in offspring and become the agency for understanding those more distant. According to Pallavicino, "Self-evident and indefinable concepts are those that come under the immediate experience of the intellect. For example, warmth and whiteness cannot be discussed with more manifest words . . . and such names are imposed on any objects we learn about by experience" (II.7). Included in this category are certain kinds of internal affect, such as anger or sadness. When we try to define them, we are not clarifying our knowledge of them, but instead adding new contexts to their nature. The occasion for these observations is a discussion of the origins of language, and while there seems to be some connection between these indefinable concepts and first apprehension, they cannot be exactly equivalent, since the former seem to involve some decision about their place in our experience. First apprehension is, to repeat, a stage of consciousness prior to the fashioning of any such decision.

On a scale of value, first apprehension is the least worthy, but in our dealings with the world of concrete detail it is the source of no little enjoyment and is the mode of perception Pallavicino believes represented by poetry, something we enjoy entirely for itself:

> Do we not see it in the storytelling of the poets? Every age, sex, and condition of mortals delights in being bewitched by fables and captured by the stage. And this does not happen because they consider to be true those prodigious encounters which have been so persuasive to many learned men. Just ask those who suffer hunger, heat, and crowds to hear a tragedy, or those who rob their eyes of sleep to give them to the curiosities of the romance. Just ask, I say, if anyone of them believes that the characters who speak . . . are Belisarius or Suliman afflicted with calamities? . . . Who doubts that they would answer no?(III.49)

Although we may be willing to concede that poetry or the plastic arts or music do involve a form of initially crude, sensory perception in which we lose ourselves, Pallavicino has already let his account of our experience of the arts drift into the category of judgment. The very ability to understand right away that a story in a book, the characters in a stage play, or a statue are mimetic representations and not real people argues that first apprehension has to involve some mode of contextualizing. Being aware that fictions are not real is different from not knowing or caring whether they are real or not. Furthermore, there are obvious difficulties in Pallavicino's attempt to equate the affective consequences of a work of art with involuntary perceptions, which is what he seems to be attempting. In *Dello stile*, as we shall see, he attempts to resolve this difficulty. But here he ignores the problem and proceeds to develop the thesis that poetry touches our capacity to respond to appearances:

> Above all the unique task of the poetic fable is to adorn our intellect with images or, I mean to say, with apprehensions that are sumptuous, new, marvelous, and splendid. And this has been judged such a great benefit to the human race that it has chosen to reward poets with a glory greater than all the other professions. . . . You see with what price the world has enriched those first lovely apprehensions, though they contain no knowledge and manifest no truth. (*Del bene*, III.49)

Once again Pallavicino has touched on confusion, for it is not clear whether the terms "sumptuous, new, marvelous, and splendid" are simply the critic's attempt to explain why we respond positively or are renderings of our consciousness of art. If the latter, then the boundaries of first apprehension have been trespassed a second time. The point Pallavicino is after, however, is this: the poet may invent fables or try to imitate the actual, but the reader's motive in approaching poetry is not to judge its truth or falsehood, its status as fiction or as history. Rather, what happens to the reader or spectator must be understood as a kind of visual or aural experience both prior to and independent of such judgments. There is some resemblance between Pallavicino's theory and the concepts of perception and semiotics developed in the early eighteenth century by the German aestheticians in which aesthetic perception is conceived of as an early stage in the linear movement from sensation to the possession of clear and distinct ideas. Pallavicino's notions are not so elaborate as the later formulations, and it is unlikely that the Germans drew on him at all.[30] Interestingly,

---

30. I discuss these matters briefly in my fifth chapter, "The Irregular Fancy of the World," below. See also the first two chapters in David Wellbery's *Lessing's* Laocoon: *Semiotics and Aesthetics in the Age of Reason* (Cambridge: Cambridge University Press, 1984).

however, both systems are based on an effort to understand the affective and cognitive as mental functions that are mutually exclusive. A passionate reaction prevents the deliberateness of reasoned judgment, and the process of rational examination inhibits or weakens emotional response.

Pallavicino's position has to be defended against an objection made by the Saracen. He wants to know why poets produce a verisimilar fable if they do not wish it to be taken for the truth, a position like that of Socrates in the *Republic*. Querengo's reply is to point out that the images in a painting, however accurate, are never mistaken for the real thing. "The reason," he explains, "why poetry and painting are accurate imitators of the true is quite otherwise; such imitations dominate the feelings. The more lively the cognition, the more perfect it is and the more delightful and striking to the appetite" (ibid.).

The question of verisimilitude is of course commonplace, but Pallavicino has to deal with it, since the audience, on the one hand, demands the marvelous or unusual for its delight and, on the other, naturally enjoys and requires detailed and concrete imitations. His reasoning is unorthodox. The common answers to the question "Why imitation?" are those provided by Aristotle: we naturally enjoy imitations, and we require verisimilitude (another term for one kind of probability) to make whatever is mimetically represented credible. Pallavicino turns the issue into a discussion of vividness, rather than accuracy, and this leads him to a distinction between sensation and judgment. We should notice, also, that unlike Tesauro, Pallavicino does not subordinate emotion in dealing with audience response.

Another element in his discussion of liveliness is the way in which he treats the reader's capacity to recognize a work of art as a work of art, in other words, his ability not to confuse art and reality. In *Del bene* he uses this point to dismiss Plato's invective against imitation:

> Imitation through images does not try to create another and identical object. . . . It intends, therefore, to produce by its work some sensible effect (and especially the more prominent, such as those which are apparent to sight) which is likely to be previously experienced only in the thing imitated. When it happens that the same effects are encountered elsewhere, at once it awakens in the imagination the recollection of that sole occurrence in which it was ordinarily found, and of the other properties usually experienced in it. In this same manner the color of that rose which I see there in the distance makes me recall the odor which I do not now smell, but

which I did smell at another time, when an object of such a color is placed before my nostrils. (II. 29)

These are among the earliest comments I know suggesting that the previous experience of the reader may influence the nature of his response. The conventional notion in the Renaissance and earlier is that the faculties of the soul, its natural powers of apprehension and feeling, are passively moved or impressed by whatever strikes the senses. Moreover, Pallavicino notices that response is not a mirroring of individual senses. One does not require an image of smell in the text to remember the smell of roses. Whatever evokes the cause of the odor evokes also the memory of it. Pleasure is thus not simply a function of the contact between perceiving faculty and object or its representation but may be a form of recovery or reexperiencing which does not require the presence of the actual object but just the word or image that in our memories is the vestige of that original experience. "Now," he says later, "the greater the likeness in all the most minute particulars between the poetic fable or the painted figure and the actual object experienced at another time by him who hears the one or views the other, the greater the efficacy with which it arouses those mobile images which lie dormant in the several chambers of the memory. And from this results the most lively apprehension and the most vivid passion. But the arousing of this [affect] does not require, as you suppose, that one believe in the object as true" (III.50).

These remarks, especially the last sentence, would seem to shift attention to the reader's or spectator's experience as governing the quality and intensity of response, but Pallavicino still seems to implicate the artist, offering a motive for fidelity of detail rather different from a commitment to truth. The silent reasoning seems to be this: whatever you depict, do so as exactly as possible, not so your audience will recognize it as objectively true, but so that their own previous experience may be recalled most intensely. Or to put it another way, the work of art as an imitation becomes the occasion for the reader's experience as an imitation, not of the work of art, but of some previous experience of his own. Pallavicino shifts attention from the process of art to the process of consciousness of art.

That something of this sort may have been in Pallavicino's mind is indicated by a passage from *Dello stile* which deals with the reader's capacity to identify what is before him: "Imitation is nothing other than the forming of a work which, although distinct from its subject, is nevertheless dressed in many properties that usually particularly belong to that subject, so that the resemblance instantly draws the intellect into a recollection of the imitated thing. So recalling it for that reason, he is drawn by such a recollection to observe that this [imitation] occurs by those accidents which he recognizes especially as common to both subjects" (III.30). Pallavicino has not, it should be said, established any sort of theory of association, for he does not speculate about the way in which we acquire the mental habits that allow us to recognize the connection between original and imitation, but this unusual comment is on the threshold of that sort of psychological speculation.

Verbal form, in the guise of the familiar contest between the verisimilar and the marvelous, is still an issue of consequence. Tesauro and Peregrini emphasize the marvelous generated by wit, together with its capacity to generate novelty and surprise. In their universe the verisimilar is the sense of restraint that prevents the maker of conceits from going too far and appearing too baldly artificial or contrived. Pallavicino is more sensitive to the natural opposition between the verisimilar and the marvelous and sees them as competitors for the same ground in claiming responsibility for the pleasure of the audience. In *Del bene*, as we have just seen, imitation is a process that originates in and makes its appeal to our experience, and in addition it "means to produce by one's effort some sensible effects (and especially the most conspicuous, which are the appearances produced by sight) likely to be experienced only in the thing imitated" (II.29). The outward appearance is what convinces, and so must be accurate. The painter's imitation is the most accurate, for he "makes a work which produces a like appearance in the spectator" (ibid.). Yet it is not accuracy that is the attraction but liveliness, and liveliness is for Pallavicino the whole point of verisimilitude. As he notes later (II.38), it is not the object but our consciousness of it that pleases.

This is possible because imitation is not total reproduction; instead it is selective and aimed at the feelings, not the judgment. Liveliness is a form of intensity, and intensity dictates close resemblance in some but not all details. The greater the reliance on such details, "with so much the greater efficacy will it give rise to those moving likenesses which lie scattered in the various chambers of our memory. And from these come both a more lively apprehension and a more fervid emotion" (III.50). In quoting this assertion a second time I wish to emphasize that what Pallavicino is talking about is that quality of style that comprehends both *energeia* (a sense of living movement) and *enargeia* (a sense of visual presence.) They can be understood to encourage a kind of knowledge, a bringing into close proximity of objects or concepts that might otherwise be remote or indistinct. But in this crucial chapter of *Del bene* Pallavicino chooses to fasten on their affective power—"a more lively apprehension and a more fervid emotion." They give the speaker considerable power and authority: "first for himself and then for others he sets [the object] before the eyes so plainly that he does not narrate, but shows, and thus by being alight himself, he inflames the listener."[31] Such language and its effects amount to a kind of reality, but Pallavicino quickly reaches the point at which verisimilitude diverges from accurate copy, which is the special concern of history. Unlike history, poetry, "whose end is to make us vividly imagine the marvelous," properly employs "those minute representations of which the narrative yields more than enough and which are like the truth." But "although fiction is an imitation of the true, the expression of fiction is not an imitation of the expression of the true" (III.51). Verisimilar in detail, poetry produces wholes that are marvelous. And finally,

> Poetry intends the apprehension of that which is delightful, and delight in apprehension comes from their liveliness and the splendor of the colors in which they are depicted. Hence, poetry is not the inventor of events that might be true and useful to know, but feigns those things which happen to be false and enjoyable to imagine. And he labors to place them before the sight, designing them to the life with minute details and coloring them with the ultramarine tincture of metaphors, similes, personifications, amplifications, and other very expressive and magnificent figures. And perhaps this obviousness or *enargeia* of representation, and that detailing, which is so much debated, is characteristic of the poet and common to every individual poem. (III.51).

Verisimilitude is, therefore, just one of the means to make the marvelous

---

31. Pallavicino echoes Horace and especially Quintilian, who discourses elaborately on the orator's obligation to feel in himself the emotions he seeks to kindle in the audience. "But how," he asks, "are we to generate these emotions in ourselves, since emotion is not in our own power? . . . There are certain experiences which the Greeks call *phantasiai* and the Romans *visiones*, whereby things absent are presented to our imagination with such extreme vividness that they seem actually to be before our very eyes" (*Institutio Oratorio*, VI.ii.26). *Enargeia* is effected by elaborating circumstantial detail, and presumably it is the ability to evoke the concrete that enables the orator to put himself in the grip of emotion. Quintilian urges orators to emulate actors: "I have seen actors, both in tragedy and comedy, leave the theatre still drowned in tears after concluding the performance of some moving role" (VI.ii.35). Pallavicino has the actor continuing offstage to feel the "boiling of the aroused passions" (III.50). For Diderot's quite contrary theory of theatrical emotion, see chapter 6, pages 200–205, below.

present to the mind. This particular juxtaposition of the two terms has led a number of critics to see baroque style as a form of "illusionism,"[32] and Pallavicino seems to confirm this judgment a few pages later where he notes that dreams may be insubstantial while their vividness leaves an intense reaction in the dreamer which has nothing at all to do with judgment. As I have indicated, among the more important consequences of the connections he makes here between vividness and affect is precisely the notion that affective reaction is distinct from thought or judgment. If the reader, like the dreamer, is led by "such a vision or vigorous apprehension to suppose it present by an act of judgment, nevertheless the taste for beauty insofar as it is beauty does not arise from judgments so made but from that seeing or lively apprehension which stays with us enhanced by the deception of belief" (III.51). The argument here is that the illusion of presence is necessary so that aesthetic response, "the taste for beauty," occurs spontaneously when the object is close at hand. This was to become a much discussed issue in the eighteenth century.

Pallavicino senses that to assign the experience of art to a process of rational judgment is to empty it of affect, and in so doing he makes us aware of a problem Tesauro, in his enthusiasm for the intellectuality of wit and our response to it, largely ignored. In proposing a radical distinction between perception and judgment and in assigning aesthetic experience to perception, he separates art from the cluster of motives and purposes historically and customarily attached to it. In this formulation there is for the reader or viewer a self-sufficient pleasure in the contemplation of beauty, and although Pallavicino does not develop the implications of what he has said, and does not at all address the question of variations in taste, he anticipates quite markedly later theoretical efforts to establish a discrete type of aesthetic experience uncorrupted by interest or ulterior motive, as well as the attendant concept of a special faculty of aesthetic perception.

Pallavicino's next book, *Dello stile*, examines literature and art in rhetorical and generic contexts. His attention is thus more obviously drawn to matters of form and to questions of the propriety of stylistic ornament in historical and scientific, as well as literary texts. Each discipline, he notes, has a different attitude toward its audience, but whenever in any of them

---

32. See, for example, Giuseppe Conte, *La Metafora barocca*, 100. See also Jean Rousset, *La Littérature de l'âge baroque en France: Circé et le paon* (Paris: José Corti, 1983), 66–78, for a discussion of theatricality in the theater. The ancient concept of *enargeia* amounts to a claim that proximity, bringing something before the eyes, tends to encourage belief in its reality or truth, but this is less a logical than a psychological account of credibility.

there is a desire to influence the will, then ornament may be employed. Even the scientist wants to be believed and so must seek to please. Thus, Pallavicino maintains the basic, almost atavistic connection between perception and delight and makes the controlling theme of his book an examination of the interplay between two stages of affective experience, perception and judgment. Judgment is no longer out in the cold, as it were, but is now arranged as part of a sequence of responses. These observations land Pallavicino back in the camp of the classical rhetoricians, implying that affect is mainly a function of the poet's manipulation of form.

His approach can be encountered first in remarks in chapter 3, where he attempts to specify the relationship between formal utterance and pleasure. "First," he declares, "it is proper to note that we are talking here of eloquence, not as it procures belief or kindles the passions, but insofar as it is an artifice of style. In such a context the principal prerogatives are the light moving of the softer affections, amplification, splendor of utterance, variety of figures, number, sentence, similes, conceits. Wherefore eloquence, insofar as it belongs to style, is nothing other than a sweetness given to things by means of expressions with the end of rendering them more delightful to the listener. But delight is likely to proceed from hearing or touch, and this derives from interesting the reader by exciting his emotions" (chap. 3, par. 1). These may be aroused by various means, either by emphasizing an object through amplification, creating beauty by dazzling speech, using variety and liveliness of figure to amuse, employing the enticement of rhythm, and finally, as Aristotle notes in both the *Poetics* and the *Rhetoric*, offering the audience the chance to learn something new. This last occurs in three ways: providing some universal truth about human life (by means of "sentences"), demonstrating the affinity between two things normally unconnected, and the surprising appearance of some marvelous insight.

All this bounty is provided by the conceits of style, but some of them are often forbidden to disciplines such as history, especially amplification and the ways of influencing the emotions: they may "conceal the truth, which does not have so great a power to influence the judgment and incline it to believe one side over the other" (chap. 3, par. 3); yet, he continues, the figures that affect the feelings are often used. The recognition that whatever the historian or philosopher wishes to teach must be presented attractively, though without "partiality," because of the limitations of the human understanding and will, is hardly new, and Pallavicino, who otherwise seeks to give a more positive value to verbal affect, is not above using the argument to establish the general necessity of ornament.

Now, his goal is to join emotion and learning as cooperative, rather than opposed, responses. Echoing Aristotle's justification for metaphor, he asserts that the intellect naturally thirsts for knowledge, which comes in two ways, absolutely, when the mind "contemplates an object as it is in itself" (chap. 7, par. 1) and comparatively, through differences, correspondences, cause and effect, proportion and disproportion. This second mode of cognition "better appeases the appetite of the intellect, in that it understands the object more exquisitely and enjoys passing from one truth to another. It is therefore a more effective instrument of knowledge. For that reason, Aristotle said that he found similitudes to be an index of a great wit. They are incredibly delightful to the reader, since delight is always more intense when many delights are brought together at the same time in one place and in one act; the reader then receives in one cognition and at one point various delights from various known truths. And together with the marvelous (which only adds to the delight) he is made to perceive a certain unity among things which at first seemed to have no exact correspondence" (ibid.). The achievement of the verbal artist is therefore double: not only does he reconcile disparate objects in the embrace of conceit but also makes it possible for clarity or perspicuity to dwell side by side with feeling or "affection" undamaged in the reader's mind.

What Pallavicino argues in *Dello stile* is that the complexity of the contemplated object guarantees a complexity of pleasurable response, and behind his distinguishing between the simple and complex object is an implied distinction between nature (the realm of the simple object) and artifice (the object whose complexity is dictated by the artificer). At this point his position is close to that of Tesauro, even though he never subordinates emotive response. Pallavicino thus locates delight in a form of structural coincidence which is perceived as artificial and unnatural. However, he does not abandon his concept of "first apprehension," the spontaneous and unreflective response of the mind to sources of pleasure. Rather in chapter 5 he elaborates two stages of aesthetic experience. The first stage he explains in terms of metrics, where the appropriate mixture of movement and repose touches just the right sense of balance in the sense organ. But there is a greater pleasure that comes from reflection, a pleasure that "the intellect secretly takes in that uniform and well-ordered variety it discerns in the object" (chap. 5, par. 3). This reflective consciousness of the object amounts to a judgment of structure. Pallavicino thinks it is exemplified by our delight in musical order or in rhyme, and he separates it from our more basic response to tone of voice in singing. Presumably, that response is to a simple rather than to a complex object. Reflection amounts to an "innate perspicacity in perceiving the art of the proportion of correspondences. And it is at its highest with discourse that offers some novel gain in truth, as Aristotle observes divinely of the delight occasioned by antithesis" (chap. 5, par. 4).[33]

Metaphor, the "queen" of all the figures, the predication of something that is not, is also complex, the naming of a thing by something other than itself, and because the joining of unlike things is a form of work, as well as a mode of brevity and condensation, it exhibits a kind of energy. For this reason it is suited to passionate expression and is thus often found in tragedy. In discussing the comparative mode of knowing or understanding to which metaphor and simile cater, Pallavicino talks of it as an appetite or need. The artifices of the conceited style not only produce knowledge, they also generate life and movement, offering a rather special pleasure to the audience: "This occurs when the similarity is such that by means of things known and sensible they are made to have a lively concept of an insensible truth previously unknown to the perceiver; or when by analogy to an effect familiar in our experience we are brought to notice a truth that before would have seemed incredible" (chap. 7, par. 1). Although he discusses similes as a form of truth (ibid.), he is really interested in truth as a source of delight, not as certainty or conviction. This bias prepares us for the terms on which he allows the poet greater license than the orator or philosopher in the use of figures.

The poet, he maintains, has as an objective the "delight of readers by exciting in them the lively apprehension of noble and remarkable objects" (chap. 9, par. 10) and realizes this aim largely by means of similes.[34] The poetic metaphor is chiefly responsible for surprise. Since surprise is bound up with the marvelous, we must pay close attention to it as an element in Pallavicino's aesthetic psychology: it separates the poet definitively from the orator or philosopher. (Tesauro, in contrast, pays little attention to such distinctions, placing all artificial discourse and its effects more or less on the same level.)[35] The surprise the poet practices is a kind of ambush, for as a

33. Cf. *Rhetoric* III.x.5
34. By way of illustration he mentions a simile of Virgil's about the tossing and turning of Aeneas's mind being like a vase of water with the rays of the sun or moon striking it (*Aeneid* 8.30–34).
35. Once again the *Aeneid* (4.130ff.) is the source of example: Aeneas, dressed for the hunt,

type of experience the marvelous amounts to our being surprised by something we had not previously known, not simply being treated to an unexpected manner of expression. As Pallavicino points out, the greater our ignorance or the more surely something is contrary to what we had believed, the more marvelous it is and the more we take pleasure in having learned what was until that moment remote and unanticipated (chap. 10, par. 2). This way of dealing with the marvelous balances the emphasis on subject matter or theme with the mode of presentation and the conditions of reception. As he says, "that which we call the *conceit* gets its value from the wounding of the soul of the listener with some particular marvel" (chap. 10, par. 4). In this he differs from Peregrini, who lists beauty as one of the conditions of the marvelous and of conceits. For Pallavicino the ridiculous is a conceit: "The sight and the fancy, which is close to sight in name and in nature, and not the intellect, has the task of being delighted by beauty. Hence that which is unpleasant to see but agreeable to know. In sum, as I have shown in another book, although the intellect takes pleasure in contemplating the beautiful according to the simple operation of apprehension, nevertheless according to that nobler and more delightful act of judgment is charmed only by what is true. Its pleasure is greater as there is more of the true, or the universal, or the necessary" (ibid.).

Pallavicino's effort to discriminate between the beautiful and the marvelous and likewise between the mental operations involved in registering those qualities persists throughout *Dello stile* and constitutes the heart of his theory, which is for its time a substantial achievement. Though it is doubtful that Addison knew Pallavicino's work, his concept of the difference between the reader's or spectator's imagination and judgment is not unlike it. Moreover, Pallavicino's method of approaching a theory of style is grounded in an effort to be precise in examining the nature of response. It is such an examination, he implies, that will explain the workings of various forms of artificial discourse. And we should note that like his companions, Peregrini and Tesauro, the kinds of pleasure he is interested in discussing are all derived from artifice. On these grounds he gives his attention to imitation and the verisimilar only as they serve to make the marvelous acceptable or credible. As to the ancient topic of poetic instruction, Pallavicino is quite

---

resembles Apollo. The poet's aim, according to Pallavicino, is to fashion more lovely and remarkable conceits from the events he narrates, rather than to clarify. Certainly this simile would seem to serve that purpose, since the only likeness of Apollo would itself be an artistic representation.

clear. He notes that it is not the ignorance and error of men that is the target of poetry, but their pleasure, and "not whatever delights them, obviously, but that which they derive from conversations or writings where marvelous things are discovered by the author" (chap. 30, par. 15). Though truth may offer a higher sort of pleasure to the reflecting mind, this is only so in the context of artifice, as the end result of a conceit.

Pallavicino, for all his attention to the audience, never forgets that it is an audience not for what is natural but for what is fashioned and created; the poet, he says in paragraph 15, is both imitator and inventor, and even as imitator he puts into words things taken from an entirely different medium. Even so, his attention to reflection and judgment edges thinking about affect into territory that later theorists, hostile as they were to the baroque as they knew it, claimed as their own. The conviction that the baroque aesthetic was even more artificial than its apologists claimed persuaded neoclassical critics such as Bouhours, Dryden, and Addison to their one-sided but generally successful repudiation of those who championed the ornamental styles of the late Renaissance.

2 "Contre le Baroque"

Bouhours and Boileau

Il n'y a pas de doute, c'est bien contre le Baroque que les artistes classiques se définissent.
—*Jean Rousset,* La Littérature de l'âge baroque en France

There is no Knowledge of Things conveyed by Men's Words, when their Ideas *agree not to the Reality of Things.*
—*John Locke,* An Essay Concerning Human Understanding, III.x.25

The literary audience, according to baroque theory, responds to ornament and evident artifice and admires artists whose ingenious conceits and clever management of verbal surfaces continue to surprise and amaze. By such means artists put themselves—insofar as they exist in the ornaments they devise—between reality and the audience, and what the audience beholds is either the creation of the artist or the reality expressed through that creation so that it is not itself, so to speak. The motive for this indirection is to be found in our impatience and our boredom, in our need for entertainment and diversion.

To successors, the baroque writer's language was a betrayal of language, and they failed to notice how fundamentally they shared with the rhetorical critics examined in the previous chapter a series of basic interests about art, most prominently the value of art as essentially, and in some cases even totally, pleasurable, and the belief in two modes of language, each assigned to aspects of mental activity rather crudely distinguished as thought and feeling. The reaction against the baroque interest in style tended to obscure whatever common ground we can discern today. That reaction, a disapproval of an open avowal of style as artifice, leveled the accusation that earlier writers neglected their duty to reflect truth. This often amounted to a charge that poets (it was usually poets whose work was at issue) interposed themselves between the reader and whatever general human experience they sought to address, and we may therefore understand that what neoclassical critics and theorists were urging was a different sense of what would please. This in turn meant a different sense of language, not only as style, but as a reflection of the poet, even of his moral character.

It is with these general points of difference in mind that I wish to look at some documents conventionally associated with French classicism in the later seventeenth century. The centerpieces of this arrangement are the several works of Dominique Bouhours, mainly *Les Entretiens d'Ariste et d'Eugène* (1671) and *La Manière de bien penser dans les ouvrages de l'esprit* (1687), who most fully articulates the reaction against wit and open artifice, and of Boileau, whose *Art poétique* (1674) and translation of Longinus (1674), together with the subsequent *Réflexions critiques* (1674–1711), developing Longinus's concept of the sublime, open up a discussion of language and affect opposed to the postures of baroque theory and potentially destructive of traditional rhetorical orthodoxy as well.

The way to Bouhours was prepared by writers and critics such as Guez de Balzac, Jean Chapelain, and Corneille, all of whom encouraged principles of orderly plotting, a strict, though significantly not a total, adherence to what they conceived to be classical conventions of genre, a fairly consistent verisimilitude (that is, *vraisemblance*, or probability), and, what is most crucial to their sense of the way in which a text ought to mediate between author and audience, restraint in the use of figured or artful style. At first, however, it is not against the baroque theorists that the French critics take issue, but against the classicism of the sixteenth century. One of the best known instances is Balzac's harsh treatment of Ronsard, whom he portrays as having abused his talent in random and clumsy expression. Here is the heart of the indictment: "Of naturalness, of imagination, of facility, all one could wish; but little order, little economy, no discrimination either for words or for things; an insupportable audacity for change and innovation; a prodigious license in fashioning bad words and bad expressions; in employing indifferently whatever occurs to him . . . and if one does not say absolutely that he lacks judgment, one does him a favor in being content to say that in most of his poems judgment is not the dominant part nor that which governs the rest."[1]

Balzac's requirements include many of the familiar standards of French classicism, most of which need not be explored here. What I wish to emphasize is that all the positive criteria implied in his list of Ronsard's deficiencies—a sense of order, economy of diction, evidence of careful discrimination in choosing words as well as subjects, a resistance to innovation, and that quality of mind that seems to embrace them all, judgment—are uttered arbitrarily, as absolutes, almost as metaphysical laws, and without any sense that they might form a set of principles useful to grasp the attention of the audience and serve its demands. The classical spirit defines itself in combat against principles and practices it dislikes, and although later critics both in France and England developed not only a better sense of the literary audience but also a genuine interest in the nature of its responses, the concept of firm and even ideal standards governing the judgment of both artist and audience remained.

The rhetoric of seventeenth-century classicism is negative in particular ways. Perhaps the most familiar is the call for restraint in the use of language. Judgment is more than choice or selectivity in diction; it also involves the rejection of verbal abundance. Only those ornaments appropriate to some governing principle can be tolerated in a proper work of art or in correct discourse. Thus, a powerful principle of exclusion or paring down is embedded in French classicism, even when expressed as a positive principle, as in the term *bienséance*; utterance, like the work of art as a whole, must be fashioned to conform to something outside itself, either to nature or to a social standard, as if the abundance of language threatened to darken the very objects it meant to represent. Moreover, Balzac's criticism of Ronsard is a scarcely concealed attack on the baroque cultivation of authorial ego, a reaction against the notion that the presentation of the work is a presentation of the poet's pyrotechnic skill. On these terms classical poetics amounts to a moral indictment of the exercise of the will and a vote for the disciplines of nature and convention. By extension, the poet's audience is also constrained, however often the poet or critic is urged to cater to its pleasure.

1. Jean-Louis Guez de Balzac, *Les Œuvres*, 2 vols. (Paris, 1655), 2:670 (Dissertation XXIV, "Comparaison de Ronsard, et de Malherbe").

The Jesuit Dominique Bouhours is perhaps the most patient of the theorists of his generation in cultivating the territory of style. He is also the writer who most clearly shows the ways in which the classical position seeks to distance itself from what it conceives to be the baroque point of view. This distancing occurs primarily in *La Manière de bien penser dans les ouvrages d'esprit* (1687), a lengthy set of four dialogues on style.[2] The two participants are Eudoxus (representing the classical position) and Philanthus (an apologist for baroque aesthetics). Bouhours clearly favors the views of Eudoxus, but his work fully characterizes both doctrines.

The main point at issue is not so much which of two styles to prefer as it is which attitude toward style should command the allegiance of a man of taste.[3] One attitude is the appreciation of style for the pleasure it brings; the other more soberly cultivates language as the expression of truth or nature. The opposing views reveal themselves in all sorts of ways, almost always illustrated by literary example. For instance, late in the first dialogue Eudoxus quotes an epigram of Saint-Amant to underline his disapproval of "quibbles" (*équivoques*) or puns:

> Certes l'on vit un trifle jeu;
> Quand à Paris Dame Justice
> Se mit le Palais tout en feu
> Pour avoir mangé trop d'épice.[4]

Philanthus rashly asks, "Why, can there be anything happier or prettier?" only to be told, "There can be nothing more empty or more frivolous. . . . These are only words in the Air which have no manner of Sence; it is all over false" (15). The puns that offend Eudoxus involve *palais* (i.e., both palate and palace) and a double meaning for *épice*, which is both spice and, colloquially, the gifts offered to judges by litigants. Eudoxus maintains that "what is called spice in the *Palais* has no relation to burning"; strictly speaking, it is of course true that institutional corruption did not bring on the fire; as an occasion to comment on corruption the fire is contingent but

---

2. My references are to the first English translation, entitled *The Art of Criticism: or, the Method of Making Right Judgment on Subjects of Wit and Learning* (London, 1705).

3. An earlier work of Bouhours, *Les Entretiens d'Ariste at d'Eugène* (Paris, 1671), contains a dialogue on the "Bel Esprit" or gentleman of taste.

4. "A sad sport it was / When in Paris Dame Justice / Ate too many sweeteners / And caused a Palate-ial fire"; the version is that of John Sturrock in his translation of Victor Hugo, *Notre Dame of Paris* (London: Penguin, 1978), 4.

convenient. It is not that Bouhours and his mouthpiece miss the point; rather, they prefer wit to derive more directly and evidently from some concept. Philanthus, on the other hand, enjoys the play of wit, its impulse to go beyond the actual, even its gaiety, while Eudoxus wants it only to make sense. This is made clear earlier in the dialogue when he says, "I would have all ingenious Thoughts . . . as sound as they were true: as surprising, as out of the way; in short, they were as natural as they were far from all that Lustre which has nothing in it that is not frivolous or childish" (6).

This reaction against brilliance is a conviction about what in language should command attention:

> Thoughts . . . are the images of things, as words are the images of Thoughts: and generally speaking, to think is to Form in ones self the Picture of any Object spiritual or sensible. Now Images and Pictures are true no further than they resemble; so a thought is true when it represents things faithfully; and it is false, when it makes them appear otherwise than they are in themselves. (7)

This would appear to limit correct thinking to "things," to what is outside the self but still capable of being known, and to forbid imaginative thinking. But there is, as we shall see, a major exception to this rather severe pre-Lockean confidence that language and ideas in the mind can be governed by what they signify. More immediately, Philanthus's response is that the falsity in a statement is what makes it attractive: "I can scarce persuade my self that a witty thought should always be founded on truth. . . . Nay, do we not see what strikes most in epigrams, and in other things where the wit gives all the beauty, generally turns most upon fictions, upon ambiguities, upon hyperboles, which are but so many lies?" (9).

Eudoxus argues rather obviously that fictions are not lies: poetry is exempt, up to a point, from the requirement of a strict mimetic connection between word and thought or object, and the door is thus opened to admit metaphor. Even so, a responsible poet will ground whatever is fictitious, marvelous, or fabulous in some sort of truth: "Poets ought never to destroy the Essences of things, when they would raise and adorn them" (9). That the poet, and presumably also the audience, knows the "essence of things" is taken for granted. Poetry is not, in Bouhours's dispensation, required to discover or demonstrate truth; it must simply reflect it, just as everywhere in the dramatic criticism of the seventeenth century *vraisemblance*, or probability, is not a logical proposition but a concession to what is thought to be the general experience of the audience.

Truth or nature are thus confirmed by intuition rather than argument, but they are nonetheless presented as objective and immutable standards controlling the individual fancy of the writer and reminding readers or listeners that they must attend to something more fundamental than ornament. But Eudoxus never explains how it is we are to distinguish between the ornamental grounded in nature and that which, in his words, "spoils and quite destroys it" (7), though as the debate proceeds to include quotations from Ariosto and Tasso, we may suspect that hyperbole, which for Bouhours sometimes appears to be synonymous with Italian poetry, is the sticking point. This too encourages the conclusion that the dispute is between two modes of taste, just as much as between truth and frivolity.

Such a judgment is supported by the crucial exchange on metaphor that grows out of the review of Italian hyperbole (9–10). The instance is Tasso's description of the death of Argante, "Superbi, formidabili, feroci / Gli ultimi noti fur', l'ultimi voci" ("Proud, strong, fierce were his last movements, his last words"). Philanthus maintains that Tasso's account is consistent with a heroic death: "I believe *Tasso* intended to describe *Argante* in a rage against *Tancred* . . . and so did not barely say that he dyed: but that his Fury and his Anger [in] some measure took away his faintness and made him appear vigorous." Eudoxus has already commented that "in advancing the Hero, [Tasso] destroys the man," in itself a witty exaggeration dangerously close to Bouhours's borderline. The description is, in effect, unrealistic because Argante does not faint before he dies. And when Philanthus remarks that Tasso wished to convey the intensity of Argante's rage, Eudoxus contemptuously replies that it's too bad he didn't explain himself better.

Eudoxus's inclination to the literal and prosaic thus introduces the topic of metaphor, which more than anything else focuses the dispute. Philanthus summons Macrobius, Seneca, Aristotle, and Tesauro in the cause of metaphor as entertainment:

> Not to speak of *Macrobius* and *Seneca* who call those things pleasant Sophisms, which we term strokes of Wit, and the *Italians vivezze d'ingegno*, and the Spaniards *agudezas*; Aristotle reduces almost the whole Art of thinking ingeniously to the Metaphor, which is a kind of fraud, and the Count Tesauro says, according to that Philosopher's Principles, that the subtlest and the finest Thoughts are only

figurative Enthymemes, which equally please and impose upon the understanding. (11)

Philanthus's first interest is in the affective powers of metaphor, and he summons some of the voices of baroque theory in support. Eudoxus is more interested in formal and semilogical properties. "What is figurative is not false, and Metaphors have their Truth as well as Fictions," he solemnly pronounces. But truth may be no more than a fairly obvious form of coherence, a point that Bouhours makes in an earlier work: metaphor, "being an image and painting that represents things in unusual colors, metaphorical utterances like paintings should have a form of unity, so that the different words of which they are composed will be proportionate to one another and, as it were, made for one another. Nothing is more irregular than to combine words that convey to the mind diverse or contrary ideas, for example *tempest* and *ruin, shipwreck* and *fire*."[5] In his *Entretiens d'Ariste et d'Eugène* (1671), he writes: "One should not join together figures ordinarily diverse and without any link between them, such as three birds lined up in the air like an arrow. . . . [A device] ought to be based on something real and certain, rather than chance."[6] Coherence must also serve clarity. To return to *The Art of Criticism*, Bouhours orients all figurative discourse toward its objects. Language as language is secondary: "We may say then," Eudoxus continues, "that Metaphors are like transparent veils, thro' which we see what they cover; or like the Habits of a Mask under which the Persons who are disguised are known" (12). Not only is metaphor supposed to be transparent, it must also be unequivocal in signification. We might at this point agree with Philanthus's comment that "Ambiguity and Truth can never agree according to your principles" (ibid.).

We may wonder if Bouhours hasn't in effect eliminated any reason for metaphor at all in his system, for if it is designed entirely for clarity and its

---

5. *Doutes sur la langue françoise* (Paris, 1675), 80–81. The marginal note refers to Aristotle, *Rhetoric* III.xi, a chapter largely devoted to *enargeia* and jokes, but it also repeats the concept of proportionality: "metaphors should be drawn from objects which are proper to the object, but not too obvious" (III.xi.5).

6. Amsterdam ed. (1682), 271–72. For a more detailed view of "devices" or mottos, see Pierre Le Moyne, *De l'Art des devises* (Paris, 1666). Le Moyne distances himself from Tesauro and argues that the device is based in simile, that is, in likeness or a metonymic relationship, whereas the emblem is pictorially metaphoric and requires nonfigurative language to interpret it (38–41; 161–63). The distinction is that the device characterizes an individual; we can thus tolerate a kind of figurative language that performs this function. The emblem, on the other hand, is aimed at some general truth or aphoristic wisdom and therefore must be given an interpretation or decoding if its message is to be understood.

referent is already known, isn't it superfluous and perhaps frivolous in itself, not just in its misuse? This is the dilemma confronting the dominant seventeenth-century doctrine of literary style. Classicists define their position by what today would be considered a rigid logocentrism or what could be called a pre-aesthetic doctrine that language in its basic, natural form is the application of single words to single thoughts and objects. Moreover, the assumption is that properly used these terms convey the essential nature of the thought or thing. Notice Bouhours's warning that ornament must not be allowed to "destroy the Essences of things" (9).[7] Yet fiction and metaphor (which are in Bouhours's thinking just as nearly synonymous as they are in that of Tesauro) are nevertheless finally tolerated so long as they are properly dressed for the occasion. The concession comes well into the second dialogue: metaphor "is of its nature a spring of agreeableness" (99), but later it is noted that the pleasure we take in represented things comes not from the object itself, but from our mental reflection on the resemblance (108). And there is a remarkable concession at another point when Eudoxus admits that the truth is not sufficient for ingenious thoughts: "something extraordinary must be added over and above to strike the Mind" (53). The example given on the following page, "Pale Death knocks equally at Kings' Palaces and poor Men's cottages" (instead of the less striking "Death spares no man"), is offered as sublime, though we might think it approaches the kind of grandiloquence so persistently challenged by Boileau.

In a separate dialogue, "Le je ne sais quoi," Bouhours seeks to accommodate what he variously presents as grace, charm, something known certainly without knowledge or known only by its effects, the marvelous, veiled beauties, that which astonishes or overwhelms, the inexplicability of taste, mysteries, even divine grace. Louis Marin, in discussing the theories of Boileau and Bouhours with respect to the *je ne sais quoi*, contends that "it lies on the borderline of the beautiful form, at the threshold of the undefinable aspect of beauty," and its "noun status" means

---

7. This is perhaps a distant reflection of the question that arose in the later seventeenth century over whether perceptions were of ideas in the mind, i.e., intelligible concepts of the essence of things, or merely appearances that were entirely subjective. See John W. Yolton, *Perceptual Acquaintance from Descartes to Reid* (Minneapolis: University of Minnesota Press, 1984), 52–55. Bouhours's concern seems to be that ornament relate to real properties in the objects it is applied to, that there be a logical connection of some kind between figure and that which it ornaments.

that it can retain the "questioning force of the sublime"[8] It admits the extraordinary into ordinary sentient life and into art, both relieving and making equivocal the neoclassical orthodoxy we have just examined. Especially what I would want to call attention to is Bouhours's way of accommodating the *je ne sais quoi*. It is known and not known, "much easier to feel than to know," yet "incomprehensible and inexplicable."[9] In other words, it provides a certainty of presence without yielding to analysis or explanation and is thus a quality in all sorts of experiences. Its intuited certainty means that from the point of view of Bouhours it does not threaten the doctrine of utter lucidity he urges, though it does open the way to a less constrained notion of audience response.

What finally marks Bouhours and sets him off from later aestheticians such as Burke, is his fourth dialogue in *The Art of Criticism*, a caution against obscurity, an even greater fault, perhaps, than ambiguity. Philanthus, who by this time has admitted defeat, wants to know what causes obscurity. The answer, unclear thinking, is hardly a surprise. Obscurity shows itself in metaphor unrelated to idea or in too great a profusion (105). The last idea that Bouhours takes up is also quantitative: he favors understatement. The writer should "leave more to the Reader's Thoughts than we have said of them.... Giving an insight to the Reader, you may give him scope to employ his Faculties" (115). But, "Notwithstanding, remember that obscurity is very Vicious, and what appears dark to Persons of Understanding, cannot pass for Ingenuity" (116). Thus, the very terms employed here and throughout the *Art of Criticism*—"obscurity," "clearness," "insight," to mention the more obvious—argue a visual analogy for the description of the way language imposes on the mind, and this analogy is both overwhelmingly common in the seventeenth century and also, in spite of Burke's objection to it, prevalent in the eighteenth century. It is also a presentation of style that argues for what is familiar, stable, and consistent. It encourages the authority of the object, the authority of an established and shared concept of the truth that rations affect and confines it to the dimensions not of the object but of an accurate representation of the object. Insofar as Bouhours can be said to articulate one formidable aspect of French classical thinking about style, he argues that the union of word and object is not the

---

8. Louis Marin, "On the Sublime, Infinity, Je Ne Sais Quoi," *A New History of French Literature*, ed. Denis Hollier (Cambridge, Mass.: Harvard University Press, 1989), 340–44.

9. My quotations are from the selection in *The Continental Model*, ed. Elledge and Schier, 183.

beginning of the reader's response to verbal art but its entire territory and limit.[10]

This is not exactly the doctrine of Boileau, though at first such may seem to be the case. Poetic composition, as he reminds his audience in *L'Art poétique* (1674), is a difficult and perilous business. It involves a sure knowledge of one's talents and limitations and an ability to grasp what the audience will tolerate: "He cannot Write, who knows not to give o're" (I.64).[11] The dangers of abundance are legion and involve either a pride such as Ronsard's or a tendency to indulge in words badly secured with thought: "If in your loitring Verse your Sense decays, / My Patience tires, and my Attention strays" (I.143–44), and careful, correct diction must be maintained, since

> A barb'rous Phrase no Reader can approve;
> Nor Bombast, Noise, or Affectation love.
> (I.159–60)

Boileau marks certain forms of ornament as verbal display for its own sake and associates this trait not just with barbarism in diction but also with the moral failing of authors who seek attention for their art, not their subject. To make the point Boileau assumes the role of a member of an audience bored and discontented with habits of expression associated with late Renaissance verse.

Boileau would not have shared Descartes's radical sense of the surfeit of literature, especially that of the Ancients, but there is a common ground in the discovery of the vanities attendant on literature. Descartes recalls: "I thought that I had already given enough time to languages and likewise to reading the works of the ancients, both their histories and their fables . . . . But . . . one who is too curious about the practices of past ages usually remains quite ignorant about those of the present. Moreover, fables make us imagine many events as possible when they are not."[12] Too much fable, and above all a belief in its promises, affects the sense of reality.

---

10. On this point, Bouhours shares the views of Port-Royal. See Antoine Arnauld and Pierre Nicole, *La Logique, ou l'art de penser* (1662), ed. Pierre Clair and François Girbal (Paris: Librairie Philosophique J. Vrin, 2d rev. ed. 1981), I.xi. This section remarks on the ambiguity or vagueness of general terms such as "soul," "sense," and "sentiment," in a fashion similar to that which Locke was to employ.

11. The anonymous English translation appears in *The Works of Monsieur Boileau*, 2 vols. (London, 1722); for the original I quote the Pléiade ed.

12. *The Philosophical Writings of Descartes*, 1:113–14.

Poetry, according to Bacon, may delude us, "submitting the shews of things to the desires of the mind; whereas reason doth buckle and bow the mind unto the nature of things."[13] And to underscore the fairly widespread disposition in the seventeenth century to court a sense of reality that excludes all but the most restricted, simple, and unequivocal employment of language, there is Pascal's *esprit de netteté* in the appropriately concise *Esprit de la géométrie* and its companion piece, *De l'Art de persuader*, a rejection of traditional rhetoric with "all the sophisms and all the ambiguities of captious arguments."[14] Pascal sets language determined by its referent absolutely against language catering to desire, wish, or pleasure. His disposition, like that of Descartes, of Bacon, and, later in the century, of Locke, is to seek the reduction of ambiguity and uncertainty. As a poet Boileau is of course otherwise committed, but the influence of Descartes and the Port-Royal attitudes toward language, as well as their insistence on a clear, basic, "natural" understanding of certain kinds of truth, can be sensed in Boileau's very strong, and at times shrill, harping on clarity and restraint.

Yet there is in Boileau and in other classical critics in the seventeenth century a different and often opposite tendency most obviously expressed in their concern for the pleasure of the audience. It is a commonplace of the modern reading of French classicism that its partisans are at heart committed to the Horatian doctrine of literature as *utile*, by which is usually meant moral relevance. There is no poverty of remarks to cite in support of such a position, but on the whole, one finds very little attempt to spell out the usefulness of poetry in detail, whereas the attention to the ways in which the poet must seek to please is more patient and extended. Chant III of *L'Art poétique*, which examines tragedy, epic, and comedy, is a long lesson in catering to an obviously cultivated and discriminating seventeenth-century French audience. Its opening lines echo the *Poetics*:

> There's not a Monster Bred beneath the Sky
> But, well dispos'd by Art, may please the Eye:
> A curious Workman, by his Skill Divine,
> From an ill Object makes a good Design.
> Thus, to Delight us, TRAGEDY in Tears,
> Provokes for *Oedipus* our Hopes, and Fears,

---

13. *The Advancement of Learning* (London: Dent, 1973), II.iv.2.
14. Blaise Pascal, *L'Esprit de géométrie et de l'art de persuader*, ed. with commentary by B. Clerté and M. Lhoste-Navarre (Paris: Editions Pédagogie Moderne, 1979), 19, 43.

> For Parricide *Orestes* asks Relief;
> And, to encrease our Pleasure, causes Grief.

What I want to indicate here is Boileau's enthusiastic commitment to literary emotionalism, to the poet's need to hold the audience and constantly to "please and touch" them. In tragedy this amounts to the cultivation of probability, to the rapid and precise establishment of place, circumstance, character, and the direction of the plot, but in the epic the poet is encouraged to different resources:

> Thus in the endless Treasure of his Mind,
> The Poet does a Thousand Figures find,
> Around the Work his Ornaments he pours,
> And strows with lavish Hand his op'ning Flow'rs.
> (III.173–76)

Methods and styles are governed by genres, and genres are equivalent to the expectations of an audience trained to associate certain features to certain types of poem. Modes of verbal abundance are therefore appropriate to the epic. Variety, exaggeration, and embellishment are what prompt the reader's delight; judgment, tasteful discrimination, or a nice sense of the limits of style, not to mention a concern for the natural or probable, seem to have no home here. Moreover, the epic, with Boileau's approval, encourages mythology and avoids the harsh reminders of Christian machinery, in order that it may "surprise, strike, seize, and bind" (*surprend, frappe, saisit, attache*).[15] Something like rapture is the effect Boileau wants from poetry in general, as we discover from his translation of and comments on Longinus.

Jules Brody has noted that in addition to his interest in the powerful effects of poetic language, Boileau underlines its capacity in the hands of the greatest writers to create illusion: he adds in his translation of Longinus a clause "which not only stresses the power of Demosthenes' apostrophe to stir the emotions, but also points up its ability to engulf the hearer in an illusion so perfect as to blind him to the potentially disturbing fact that the orator is even trying to arouse him."[16] Boileau follows Longinus in insisting

---

15. My translation here. The eighteenth-century English text is much blander: "These are the Springs that move our Hopes and Fears" (III.188).

16. Jules Brody, *Boileau and Longinus* (Geneva: Librairie Droz, 1958), 126. The passage is as follows in the Loeb translation of Longinus: "he [Demosthenes] has filled his judges with the

that this form of affect is entirely different from persuasion, that it is one in which the listeners become so absorbed in what is happening that they are unaware of words as words, of style as style, and are momentarily convinced that they are in the presence of utter actuality. Used by a master, language thus has the power to make itself disappear. Boileau may here seem to have returned to the neoclassical commonplace of perspicuity, but the more important issue is the preemptive force of affective emotion, the listener's or reader's diversion from one kind of possible response to the experience of quite another.[17]

Yet in spite of Boileau's (and Longinus's) claim to a style in which there is little or no evidence of artifice, and in spite of the effort to insist that the sublime is primarily the result of greatness of soul and of thought, the sublime is still at this stage of its career a question of style, a use of language according to rules and, however simple, a mode of language still shaded by ornament, still a powerfully formal presence, understood as deliberately fashioned and shaped. In contrast to Bouhours, Boileau promotes a simplicity of expression yoked to abundance of figure. Much the same movement of thought reaches from an initial emphasis on perspicuity to a rather different encouragement of emotional power to be gained through figures. According to Rapin,

> Poetry demands a more clear Air, and what is less Incomprehensible. The third Quality is, that it be *Natural*, without Affectation, according to the Rules of *Decorum* and good *Sense*. *Studied Phrases*, a too *florid Style, fine Words, Terms strain'd and remote*, and all *extraordinary Expressions* are *Insupportable* to the *true Poesie*; only *Simplicity* pleases, provided it be *sustain'd* with *Greatness* and *Majesty*.

---

spirit of those who bore the brunt there [at Marathon]: he has transformed his argument into a passage of transcendent sublimity and emotion, giving it the power of conviction that lies in *so strange and startling an oath: and at the same time his words have administered to his hearers a remedy and an antidote*" (XVI.2). Boileau translates: "Il inspire à ses Juges l'esprit et les sentiments de ces illustres Morts, et, *changeant l'air naturel de la preuve en cette grande et pathétique manière d'affirmer par des sermens si extraordinaire, si nouveaux, si dignes de foi, il fait entrer dans l'âme de ces auditeurs comme une espèce de poison et d'antidote qui en chasse toutes les mauvaises impressions*" (XIV[Boileau's chapter numbering]). The phrases Brody has in mind are indicated by my italics.

17. See Marian Hobson, *The Object of Art: The Theory of Illusion in Eighteenth-Century France* (Cambridge: Cambridge University Press, 1982), 217–19. According to Hobson the illusion Boileau mentions is a kind of deceit, or in terms she uses elsewhere, "hard illusion," a state in which the audience is totally in the power of the medium and thus unconscious of any difference between art and reality.

But poetic expression must also be lofty and splendid:

> Finally, the Poet must above all things, know what *Eloquence* has of *Art* and *Method* for the use of Figures: For it is only by the Figures that he gives Force to the Passions, Lustre to the Discourses, Weight to the Reasons, and makes Delightful all he Speaks. 'Tis only by the most lively Figures of Eloquence that all the *Emotions* of the Soul become Fervent and Passionate.[18]

This earlier version of Pope's doctrine that art is nature methodized makes sense up to a point, but the figurative and the simple are still considered opposed, as we discover in Rapin's statement that "There is a particular *Rhetorick* for *Poetry*, which the *modern Poets* scarce understand at all; this Art consists in discerning very precisely what ought to be said *Figuratively* and what ought to be spoken *simply*" (II.172), a distinction that is fundamental to the tradition of rhetoric, even if it seems to serve a contemporary thesis. According to this thesis, Tasso lacked this ability and Guarini and Bonarelli have their characters speak wittily rather than naturally. Boileau, we should remember, discovered in his perennial opponent Charles Perrault an opposite fault, a persistent and pedestrian prosiness he carped at over the years in his *Réflexions* on the translation of Longinus.

Bernard Lamy proposed ideas similar to those of Boileau and Rapin. A Cartesian and a Jansenist, he had double reasons for preferring language aimed at rendering objects clearly, accurately, and simply. Yet in his *De l'Art de parler* (1675), he concedes that artifice and even ornament are necessary to convey ideas and sentiments naturally, clearly, and pleasurably. He is also aware of the problem that was to preoccupy Locke, that "Words do not give the same Idea of things that they signifie, and that to make us understand the Form of our Thoughts, we ought to use among our Terms such as represent their true lineaments, and their natural Colours, that is to say, such as awaken in the Minds of other people the same Ideas, and the same Sentiments as we have in ours."[19] That there is more to oratory, rhetoric, or poetry than accurate representation and communication does not concern him here, and he does not go into the problem that different individuals may

---

18. René Rapin, *The Whole Critical Works*, 2 vols. (London, 1706), 2:163, 166. The translation is Thomas Rymer's, first published in 1674.

19. Bernard Lamy, *The Art of Speaking: Written in French by the Monsieurs of Port-Royal*, 2d English ed. (London, 1708), 201.

understand utterly different ideas by the same word, no matter how carefully chosen. Instead, he requires of the speaker or writer a good imagination in order to appeal to the audience's need for concrete, sensory representation, and in the course of pursuing this point he runs into a difficulty he is unable to sort out. Indeed, it is not clear that he is aware that there is a difficulty.

The problem is this. Lamy insists that appropriate style must be determined by the "matter" to be articulated—an ordinary enough truism on its face—but as he develops it, it becomes evident that he is urging opposed and contradictory imperatives, that is, rules for styles that are at once natural, affectively powerful, inartificial (or seemingly so from the point of view of the audience), and yet the result of the most carefully deliberated contrivance. Consider the following:

> If the Matter it self be unworthy, if it be great only in the Imagination of the Author, his Magnificence turns to his Prejudice, and shows the weakness of his Judgment, in putting a Value upon that which is only worthy of Contempt. Figures, and Tropes, unknown to the natural order of Discourse, discover likewise the motion of the Heart; but that these Figures may be just, the Passion, of which they are the Character, ought to be reasonable. There is nothing comes nearer Folly, than to be transported without Cause; to put oneself into a heat for a thing that ought to be argu'd coolly:[20] each Motion has its Figures: Figures may enrich and imbellish a Style, but unless the Motion that causes them be laudable, the Figures cannot be worthy of Commendation. (218–19)

On the one hand, Lamy wants expression that is the accurate and appropriate manifestation of emotion, a mimetic connection between feeling and its outward show, but then, on the other hand, an emotion that is unreasonable (unmotivated? unworthy?) will not produce appropriate figures. There would seem to be a confusion of technical and moral issues.

---

20. The notion that passions should be logically, rather than probably judged, may be explained by Lamy's strict Cartesianism. See Douglas Lane Patey, *Probability and Literary Form: Philosophic Theory and Literary Practice in the Augustan Age* (Cambridge: Cambridge University Press, 1984), 64–65. Patey is discussing an educational tract, but the point is important: "Lamy's Cartesian rejection of sagacity and judgment in favor of mathematical demonstration is essentially the programme also of Arnauld, Nicole, Pascal, Malebranche, Le Clerc, and Crousaz" (65).

There is also a less evident problem. Lamy, like most of his contemporaries, expects passion, if properly communicated, to result in the audience's absorption into the text, producing a seizure or rapture that Boileau claims for the sublime and that takes place in such a way that the audience is not conscious of style and so does not make judgments about the propriety of figures. (In response to this problem Addison, for example, radically separates the "pleasures of the imagination" from those of judgment.) There is also the apparent anomaly that figures and tropes, artificial departures from "the natural order of Discourse," are nevertheless believed to have what looks suspiciously like a natural relationship to feelings. In other words, anger should give rise to one kind of trope, jealousy to another, and love to yet another, and so on. This is precisely what Lamy has in mind.[21]

Whatever his problems with coherence, Lamy exemplifies the thinking that seeks an exact and proportionate correspondence between language and its objects as the standard against which to measure forms of discourse, as if for every category of idea there could be terms that convey it unchanged from one mind to another. Much the same kind of undistorted, systematic communication is proposed for tropological language expressive of emotions.[22]

Another kind of formal problem shadows neoclassical thinking about language: the possibility of a discrepancy between the object and the words used to represent it. As I have phrased it, this is another way to approach the concept of the sublime. Boileau's several remarks appear to diminish the importance of language in relation to its object. He anticipates a line of thought in the eighteenth century—and especially in England—that sought virtually to liberate thought and feeling from their bondage to words. Boileau's *Réflexions critiques* returns again and again to Longinus's example of the sublime in Genesis: "And God said, Let there be light; and

---

21. The association of tropes and figures with the prompting of emotional reactions in the audience is traditional from the beginning of formal rhetoric. Cf. Brian Vickers's chapter, "The Expressive Function of Rhetorical Figures," *In Defence of Rhetoric* (Oxford: Clarendon Press, 1988). Vickers states categorically: "Thus from Aristotle to the end of the eighteenth century the figures and tropes were regarded mimetically, as capturing specific and clearly defined emotional states" (304–5).

22. Vickers, *In Defense of Rhetoric*, 298, cites a passage from Longinus on inversion (*hyperbaton*) which claims that people in the grip of strong emotion are apt to "lay their words and thoughts first on one tack then another, and keep altering the natural order of sequence into innumerable variations" (22.1). The rhetorician must be artful in such instances to give the illusion of nature.

there was light." His last and most extended comment in "Réflexion X" most completely articulates the point I wish to draw attention to. The essay, entitled, "Réfutation d'une dissertation de Monsieur Le Clerc contre Longin," was composed sometime between 1710 and 1711, the year of his death. It was first published in 1713.

Throughout the piece Boileau harps, sometimes at tedious length, on his belief (and up to a point that of Longinus) that sublime events or thoughts are best presented in simple language. (Jean Le Clerc and Pierre-Daniel Huet, opponents whom Boileau treats with more courtesy, had argued that the language of the Mosaic original was merely everyday conversational utterance). The sublime, he notes in a remark similar to the observations of Bouhours, "is not properly something for proof or demonstration; rather it is a marvel that seizes and strikes and makes itself felt."[23] It is not well served by grand words, elevated diction, or stately rhythms. Rather tritely, indeed, Boileau resorts to a formula, insisting on the "je ne sais quoy du sublime." But at the heart of his argument is the concept of radical disproportion between the sublime and the language used to represent it. Quoting once more from Genesis—"the Spirit of God hovered on the waters" ("Et l'Esprit de Dieu se porter sur les eaux")—he notes that the words "have something magnificent in them, and their elegant and majestic obscurity makes us imagine many things beyond what the words seem to say" (551).

Although Boileau may seem to be merely arguing for one style in preference to another, his emphasis is really on affect, on the necessity of removing or blocking the kind of language that interests the auditor in words as words, rather than in the things they are meant to convey. Auditors should neither reason nor judge; they should instead be ravished, seized, transported, in other words powerfully and completely dominated by whatever is being represented, and the best way, paradoxically, to guarantee that experience is to employ a style utterly opposite from a conventional point of view to the grandeur of the event. The logical extension of this view of style is to eliminate language altogether and make the sublime an almost totally subjective experience. For that we must wait for Addison.[24]

As I have suggested, the seventeenth-century French concept of form

---

23. The text for this essay is Nicolas Boileau Despréaux, *Oeuvres Complètes* (Paris: Gallimard, Pléiade ed., 1979), 546.

24. It is unlikely that Addison knew this essay, since his pieces on the "Pleasures of the Imagination" were written in June and July 1712. He does, however, quote from Boileau's much earlier translation of Longinus.

has its ambiguities. On the one hand, it vigorously champions an idea of literary and linguistic structure in which form responds to something prior to it, and from the point of view of the audience, more important than it. That something is variously grouped under notions of nature or idea, anticipating its appearance in language. It has a certainty and an endurance that require constant attention and reminder. Even so, there is no need to argue its existence. The effort required is, instead, one of presentation. This motive calls first for perspicuity, for language that is so far as possible a clear mirror of its object. Yet those who take this line concede that "naked" truth is often dull or uninteresting. It must occasionally be dressed in the colors of surprise or novelty (which means, usually, metaphor) but never overdressed.

Such a doctrine of form is unlikely to find much favor today, not because we have a gaudier taste for language, but because we hold to a different concept of language. The neoclassical doctrine assumes an original or primal similarity between word and thing; it also assumes the existence, even the presence, of the nonverbal thing or idea, when in fact (from our viewpoint) these exist only as functions of language. Moreover, the neoclassical view risks self-contradiction in arguing, on the one hand, for the commonsense pairing of word and thing and, on the other hand, for the rarity of the talent or "genius" required to present the object in all its colors as a natural, living, authentic thing. Much of the critical literature from Guez de Balzac to Pope and beyond is pointed at a supposed epidemic of imperfect, dull, boring, extravagant, indecorous, misdirected verbal art. In Boileau's harsh terms,

> Most Writers, mounted on a resty Muse,
> Extravagant, and Sensless Objects chuse;
> They Think they err, if in their Verse they fall
> On any Thought that's Plain, or Natural:
> Fly this Excess; and let *Italians* be
> Vain Authors of false glitt'ring Poesie.
> (*L'Art poétique* I, 39–44)

There is another ambiguity in neoclassicism's dealings with ornament. We have seen how Bouhours reacts against the purely ornamental, a position he attributes fairly enough to Tesauro and his companions. We have also seen that Boileau, when he discusses tragedy and epic, justifies formal procedures determined by the audience's need for emotional intensity and imaginative wish fulfillment. Indeed, much of his attack on Charles Perrault is an attack on realism. We have already noted that, for Boileau, tragedy, however firmly anchored in probability, becomes the occasion for abundance and intensity of feeling, and that he believes the epic lends itself to formal extravagance in a distinctly nonrealistic play of fancy. According to Gordon Pocock, this cultivation of emotion is under strict limits and is at the same time symptomatic of a broad social tension. Boileau "represents, though in pure form, the characteristic of French seventeenth-century literature which gives it its peculiar intensity: a tension between the social facade and the passion behind it, a sense of anarchy pressing against immovable discipline."[25] This condition is compellingly expressed in the structure and themes of Racinian tragedy. But on the level of language it is not quite so simple: from Boileau's point of view there are two kinds of relationship between language and the larger realities it expresses. On the one hand, in tragedy one finds language used abundantly in the service of tears, and the containing medium or control is not a doctrine or style but the theater. On the other hand, in lyric poetry or in Scripture we expect a simplicity of language linked in an asymmetrical embrace with emotionally and conceptually powerful situations. In the case of the sublime it is not emotion calling forth emotion, exactly, but rather the impression of the presence of great and powerful events, the Creation in its vastness or a chariot race in its intensity. The notion that simplicity of language matched to magnitude of event is somehow reasonable and appropriate to the general psychology of the audience—a proposition that Boileau hammered home year after year—has the result of encouraging a distrust of language as style, and of suggesting that there is a reality independent of language and prior to it that is presumably susceptible of being experienced in some other way, perhaps even logically. Yet, of course, everything Boileau says about the sublime suggests that this is not really so, that language is virtually the only approach to this reality that guarantees it a kind of independence from the author. Boileau thus seems to hesitate between restraint and abundance, between judgment and feeling, and between a desire to make language secondary and an almost unconscious sense that it is of paramount importance. At the surface of critical doctrine neoclassicism presents itself as an effort to bring the mind of the literary audience and the practice of the writer into a symmetrical match with the order of nature, but its interest in the sublime and in linguistically induced states of emotion works against this match and produces a division of critical sympathy that points even further beyond a literary theory centered in formal questions.

25. Gordon Pocock, *Boileau and the Nature of Neo-Classicism* (Cambridge: Cambridge University Press, 1980), 126.

3 Addison and the "Helps and Ornaments of Art"

> *Some to conceit alone their taste confine,*
> *And glitt'ring thoughts struck out at ev'ry line;*
> *Pleased with a work where nothing's just or fit;*
> *One glaring chaos and wild heap of wit.*
> *Poets, like painters, thus unskilled to trace*
> *The naked nature, and the living grace,*
> *With golds and jewels cover ev'ry part,*
> *And hide with ornaments their want of art.*
>   —*Alexander Pope*, An Essay on Criticism

Some years ago Marjorie Hope Nicolson concluded that Addison based his aesthetic system in the experience of natural scenery rather than art,[1] and in support of this view we should note that he begins one of the early pieces on "The Pleasures of the Imagination" (1712), *Spectator* 414, by saying, "If we consider the workings of Nature and Art, as they are qualified to entertain the imagination, we shall find the last very defective, in comparison of the former."[2] Although Wimsatt and Brooks have pointed out that

---

1. Marjorie Hope Nicolson, *Mountain Gloom and Mountain Glory: The Development of the Aesthetics of the Infinite* (Ithaca: Cornell University Press, 1959), 308.
2. My text for Addison's *Spectator* papers is *Critical Essays from* The Spectator *by Joseph Addison*, ed. Donald F. Bond (Oxford: Oxford University Press, 1970).

Addison ranges himself on both sides of the question,[3] Nicolson's eccentric reading is nevertheless useful in underlining his effort to modify radically the role of language in literature—to modify it by virtually denying its validity as ornament, on the one hand, and, on the other, endowing it with the most extraordinary affective power. In the first instance language must be compelled to hide its character as language to become transparent.[4] This is especially the case with figurative language. Then in the second instance it must serve to stimulate the imaginative experience in the reader Addison so persistently seeks to encourage. If, as Addison claims, the reader or spectator can be prompted to range in spirit beyond the limits of immediate situation or conventional thought, we must wonder at his acceptance of routine notions of genre, as in his papers on English drama. It is in the context of these apparent contradictions in critical sympathy (not unlike the alternations of freedom and restraint in French classical theory discussed in the previous chapter) and of his approach to questions of artistic language generally that I will treat Addison's criticism, including with "The Pleasures of the Imagination" the papers on taste, wit, the ballad, and *Paradise Lost*.

His concern for language in the essays on wit (*Spectator* 58–63) takes the form of an attempt to reduce and confine the role of figurative expression in poetry. Near the beginning of #58 he says that his goal is "to establish among us a taste for polite writing," and with that in mind he itemizes the types of false wit in vogue: pattern poems, acrostics, lipograms, rebuses,

---

3. W. K. Wimsatt and Cleanth Brooks, *Literary Criticism: A Short History* (New York: Knopf, 1967), 255.

4. The concept of linguistic transparency gets its most extensive and systematic treatment in German Enlightenment aesthetics; cf. David E. Wellbery's *Lessing's* Laocoon: *Semiotics and Aesthetics in the Age of Reason*, 72. The principle of transparency "consists in the demand that the linguistic level of the poetic text, that is, the level of the signifiers, not emerge into the foreground of consciousness, that the cognition which the poetic text transmits not remain a symbolic cognition but rather be actualized as intuition, as the experienced presence-to-mind of the represented object. . . . Poetic language is diaphanous; it presents its object to intuition." Wellbery implies that this understanding of artistic language is an innovation for which the German philosophers are responsible, but I think the concept is already well established in seventeenth-century French and English classicism in texts familiar to the Germans, especially to Mendelssohn, who had read, among others, Locke and Addison. Michel Foucault regards the theory of transparency as dominant after the Renaissance: "The language of the Classical age is much closer to the thought it is charged with expressing than is generally supposed; but it is not parallel to it; it is caught in the grid of thought, woven into the very fabric it is unrolling. . . . And, because of this, it makes itself invisible, or almost so. In any case, it has become so transparent to representation that its very existence ceases to be a problem"; *The Order of Things: An Archaeology of the Human Sciences* (New York: Vintage Books, 1973), 78–79. The last, and quite extreme, statement in this passage is exactly opposite to what I trust my thesis reveals.

anagrams, and puns. These have an ancient, and to him discreditable lineage, rising in antiquity and enjoying a medieval, "monkish" revival that survives into his own time, attracting minor talents whose deficiencies in genius oblige them to seek out "foreign" ornaments: "I look upon these writers as Goths in poetry, who, like those in architecture, not being able to come up to the beautiful simplicity of the Greeks and Romans, have endeavoured to supply its place with all the extravagances of an irregular fancy" (*Spectator* 62).

Addison distinguishes true from false wit by saying that the former must involve a resemblance of ideas, while the latter is mere wordplay. But the distinction must have been in practice a hard one, for he fails to offer a single example of true wit, invoking Cowley instead to demonstrate mixed wit which, not surprisingly, "consists partly in the resemblance of ideas, and partly in the resemblance of words." His next remarks betray a scant regard even for this compromise: "This kind of wit abounds in Cowley, more than in any author that ever wrote. Mr. Waller has likewise a great deal of it. Mr. Dryden is very sparing in it. Milton has a genius much above it. Spenser is in the same class with Milton. The Italians, even in their epic poetry, are full of it. Monsieur Boileau, who formed himself upon the ancient poets, has everywhere rejected it with scorn" (*Spectator* 62). These judgments are the familiar Augustan reaction against the Metaphysical style and Italian baroque aesthetics,[5] but for Addison the posture is by no means just a rehearsal of the common bias; it is primarily an effort to encourage one mode of art and discourage another in terms of their affective results. The negative qualities of "Gothic" wit are precisely those that declare the presence of language.

In these essays and later in *Spectator* 411 and 416, he associates wit with the diminutive, that is with epigram and other forms of short poem. Its effects are quickly achieved and quickly disappear; they lack power, depth, and duration. A witty style fails in perspicuity, it fails, in other words, to employ language that transparently displays its object. The Gothic, in language as in architecture, swarms with detail, in contrast to a building such as the Pantheon. When the viewer first sees the Pantheon, "his imagination is filled with something great and amazing" (*Spectator* 415); a Gothic cathedral, however massive, lacks this power to astonish, instead distracting the viewer with interrupted outline and fussy detail. Everyone, Addison believes, prefers round pillars and vaulted roofs: "The reason I take to be

---

5. For example, Dryden; cf. *Of Dramatic Poesy and Other Critical Essays*, ed. George Watson, 2 vols. (London: Everyman's Library, 1962), 1:39–40.

because in these figures we generally see more of the body than in those other kinds. There are, indeed, figures of bodies, where the eye may take in two thirds of the surface; but as in such bodies the sight must split upon several angles, it does not take in one uniform idea, but several ideas of the same kind" (*Spectator* 416).

In the final paper on wit, #63, Addison drives home the difference between the Gothic and the classical by concocting a mock dream allegory in which he enters a "Region of False Wit" governed by the Goddess of Falsehood, a landscape of artificial shrubbery and contrivances such as birds with golden beaks and human voices. In a grove there is an edifice "built after the Gothic manner, and covered with innumerable devices in that barbarous kind of sculpture." These and similar details are set against the figures of Truth and Wit, who are beautiful and shining, though not otherwise described. Simplicity, grandeur, and uniformity are celebrated; we are encouraged to favor whatever presents the object in its wholeness and essence, while unnatural or artificial combinations are mocked.

There are a number of things to be said about Addison's views as I have summarized them: they center in a strong distaste for the symbolic and iconographic; there is an obvious preference for artistic language as close as possible to perception or concepts in the mind ("ideas" in the philosophical jargon of the time[6]); one notices a companion reaction against whatever smacks of human contrivance in the form of nature altered; and running through the whole series on wit is a distrust of the verbal in itself, an attitude that has its origins in Addison's reading of Locke.

Locke says that quickness of wit does not always go with "the clearest judgment, or deepest reason. For wit [lies] mostly in the assemblage of ideas, and [puts] those together with quickness and variety, wherein can be found any resemblance or congruity thereby to make up pleasant pictures and agreeable visions in the fancy."[7] These remarks are part of a passage

---

6. I do not mean to suggest that the topic is a trivial one. For an account of the theory of ideas in the later seventeenth century, centering in Arnauld and Locke, see John W. Yolton, "Ideas and Knowledge in Seventeenth-Century Philosophy," *Journal of the History of Philosophy* 13 (1975), 145–65. Yolton's *Perceptual Acquaintance from Descartes to Reid* considerably elaborates the topic.

7. John Locke, *An Essay Concerning Human Understanding*, ed. Peter Nidditch (Oxford: Oxford University Press, 1975), II.xi.2. All my references to the *Essay* are to this edition. The paragraph quoted pursues the notion of imagination in terms Addison may well have had in mind: "*Judgment*, on the contrary, lies quite on the other side, in separating carefully, from one another, *Ideas*, wherein can be found the least difference, thereby to avoid being misled by Similitude and by affinity to take one thing for another. This is a way of proceeding quite

Addison quotes with approval in *Spectator* 62, though he fails to mention that in context Locke's point of view is one of dismissal. A further and more serious problem is Locke's contempt for fancy, the very faculty Addison later puts at the heart of his account of imaginative pleasure. For Locke, wit caters to fancy by its association with wish and fiction-making. By inference wit has nothing to do with the accurate observation of the phenomenal world or a decision as to the real nature of things. It differs markedly from judgment, which is concerned with establishing differences and distinctions, and it employs metaphor and allusion, "wherein, for the most part, lies that entertainment and pleasantry of wit which strikes so lively on the fancy, and is therefore so acceptable to all people" (*Essay* II.xi.2).

These remarks are part of Locke's effort to reform the way in which language is used to define and classify knowledge. His concern was to bring our understanding of the natural world, and the language employed to record and communicate it, as closely together as possible, and this program specifically means the elimination of figurative language from serious discourse, as the following passage makes plain:

> Since Wit and Fancy finds easier entertainment in the World, than dry Truth and real Knowledge, *figurative Speeches*, and allusion in Language, will hardly be admitted, as *an* imperfection or *abuse* of it. I confess, in Discourses, where we seek rather Pleasure and Delight, than Information and Improvement, such Ornaments as are borrowed from them can scarce pass for Faults. But yet, if we would speak of things as they are, we must allow that all the Art of Rhetorick, besides Order and Clearness, all the artificial and figura-

---

contrary to Metaphor and Allusion, wherein for the most part, lies that entertainment and pleasantry of Wit, which strikes so lively on the Fancy, and is therefore so acceptable to all People; because its Beauty appears at first sight, and there is no labour of Thought to examine what Truth or Reason there is in it." Addison in *Spectator* 411 says, "The colours paint themselves on the fancy, with very little attention of thought or application of the mind in the beholder." The crucial difference between Addison and Locke is that Addison has no intention of setting the fancy to one side. There is a detailed discussion of this point by Clarence D. Thorpe, "Addison's Theory of the Imagination as 'Perceptive Response,'" *Papers, Michigan Academy* 21 (1936), 519–22, though Thorpe does not connect the treatment of imagination to a concept of language, a matter of importance for both Locke and Addison. For Locke's theory of ideas, see Knowlson's essay, "Ideas and Knowledge in Seventeenth-Century Philosophy," and Yolton's *Perceptual Acquaintance from Descartes to Reid*, 88–104 and passim; also Stephen K. Land, *The Philosophy of Language in Britain: Major Theories from Hobbes to Thomas Reid* (New York: AMS Press, 1986), 31–77, especially 74–77, which argues that Locke's system is primarily a theory of propositions.

tive application of Words Eloquence hath invented, are for nothing else but to insinuate wrong *Ideas,* move the Passions, and thereby mislead the Judgment. (*Essay* III.xi.34)[8]

This division of labor, together with Locke's evident contempt for the imagination and figurative language, is one of the consequences of the growth of scientific empiricism in the seventeenth century. The reaction is against the rhetorical tradition as a basis for understanding language, to reform it by a forced marriage between objects and words.[9] I recall it here

---

8. Paul De Man in his article "The Epistemology of Metaphor," *On Metaphor,* ed. Sheldon Sacks (Chicago: University of Chicago Press, 1979), 11–28, has a provocative study of this passage. He argues that Locke in his account of language fails to grasp the following problem: he says that words designating simple ideas are more or less identical with the things they refer to, but they can't be defined. Therefore, only those ideas that can be defined are useful to the understanding. But the process of definition, for Locke the difficult and not always successful effort to turn original terms into other words that genuinely explain or contribute to our understanding of the truth of the things we contemplate, is for De Man a closet theory of metaphor. He suggests that Locke's effort to establish a purely denotative mode of language is futile because the very act of definition is the contrary of what it pretends to be: it is a deferring of accurate meaning by the continual process of substitution or translation. Followed to its end, De Man's critique might provoke the conclusion that if all language is metaphor, there can be no meaningful distinction between the faculties of judgment and fancy; therefore, all thought is fancy. Addison could not have accepted such a conclusion, for his interest in language is really a function of his interest in affective response as one among other kinds of response. Furthermore, De Man's disposition to think of metaphor as substitution ignores its pictorial or the expressive functions, and with these most seventeenth- and eighteenth-century critics were persistently concerned.

9. See, for example, Francis Bacon, *Novum Organum* LIX–LX (the "Idols of the Marketplace") and *The Advancement of Learning,* II.XII.1, and Thomas Hobbes, *Leviathan,* I.4 ("Abuses of Speech"). Some of the consequences of assigning one mode of language to fact and another to human wish and illusion are discussed by R. F. Jones in several essays in *The Seventeenth Century: Studies in the History of English Thought and Literature from Bacon to Pope* (Stanford: Stanford University Press, 1951), 41–160. Hans Aarsleff notes that "with Locke's *Essay* laying the foundations of the modern study of language, the origins of this study become tightly intertwined with the major intellectual event in our centuries [the seventeenth through the twentieth?], the rise of the new science in the seventeenth century," *From Locke to Saussure: Essays on the Study of Language and Intellectual History* (Minneapolis: University of Minnesota Press, 1982), 27. One important side to the scientific effort was the movement to establish a universal language, one that not only would eliminate metaphor and erase the miscommunications and misunderstandings caused by national languages, but also one in which words became identical with the objects they designated. James Knowlson, *Universal Language Schemes in England and France 1600–1800* (Toronto: University of Toronto Press, 1975), says that the projected language would "provide a universal character that through the actual composition of its 'words' would accurately mirror the various qualities of natural things and the relations between them. In this way, language would not only be a means of acquiring knowledge; it would itself *be* knowledge, since each 'word' would provide an accurate

for the point it gives to the direction of Addison's thought, as well as for its reminder of comparable attitudes in Bacon and Descartes.

Had he accepted Locke's coupling of audience imagination and figurative language entirely, Addison might well have exhibited a rather different attitude toward wit and metaphor, but in fact, as we have seen, he joins Locke in disparagement of wit, approves of a mode of style as close as possible to the objects and perceptions it is meant to express, and yet claims for the reader that "Pleasure and Delight" to which Locke so clearly assigns a secondary importance. The kind of style Locke approves for "Information and Improvement" Addison promotes not to generate sound judgment but for the sake of powerful affect.

He pursues his interest in perspicuous style most diligently in the papers on the ballad, *Spectator* 70, 74, and 85. The burden of these essays is the rather strained notion that the ballad of Chevy Chase should be thought of as a kind of epic poem. The argument turns in part on the familiar distinction between the affectation of "Gothic" wit and a style of severe simplicity, the former pleasing only those who have cultivated "a wrong artificial taste, [formed] upon little fanciful authors and writers of epigram" and the latter appealing to "all kinds of palates" (#70). He also equates naive directness with impressiveness of style: there are "several places [in the ballad] where not only the thought but the language is majestic, and the numbers sonorous"; he later quotes four stanzas "which have a great force and spirit in them, and are filled with very natural circumstances" (#74). In #85 the attachment to naiveté is even more decisively expressed in an aesthetic formula that equates authenticity with transparency of language. Of an old ballad, "Two Children in the Wood," he says:

> This song is a plain simple copy of nature, destitute of all the helps and ornaments of art. The tale of it is a pretty tragical story, and pleases for no other reason, but because it is a copy of nature. There is even a despicable simplicity in the verse; and yet, because the sentiments appear genuine and unaffected, they are able to move the mind of the most polite reader with inward melting of humanity and compassion.

He concedes that the ballad has "a little poetical ornament; and to show the genius of the author amidst all his simplicity, it is just the same kind of fiction

---

description of the thing signified" (8). See also his account of Wilkins's objections to existing languages, 38.

which one of the greatest of the Latin poets has made use of upon a parallel occasion." As Chevy Chase invited comparison with Homer, so this song is reminiscent of Horace.

These comments make it evident that Addison's belief in the direct transcription of nature is mildly qualified and hesitant, though his distrust of ornament is equally plain. What is involved, I think, is a choice between two modes of verbal pictorialism which Jean Hagstrum calls "profoundly antithetical." One belongs to the tradition that encourages *enargeia*, or sensory vividness. This tradition is associated with antiquity and the Renaissance and retains its adherents well into the eighteenth century. The other matches pictorialism with the internal or supernatural and is characteristic of medieval and baroque symbolism. A taste for the antique is a taste for the direct, external visual image, and neoclassicism, according to Hagstrum, "was in open revolt against the emblematic expression of the seventeenth century, which it considered barbarously unnatural and inelegant."[10] As we have already noticed, this bias is evident in the writing of Bouhours, whom Addison calls "the most penetrating of all the French critics" (*Spectator* 62). In his dialogue on the "Bel Esprit" Bouhours maintains that the true role of wit is a discernment that "shows things to be what they are in themselves." It is "inseparable from common sense. . . . It is solid but brilliant matter, it dazzles but has consistency of body."[11] Similar sentiments in *The Art of Criticism* obviously impressed Addison. But Addison is interested in the visual in figurative language, though not so much because it can convey a truth but because in one way or another it is a source of affect. This side of his thinking leads us back to the influence of Boileau.

The possibility that words can almost appear not to be words at all but the objects or events they designate seems to have led Addison to his extreme praise of simplicity in ballad and epic. Simplicity in these genres entails, as we have noticed, severe limitations on the use of metaphorical ornament. This position perhaps owes something to Boileau's translation of Longinus. In chapter 13 Longinus quotes from Euripides' *Orestes*: "Ou fuirai-je? Elle vient. Je la voi. Je suis mort." Then he adds, "Le Poête en cet endroit ne voyoit pas les Furies: cependant il en fait une image si naïve, qu'il les fait presque voir aux Auditeurs."[12]

---

10. Jean Hagstrum, *The Sister Arts*, 129.
11. Dominique Bouhours, *Les Entretiens d'Ariste et d'Eugène* in *The Continental Model*, ed. Scott Elledge and Donald Schier, 161.
12. Boileau, *Œuvres complètes*, 364. It should be remembered that in *L'Art poétique*, Chant

Enargeia, the quality of style Boileau refers to, is in Aristotle's *Rhetoric* (cf. III.xi) related to the sensory aspect of metaphor. Here *enargeia* is not descriptive language but language that by its directness prompts us to imagine or picture in our minds the presence of something referred to. The process is a kind of inference-making, but it is quite different from the use of imagery with symbolic or emblematic reference. So in this context *enargeia* appeals to the kind of perception Addison identifies with imagination. Our imagination allows us, as readers or viewers, to receive those visual qualities in language Aristotle associates with metaphor but which, as the example from Longinus makes plain, is by no means confined to it. Nor is metaphor, of course, simply the presence of sensory images. With one part of his thinking Addison wants a style that conveys objects nakedly, not as signs or symbols, but at the same time he has chosen to emphasize noncognitive responses to literature and art. He reacts against metaphor as ornament, as something added to the object, an object of attention in itself and therefore superfluous. Above all he seems reluctant to accept it as presenting a complex set of ideas. This is the emphasis we have seen in his reaction to false and mixed wit as well as in his preference for unornamented style. It is also influential in the papers on *Paradise Lost* and those on "The Pleasures of the Imagination," for as that title suggests, it is the reader's imagination he seeks to cultivate. Indeed the reader's interest governs the direction of all his critical thought. Yet the imagination, we must remember, is the very faculty despised by Locke and engaged by figurative language. What we observe, then, in the greater bulk of Addison's criticism is an effort to accommodate metaphor insofar as it is affective, but to disparage or downplay it as the vehicle of witty or symbolic discourse. In one mood he tries, like Bouhours and Boileau before him, to break the hold of conventional rhetorical doctrine on poetic language, but in another he continues the alliance. The difference is that for Addison it is not language as a system of figures that calls forth our response, but language as the vehicle of objects that touch the imagination.

Addison's commitment to the word as virtually identical with its object explains why he begins the series on the "Pleasures of the Imagination" talking not of literature but of landscape. Landscape offers him the occasion

---

III, he allows the epic an indulgence in fanciful event and imagery quite different from the "naive" visualization Longinus discovers in Euripides. Addison does not comment on the example from Euripides, but it is consistent with the point he makes in the *Spectator* pieces on ballad and epic.

appropriate to his argument that sight is "the most perfect and delightful of all our senses," with the advantage over touch of giving us "a command of the material world extended beyond the body."

> It fills the mind with the largest variety of ideas, converses with its objects at the greatest distance, and continues the longest in action without being tired or satiated with its proper enjoyments. . . . Our sight . . . may be considered as a more delicate and diffusive kind of touch, that spreads itself over an infinite multitude of bodies, comprehends the largest figures, and brings into our reach some of the remotest parts of the universe.[13]

Sight is therefore first of all a compensation for our bodily limitations, bringing within the circle of our attention objects at a distance. The next point has to do with the extension of time:

> It is this sense which furnishes the imagination with its ideas; so that by the pleasures of the imagination or fancy (which I shall use promiscuously) I here mean such as arise from visible objects, either when we have them actually within our view, or when we call up their ideas into our minds by paintings, statues, descriptions, or any the like occasion. We cannot indeed have a single image in the fancy that did not make its first entrance through the sight; but we have the power of retaining, altering and compounding those images, which we have once received, into all the varieties of picture and vision that are the most agreeable to the imagination; for by this faculty a man in a dungeon is capable of entertaining himself with scenes and landscapes more beautiful than any that can be found in the whole compass of nature. (#411)

---

13. In *Essay* II.ix.9, Locke calls sight "the most comprehensive of all our senses," and in II.xi he seeks to show how simple ideas (primary sensations) become translated into complex ideas that then are represented by words. Locke's belief that all thinking begins in sensory experience and his evident influence in the literary theory of the eighteenth century have prompted the epithet "sensationalism": see Wimsatt and Brooks, *Literary Criticism*, 257, and Ernest Lee Tuveson, *The Imagination as a Means of Grace: Locke and the Aesthetics of Romanticism* (Berkeley and Los Angeles: University of California Press, 1960), 18, 73, for the view that for Locke thinking is seeing. This is challenged by John W. Yolton's review of Tuveson in *JAAC* 20 (1961), 107–9. Yolton generally argues that Locke conceives of some ideas as derived from sense perception but by no means do such ideas necessarily occur in the mind as pictures, especially when called into the mind by words.

This passage comprehends the most conventional as well as the most revolutionary features of Addison's critical writings: his reduction of the imagination to sight is not, contrary to Nicolson's belief, new;[14] but his interest in an elemental transaction between the viewing mind and material objects for the sake of affective enjoyment is radical. In such an experience understanding has no place (though he concedes that there are pleasures of the understanding and that they are "more preferable, because they are founded on some new knowledge or improvement of the mind"), perhaps because it might lead to a detached or analytical attitude toward objects.

That Addison begins his account of imaginative pleasure by testifying to the affective power of natural scenery can be misleading, for his overriding interest in all his criticism is not to denigrate the pleasures to be derived from the arts in comparison to those available in nature. His motive is instead, as my discussion up to this point has tried to suggest, to encourage a preference for modes of art based in efforts to give naked representation to the natural or the objective. The effects of such artistic modes are the "secondary" pleasures of the imagination, and it is on these that Addison fixes his closest attention.

These pleasures are produced by painting, statuary, architecture, or literature, media that come between the object and the sensibility of the spectator or reader. Statuary, we are informed in *Spectator* 416, is "the most natural, and shows us something *likest* the object that is represented." Painting, because it flattens out the image, is at a greater distance from the object, and written description "runs yet further from the things it represents than painting; for a picture bears a real resemblance to its original, which letters and syllables are wholly void of." All language, Addison might have said, is metaphorical, at least to the extent that there is in all metaphor some degree of difference between tenor and vehicle. But for him, as for almost everyone else who had discussed imagination as a source of metaphor and a faculty for appreciating it, the faculty discovers and notices resemblances, more readily than differences.[15] Most of *Specta-*

14. Cf. Aristotle, *De Anima* III.iii: "As sight is the most highly developed sense, the name *phantasia* (imagination) has been formed from *Phaos* (light)," *The Basic Works of Aristotle*, ed. Richard McKeon (New York: Random House, 1941).

15. The *locus classicus* in seventeenth-century criticism is Hobbes's account in *Leviathan* I.8: "those that observe . . . similitudes are said to have a *good wit*; by which, in this occasion is meant a good *fancy*. But they that observe their differences, and dissimilitudes . . . are said to have a good *judgment*." See also his remark in the "Answer to Davenant" that "Judgment begets the strength and structure, and Fancy begets the ornaments of a Poem." Before the seventeenth century, the imagination is usually understood as the power to call images into the

tor 416 is devoted to reminding us that the plastic or verbal arts are mimetic and that our pleasure in them comes from being able to compare the "ideas" we get from "statues, descriptions, or any the like occasion" with "places, persons, or actions, in general, which bear a resemblance, or at least some remote analogy with what we find represented."[16]

Through Hobbes and Locke, Addison inherits the notion that all meaning in language is arbitrary, a social convention.[17] He illustrates this generalization by the fact that different linguistic cultures have different words and sounds for the same object. Therefore, the scale that separates the various media from the objects they represent is not only one of distance; it is also the difference between what Addison considers a "natural" or universal knowledge and that which is artificial. And language is the essence of artifice:

> Colours speak all languages,[18] but words are understood only by such a people or nation. For this reason, though men's necessities

---

mind and combine them; cf. *De Anima* III.iii. Most rhetorical treatises, including the *Rhetoric* and Cicero's various essays, describe the structure and effects of metaphorical language without specifically deriving it from a single mental faculty. The overt linking of judgment to nonmetaphorical language and of fancy to metaphorical language may well be an innovation of the seventeenth century. It appears, for example, in a statement of Tesauro's: "When we cause another to imagine that which is not, we form a fiction, a very lively figure" (*Il Cannocchiale aristotelico*, 219). Although metaphor involves the simultaneous perception of difference and likeness, Addison tends to think of metaphor as analogue, except when he is criticizing "Gothic" wit. See also note 6 above.

16. The unspoken corollary to this is that the more we have experienced the primary pleasures of the imagination—in other words, the more we know of objects that represent nothing but themselves—the more we have to gain from the secondary. But in *Spectator* 409, a discussion of taste, Addison says that apart from the necessity of being born with some capacity for good taste, "The most natural method for this purpose is to be conversant among the writings of the best authors." This statement would seem to undercut Nicolson's argument that Addison's aesthetic is based in the experience of nature, rather than art.

17. Cf. Locke, *Essay* III.ii.1: "Thus we may conceive how *Words* . . . come to be made use of by Men, as *the signs of* their *Ideas*; not by any natural connexion, that there is between particular articulate Sounds and certain *Ideas*, for then there would be but one Language amongst all Men; but by a voluntary imposition, whereby such a Word is made arbitrarily the Mark of such an *Idea*." The distinction was an issue in ancient Greek thought about language: see R. H. Robins, *A Short History of Linguistics*, 2d ed. (London: Longmans, 1979), 17–20.

18. This statement on the universality of color, by which Addison generally means pictures, should be compared to his comment at the end of #414 that "light and colours, as apprehended by the imagination, are only ideas in the mind, and not qualities that have any existence in matter." He gets this notion from Locke and Newton (though it may also be found in the first chapter of *Leviathan*), and it seems to suit one of his main points in his account of imaginative pleasure: that nature in itself is drab and that man's mind adorns and idealizes it. Presumably, the pictorializing faculty in man is universal, at least to the extent that we can agree on the colors our imaginations impose on matter, but Addison does not follow out the implications of the concept.

quickly put them on finding out speech, writing is probably of a later invention than painting; particularly we are told, that in America when the Spaniards first arrived there, expresses were sent to the Emperor of Mexico in paint, and the news of his country delineated by the strokes of a pencil, which was a more *natural* [emphasis added] way than that of writing, though at the same time much more imperfect, because it is impossible to draw the little connections of speech, or to give the picture of a conjunction or an adverb. It would be yet more strange, to represent visible objects by sounds that have no ideas annexed to them, and to make something like description in music. Yet it is certain there may be confused, imperfect notions raised in the imagination by an *artificial* [emphasis added] composition of notes; and we find that great masters in the art are able, sometimes to set their hearers in a heat and hurry of battle, to overcast their minds with melancholy scenes and apprehensions of deaths and funerals, or to lull them into pleasant dreams of groves and Elysiums.

It is not mimesis that interests Addison. For the listener or spectator or reader, the medium, which does not directly represent a scene, can be the start of an interior journey or a substitute for being present at some scene or event; the feelings experienced are created "artificially" and one responds as if one were there. The presence is not simply that of the object; it is also that of the spectator, the imaginative viewer that is evoked. Furthermore, if we are concerned about whether Addison values natural over artificial or mediated experience, we should note that he is insinuating here the concept of the greater precision of artificial over natural communication.

But he also seeks to retain the traditional notion that a major source of pleasure in art is the audience's opportunity to compare a copy or analogue with an original. This is the basis for a whole host of "entertainments": "for it is this that not only gives us a relish of statuary, painting and description, but makes us delight in all the actions and arts of mimicry." Even the much maligned forms of wit—false, true, and mixed—delight us because of the "affinity of ideas," and "this secondary pleasure of the imagination proceeds from that action of the mind, which compares the ideas arising from the original objects, with the ideas we receive from the statue, picture, description, or sound that represents them." Art improves on nature and provides something that nature alone does not, the pleasures of discovering analogues.

Though he does not say so, it seems to me that Addison must have sensed an insufficiency in this account of the affective purpose of art. The notion that we take pleasure in imitations is at least as old as Aristotle, but Aristotle noted that one cause of our interest is noticing the skill with which the imitation is made,[19] while Addison's disposition is to mute the influence of the artist's cleverness or ingenuity as a source of delight. So when he discusses the advantages of art over nature he attempts to state the case so that there is no suggestion that an individual display of talent is what makes the difference. The crucial passage follows:

> Words, when well chosen, have so great a force in them, that a description often gives us more lively ideas than the sight of things themselves. The reader finds a scene drawn in stronger colours, and painted more to the life in his imagination, by the help of words, than by an actual survey of the scene which they describe. In this case the poet seems to get the better of Nature; he takes, indeed, the landscape after her, but gives it more vigorous touches, heightens its beauty, and so enlivens the whole piece, that the images, which flow from the objects themselves, appear weak and faint, in comparison to those that come from the expressions. The reason, probably, may be because in the survey of any object we have only so much of it as comes in at the eye; but in its description the poet gives us as free a view of it as he pleases, and discovers to us several parts that either we did not attend to, or that lay out of our sight when we first beheld it. As we look on any object, our idea of it is, perhaps, made up of two or three simple ideas; but when the poet represents it, he may either give us a more complex idea of it, or only raise in us such ideas as are apt to affect the imagination.

The mimetic principle is observed only to be replaced by the poet's capacity to place our eyes on all sides of an object and to offer it complexly to the mind. Addison is thus reaching to a concept of art that all but acknowledges the importance of the figurative or metaphorical. In *Spectator* 418 he suggests that the human mind requires "something more perfect in

---

19. *Poetics* 4. In *Spectator* 418 Addison makes an interesting modification: "the description of a dunghill is pleasing to the imagination, if the image be represented to our minds by suitable expressions; though, perhaps, this may be more properly called the pleasure of the understanding than of the fancy, because we are not so much delighted with the image that is contained in the description, as with the aptness of the description to excite the image."

matter, than what it finds there [in nature]," and in the same essay he states that in painting there is a pleasure greater than that to be taken in a good resemblance: "the pleasure increases, if it be the picture of a face that is beautiful, and is still greater, if the beauty be softened with an air of melancholy or sorrow." Addison's interest in the affective powers of art is everywhere the dominant issue, one that certainly overrides whatever disposition to consistency he might have tried to cultivate.[20]

What he has to say directly about allegory, simile, and metaphor (or allusion, as he sometimes terms it) is not extensive, but two passages are worth attention. The first occurs in *Spectator* 303, one of the series of papers on *Paradise Lost*, and the second is from #421, the last of those on "The Pleasures of the Imagination." The latter piece, which I will take up first, begins with a concept of metaphor that at first seems conventional in discussing trope as a process in which abstract concepts are dressed out in images. But there is an emphasis that is Addison's own. He describes a general class of writing "to be met with among the polite masters of morality, criticism, and other speculations abstracted from matter; who, though they do not directly treat of the visible parts of nature, often draw from them their similitudes, metaphors, and allegories. By these allusions a truth in the understanding is as it were reflected by the imagination; we are able to see something like colour and shape in a notion, and to discover a scheme of thoughts traced out upon matter."

It may be confusing to find him assigning metaphor to what seems to be conceptual purpose, but his point is unexpected: it is that for the reader or spectator it functions exactly like landscape or description. Allegories, properly done, "are like so many tracks of light in a discourse, that make everything about them clear and beautiful." A "noble" metaphor "casts a kind of glory around it and darts a lustre through the whole sentence." Presumably it explains nothing and has nothing to do with accuracy of thought. Instead figure turns all thoughts into objects to be seen, drawing upon nature, not upon other arts and sciences. "It is this talent," he continues, "of affecting the imagination, that gives embellishment to good

20. In #413 Addison comments at length on the proposition that beauty is something the human mind adds to nature. This is the sort of treatment that bothers some modern critics. For example, Ernest Tuveson concludes: "Beauty, now an illusion rather than a kind of knowledge, serves to arouse delight and to reconcile us to living in the universe (itself a dull place) rather than to arouse us to ideal aspirations"; *Imagination as a Means of Grace*, 107–8. Tuveson's view of Addison and the direction in criticism he represents is heavily colored by the desire to find in art the elements of religious instruction and inspiration.

84   Terms of Response

sense, and makes one man's compositions more agreeable than another's." And finally, rising to an unaccustomed pitch, he triumphantly vindicates figurative composition, though once more on his own terms:

> It has something in it like creation; it bestows a kind of existence, and draws up to the reader's view, several objects not to be found in being. It makes additions to nature, and gives a greater variety of God's works. In a word, it is able to beautify and adorn the most illustrious scenes in the universe, or to fill the mind with more glorious shows and apparitions, than can be found in any part of it.

What should be carried away from this passage is a sense of how deeply Addison is committed to a theory of language as an object. Though he may have changed his mind about metaphor,[21] his conviction about the psychological importance of this view of language is very much the same as when he composed the papers on wit. As objects working on the mind metaphors transform the world into color or make palpable that which can only be fancied, just as seen things work upon the sight. The notion is, of course, almost as ancient as rhetoric itself, but Addison's way of understanding it is different. Figurative speech is not employed in the service of persuasion; the vividness and presence of verbally mediated objects are not avenues to thought or truth. They are there simply to be enjoyed. If we did not know better, we might think Addison had somehow brought himself to accept some of the principles of baroque aesthetics.

The point is made more elaborately in *Spectator* 303, and concerns Milton's affective power:

> There are also several noble similes and allusions in the first book of *Paradise Lost*. And here I must observe, that when Milton alludes either to things or to persons, he never quits his simile till it rises to some very great idea, which is often quite foreign to the occasion that gave birth to it. The resemblance does not, perhaps, last above

---

21. A full and interesting account of Addison's inconsistencies about the value of poetic ornament is David A. Hansen's "Addison on Ornament and Poetic Style," *Studies in Criticism and Aesthetics, 1660–1800: Essays in Honor of Samuel Holt Monk*, ed. Howard Anderson and John S. Shea (Minneapolis: University of Minnesota Press, 1967), 94–127. I share many of Hansen's judgments, but I would interpret the record he surveys as demonstrating Addison's partial break with a conventional interest in matters of form and his movement into a dominant interest in affect.

a line or two, but the poet runs on with the hint, till he has raised out of it some glorious image or sentiment, proper to inflame the mind of the reader, and to give it that sublime kind of entertainment, which is suitable to the nature of an heroic poem.[22]

If this passage seems to indicate a shift in emphasis from the attitude toward figure in the papers on wit and the ballad, in #279 he praises Milton's thoughts or "sentiments" for being natural and sublime, and in the same place takes him to task for the wordplay in *Paradise Lost* VI.607–29. And a similar attitude is at work in #297 where he discusses Milton's faults, his occasional use of allegory, puns, mythological allusion, an "unnecessary ostentation of learning," and overuse of foreign idiom. Whatever concessions Addison makes to figure are proposed on grounds of affect, "to inflame the mind of the reader."

In his attention to the formal characteristics he considers appropriate to epic Addison stresses two things, their contribution to magnitude or "greatness" and their power to affect the reader's imagination dynamically, to set the mind in motion. A remark of Jean Hagstrum's about Addison's concern for imagery is suggestive: "Under impulses from the new psychology [that derived from Hobbes] *enargeia* now arises from the process of seeing and no longer resides in the thing seen."[23] If this distinction is applicable, and I believe that it is, it helps to explain Addison's interest through the agency of Bouhours and Boileau in Longinus, for Longinus offers not just an authoritative account of style that praises grandeur and simplicity and dispraises artificiality and ostentation; he also inevitably draws attention to the mental reactions of the audience. Even more pointedly Hagstrum's distinction allows us better to understand Addison's apparent inconsistencies concerning figurative language or ornament. He does not favor ornament that leads the mind into the intricacies of its own details; he does favor the kind that serves as a kind of release or trigger to the reader's own powers of imaginative journeying. It hardly needs to be added that the exceeding of limits is a familiar feature of the sublime.

The art that Addison prefers is composed of palpable objects to be viewed, and to a large extent these objects are meant to stand still so they can be viewed. The natural world is a gallery of pictures intended for pleasure alone. In *Spectator* 413 he tells us that such pleasures cannot be defined, at least in the sense of assigning causes to any particular

22. Cf. Boileau, "Réflexion VI," *Œuvres complètes*, 519.
23. Hagstrum, *The Sister Arts*, 137.

pleasurable experience, but he describes the dynamics of what he thinks is the proper kind of imaginative pleasure in some detail. In #411 perhaps the most central of such accounts is worth a partial second citation: "we have the power of retaining, altering and compounding those images which we have once received, into all the varieties of picture and vision that are most agreeable to the imagination; for by this faculty a man in a dungeon is capable of entertaining himself with scenes and landscapes more beautiful than any that can be found in the whole compass of nature."

The imagination stimulated by art has the capacity to extend the mind beyond the confines of the actual present. Greatness is important because "Our imagination loves to be filled with an object, or to grasp at anything that is too big for its capacity. We are flung into pleasing astonishment at such unbounded views, and feel a delightful stillness and amazement in the soul at the apprehension of them. The mind of man naturally hates anything that looks like a restraint upon it" (#412). Release, repletion, movement through unbounded space—all these inform Addison's concept of affect as the mind being acted upon. They also suggest a concept of the reader or spectator as a peripatetic, a stroller in the countryside or among monuments of architecture. He does not explore or calculate, and overreaching the influence of Boileau, Addison here transforms the concept of the sublime from a theory of linguistic expression to a subjective experience prompted as much by landscape as by art.[24]

Just as important is Addison's exploitation of a rudimentary idea of association to illustrate the impact of memory on the affective imagination: "We may observe, that any single circumstance of what we have formerly seen often raises up a whole scene of imagery, and awakens numberless ideas that before slept in the imagination; such a particular smell or colour is able to fill the mind, on a sudden, with the picture of the fields or gardens where we first met with it, and to bring into view all the variety of images that once attended it" (#417).

The imagination may be stimulated by object or language alike, as we have seen, but the mind's response to stimulus is curiously nonverbal. It may be that this omission, which is surely deliberate, is behind the occasional negative reaction of modern critics to Addison's view of art.

24. Monk, who gives Addison credit for the "first effort in the century to build up a real aesthetic," interprets the shift of attention from language to nature, to "the aesthetic apprehension of mass and space," as Addison's freedom from the "rhetorical tradition" and its overemphasis on emotion; *The Sublime: A Study of Critical Theories in XVIII-Century England* (Ann Arbor: University of Michigan Press, 1960, 1st pub. 1935), 57–58.

Tuveson, for example, faults him for emphasizing "overpowering effect, rather than discovery . . . novelty and variety of images—new experience, not new insight."[25] But the direction in which Addison's critical system points, though it is indeed partial and excludes the analytical, nevertheless is notable for giving a more complete account of art as diversion than anyone before him. Had he included the judgment in his catalogue of responses, he would then have been compelled to propose for the reader a set of reactions modeled on concepts and based in a verbal or textual "journey" rather than one in which the imagination situates him in the midst of objects. Addison's terminology, which describes the mind being filled, distracted, overwhelmed, diverted, released, transported, and surprised, implies a view of artistic experience in which the reader's attention is not only turned away from the author but also from the ordinary round of daily life and its limitations to a total preoccupation with images in the fancy. The pleasures of the imagination are both inclusive and exclusive—that is, they keep the attention away from the irritating, the laborious, from that which demands to be explained, puzzled out, or solved, and lead it into a kind of mild rapture. The mind is focused and at the same time free to ruminate; in no sense is it confined to any necessary sequence of motion or progress. The poet must have designs, but the audience need not, perhaps indeed should not, though in the essay on taste, *Spectator* 409, he mentions better and worse kinds of aesthetic response scaled to better and worse kinds of art.

Addison has entered this wide and ungoverned territory through adapting a particular view of language. It is a view, as we know, that owes a great deal to the impact of scientific thinking on concepts of language and that owes much also to the Longinian doctrine of stylistic simplicity articulated by Boileau and Bouhours. But what Addison does to establish the authority of affective pleasure is to dismiss metaphorical ornament in one of its modes, the symbolic, and readmit it to his company as visual stimulation. His supposition is that language can be stripped of its cognitive and conceptual functions, that it can be made unobtrusive, hiding its presence as language, and yet as ornament be made powerful in transporting the mind. What he achieves may well have gone beyond his intentions, for he offers us, in anticipation of Du Bos, a theory of art as almost pure entertainment. The entertainment is benign, rather than idle or vicious, but it is nevertheless entertainment, supposing conditions of response in which the authority of the artist or poet and the claims of truth and judgment are entirely obscured by the powers of ornament.

25. *Imagination as a Means of Grace*, 90.

4   "The Irregular Fancy of the World"

> *The great variety of taste, as well as of opinion, which prevails in the world is too obvious not to have fallen under everyone's observation.*
>   —David Hume, "Of the Standard of Taste"

> *If I make a drawing of a palace, or a temple, or a landscape, I present a very clear idea of those objects; but then (allowing for the effect of imitation which is something) my picture can at most affect only as the palace, temple, or landscape would have affected in the reality. On the other hand, the most lively and spirited verbal description I can give, raises a very obscure and imperfect idea of such objects; but then it is in my power to raise a stronger emotion by the description than I could do by the best painting. This experience constantly evinces. The proper manner of conveying the affections of the mind from one to another, is by words. . . . In reality a great clearness helps but little toward affecting the passions, as it is in some sort an enemy to all enthusiasms whatsoever.*
>   —Edmund Burke, A Philosophical Enquiry into the Origin of Our Ideas of the Sublime and the Beautiful

When Addison wrote that he had "endeavored in several of my speculations to banish this Gothic taste, which has taken possession among us" (*Spectator* 409), he was describing what he took to be a set of aesthetic preferences widely shared at the beginning of the eighteenth century and also defining taste as a social phenomenon. But as his essay makes clear, taste is just as much an individual disposition, and this is really his focus: it is an adjunct to aesthetic pleasure, perhaps indeed scarcely distinguishable from pleasure because it is that habit of mind that allows us to recognize objects that please us and those that do not. It is the basis of our choice of what to enjoy, and it is also, as Shaftesbury recognized, an unstable and uncertain power: "Our modern authors are turned and modelled (as they themselves confess) by the public relish and current humour of the times. They regulate themselves by the irregular fancy of the world, and frankly own they are preposterous and absurd, in order to accommodate themselves to the genius of the age. In our days the audience makes the poet, and the bookseller the author."[1] In this guise taste is a kind of blatant beast driving the public to admire now this, now that, "the alterations which happen in manners, and the flux and reflux of politeness, wit, and art," and a disposition to make whatever is fashionable in the present a standard for judgment.

It is not simply Shaftesbury's aristocratic dislike of contemporary authors that agitates the question of taste. Rather, what we can discern in the midst of almost every eighteenth-century discussion is worry over the fickleness of taste, over the difficulty in making it conform to some universal and steady principle, in other words, the desire to liberate taste from social and cultural influence while at the same time acknowledging that it must develop through education and cultivation. It is a topic that gives us access to the eighteenth-century difficulty in seeing subjective response as authentic feeling, as deriving from a genuinely valuable source. Under such circumstances, taste could be presumed to differ from our immediate emotional responses to art, responses that ought, at least in theory, to be a power to feel not subject to culture or circumstance and hence universal. This line of thinking led to Kant's situating taste under "the imagination (acting perhaps in conjunction with the understanding)" which represents objects "to the Subject and its feeling of pleasure or displeasure,"[2] but the consequence of his argument is to establish what is involved in the process of calling an object beautiful or ugly. The process may start in a pleasurable or painful reaction to an object, but it ultimately involves a mode of contemplation independent of interest, what is pleasant or gratifying (§5). In separating the judgment of the beautiful from interest, Kant at the very least attenuates its emotional side, though he offers a solution to the problem of joining particular judgment to a universal standard. In tracing some of the lines of discussion of taste, this chapter will deal with the effort to subordinate or qualify certain elements of emotion in formulating a concept of taste, to look to an ideal process of judgment. The discussion will center in the speculations of some of Kant's predecessors, Hutcheson, Burke, Mendelssohn,

1. Anthony Ashley Cooper, 3d Earl of Shaftesbury, *Characteristics of Men, Manners, Opinions, Times* (1711), ed. Stanley Green, 2 vols. (Indianapolis: Bobbs-Merrill, 1964), III, iii.3; 1:172.

2. Immanuel Kant, *The Critique of Judgement* (1790), trans. James Creed Meredith (Oxford: Clarendon Press, 1952), 41 [I.I.I.I.§1: "The Judgement of Taste is Aesthetical"].

Lessing, Hume, and Kames. In addition, this chapter focuses closely on attempts, represented by Burke and Kames primarily, to clarify audience responses to language, and the discussion here will deal also with the ways in which attention to affect can turn into an attention to form, even though ostensibly taste is the term under which most eighteenth-century discussions of audience psychology, or what Ralph Cohen simply summarizes as "innumerable problems,"[3] were gathered.

The immense popularity of the topic, and especially its affinity to psychologies of aesthetic emotion, has prompted some twentieth-century reservations about the critical interests of the Enlightenment. For Wimsatt and Brooks taste exemplifies the aesthetics of association and "sentimentalism," by which they mean that such theory mutes attention to the value of literature and art as occasions for reflection.[4] Or from another angle, the theoretical interest in audience response tends to erase the line between art and life. According to Wellek (commenting on Dennis and Du Bos), "They did not see that poetry (when reduced to communicating emotion) merges with persuasion, ceases to be art, and becomes life, excitement of experience, passion."[5] In other words, the enjoyment of one's immediate experience of a work of art—and that experience concentrated largely in emotional rather than intellectual reaction—becomes the final or end motive of the arts.

Taste is precisely the term that suggests this bias: it emphasizes the sensory, and not just as metaphor. It emphasizes also the distinguishing of good from bad on the basis of an experience of the work, and finally it emphasizes, in spite of the frequently introduced notion that individuals by birth differ in their tastes, the process of habit in the development of a fine taste. Though variability in taste was often understood as a difficulty, one has the sense that on the whole the opportunity to notice how much one man's taste might differ from another's or how one's own taste might change as one grew older was more welcome than not. At the same time, it must be said that Wellek's judgment is unfair: the concern for taste was by no means entirely confined to the emotional, though it often involved an effort to discover whether and in what ways the work of art might produce special emotions and responses. This effort was as compelling as questions of form,

---

3. Ralph Cohen, "David Hume's Experimental Method and the Theory of Taste," *ELH* 25 (1958), 276.
4. Wimsatt and Brooks, *Literary Criticism: A Short History*, 260–261, 297–309.
5. René Wellek, *A History of Modern Criticism: 1750–1950* (London: Jonathan Cape, 1955), 1:23.

for British thinkers at least, if not for numbers of their French and German colleagues. I shall examine this issue shortly. If literature and art are valued primarily as occasions to experience beauty and sublimity, and indeed if that experience is inward and private rather than communal—even though our social feelings of sympathy may well be engaged—then we ought to speculate some on the significance of such a short-circuited view of the ends of art. My own judgment is that what is at issue is the establishment of the arts not only as forms of experience (if we have a faculty for beauty and sublimity then it must be exercised), but also as substitutes for other forms of experience.

Hume's observation in "Of Tragedy" that viewing the death of someone is quite different from, and far more bearable than, being told of the death of one's own child is a vivid way of illustrating the conditions under which such an event may be not only tolerated but enjoyed. The eighteenth-century interest in artistic affect is not simply a cultivation of sensation but rather a way of experiencing that is thought to be both natural and yet inaccessible without the special conditions provided by art and, above all, by language. Language draws one away from the natural and then toward it almost at the same time.

Hutcheson

The initial problem, addressed by de Crousaz in his *Traité du beau* (1685), was how to accommodate beauty as a more or less rational concept in the mind to a theory of response. As he notes, it is quite possible to entertain the notion that an object is beautiful without being in the least affected or moved by it.[6] If beauty is simply what pleases us, both the possibility of a more precise general standard and the hope of discovering a way to join the emotive and intellectual aesthetic responses are frustrated. And, indeed, any useful concept of the aesthetic is reduced to any individual pleasurable response to any object whatsoever. De Crousaz's solution, which is really no solution, is to propose that we have both an idea of beauty in us which is not dependent upon feeling alone and a kind of sentiment that may be

6. J. P. de Crousaz, *Traité du beau* (Amsterdam, 1685), 3: "We have, then, an idea of the beautiful that does not depend on feeling alone, and that can neither be attached in the degree we would wish to what pleases us the most, nor be denied to that which pleases us the least."

entirely separate from what the intellect recognizes. There are, in other words, two sorts of pleasure that under the right circumstances may respond to the same object at the same time (7–10).

The notion that we can entertain the idea that something is beautiful is important first of all because it allows us to value an object unselfishly—that is, without regard to its utility. We are responding, de Crousaz says, to uniformity in variety, and to grandeur, novelty, and diversity (12, 74), but what really seems to govern his theory is the belief that we have in us waiting to be confirmed a set of expectations that are realized in certain aspects of the material world: even the ugly or grotesque may please because they remind us of their opposites (45). This is why for de Crousaz beauty is a term that refers to a rapport between our ideas and certain objects (4), or, when he comes to deal with poetry, a kind of rightness or realization by art that matches what we already know. Figurative language is central because it links us with a familiar world and at the same time raises us to the appreciation of the concordance of ends and means: "A figure is appropriate and produces the effect of beauty when it helps the auditor raise himself to a movement into which he was going to enter on his own and for which what he has come to understand has already prepared him, the beauty of the means turns on their harmony with the ends for which they are put in play" (170). The greatest propriety affords the greatest beauty.

De Crousaz thus establishes a number of the issues which will concern this chapter and which his successors elaborated, especially the theory of an ideal response, the union of impeccable taste and powerful affect that prompts the return of the soul to an essential beauty that stands in for a return to nature. But much of de Crousaz's text understands beauty as based in sensory experience, though his comments on poetry can be read to point beyond that limitation. Francis Hutcheson, in his *Inquiry into the Original of Our Ideas of Beauty and Virtue* (1725) first tries to establish a sense of beauty that is independent of sense experience.[7] Sensory knowledge he associates with the inquiries of the scientist and the lifeless analytical skill of the critic:

> Let everyone here consider, how different we must suppose the perception to be, with which a poet is transported upon the prospect of any of those objects of natural beauty, which ravish us even in his

---

7. On this point see Ermano Migliorini, *Studi sul pensiero estetico di Francis Hutcheson* (Padua: Liviani Edetrice, 1974), 11–17.

description; from the cold lifeless conception which we imagine in a dull critick, or one of the virtuosi, without what we call a fine taste. This latter class of men may have greater perfection in that knowledge, which is deriv'd from external sensation; they can tell all the specifick differences of trees, herbs, minerals; they know the form of every leaf, stalk, root, flower, and seed of all the species, about which the poet is often ignorant: And yet the poet shall have a much more delightful perception of the whole; and not only the poet but any man of a fine taste.[8]

The effort to dissociate aesthetic experience from reasoned or analytical knowledge, to establish taste as an emotion or, in Hutcheson's case, as a kind of felt knowledge, reflects a general belief that our primary relationship to the objects we encounter is emotional (in the sense that we are attracted or repelled or indifferent to them). It amounts at times to a desire for unmediated experience that seeks to establish our relationships to the arts in the pleasure of the senses, paradoxically attempting to exploit artificial media to achieve that ordinary state. It should also be noted that the "delightful perception of the whole" joins poet and audience in a shared vision.

But the definition of beauty constituted a major problem for Enlightenment theory. It was essentially the problem of whether, in experiencing something as beautiful or ugly, we are responding to actual properties in the object. One obvious resource, that of de Crousaz, is to propose that aesthetic experience is the conjunction of fixed objective qualities and the perceiving subject, and this is the direction taken by Hutcheson. As a post-Lockean he is careful to note that beauty is an "Idea raised in us" ("Beauty" I.9), and such a phrase might at first appear to be simply an echo of Addison's remark that "There is not perhaps any real Beauty or Deformity more in one piece of Matter than another." (*Spectator* 412). This appears to mean that beauty is entirely the result of subjective judgment. But Hutcheson's system, even though it begins empirically in a consideration of affect, is centered in the concept of an ideal or primary beauty that

8. Francis Hutcheson's *An Inquiry into the Original of Our Ideas of Beauty and Virtue* consists of two parallel essays, "An Inquiry concerning Beauty, Order, etc." (which I shorten to "Beauty") and "An Inquiry concerning Our Ideas of Moral Good and Evil" ("Moral" for short). As in previous citations, I quote from the third corrected edition of 1729. References are to section and paragraph for readers who may have other editions available. The quotation here is from "Beauty" I.xii.

finds its realization in the human aesthetic faculty. That faculty is not simply our ordinary mechanism of perceptive response to objects, nor would Hutcheson concede that we choose, from motives of habit or temperament or whatever, to declare some objects beautiful. He creates instead a psychology that guarantees a universal response to qualities in objects that are themselves universal.

The qualities to which our sense of beauty responds are the same as those listed by de Crousaz: "uniformity amidst variety." Hutcheson notes that this phrase is not a definition of beauty, but rather the cause of the perception to which we give the name. Nevertheless, he spends many of the early pages of the *Inquiry* identifying uniformity amidst variety in all sorts of objects, an obvious effort to argue for these as objective qualities. But as he recognizes, only geometric figures nakedly exhibit ideal beauty. Most of the objects to which we respond aesthetically fall into the category he calls relative beauty. Relative beauty is that "which is apprehended in any object, commonly consider'd as an imitation of some original: And this beauty is founded on a conformity, or a kind of unity between the original and the copy" ("Beauty" IV.1). Such a statement seems to indicate that Hutcheson has abandoned any attempt to identify unmediated experience.

Instead he concentrates on the nature of our response, which he says is spontaneous and unreflective, a direct and unforced reaction to the beautiful or ugly object. But in developing his concept of original and copy, he touches on a psychology that involves much more than impulsive response:

> The original may be either some object in nature, or some establish'd idea, for if there be any known idea as a standard, and rules to fix this image or idea by, we may make a beautiful imitation. Thus a statuary [sculptor], painter, or poet, may please us with an Hercules, if his piece retains the grandeur, and those marks of strength, and courage, which we imagine in that hero. ("Beauty" IV.1)

The relation, then, is between the work of art and its model either in nature or in the collective mind and developed there through a literary tradition, though Hutcheson doesn't say so. Nor does he acknowledge that once the mind takes pleasure in comparing two things—unless the comparison is simply a matter of size, shape, color, or other feature of physical detail—something beside sensation is bound to be involved. The example of Hercules would suggest that the concept of imitation Hutcheson proposes in which the work becomes an imitation of the audience's already established concept draws him toward the kind of relativism one modern critic sees him trying to avoid.[9] There is clearly an expectation upon which pleasure depends that is antecedent to aesthetic experience, and this expectation may involve a moral idea, as well as other kinds of standard such as grandeur or strength. Yet Hutcheson is at the same time committed to the priority of sensation as the process by which ideas are raised in the mind. There is an obscure acknowledgment of this difficulty in his reference to "a just representation of manners or characters as they are in nature" ("Beauty" IV.6). It is hard to know how we could decide such justness without bringing prior experience and judgment to our perception, and this of course puts his concept of an aesthetic sense at risk.

The theory of relative beauty nevertheless has the advantage of permitting Hutcheson to establish man-made beauty as the center of aesthetic experience. There are several conveniences. A representation of something that is not beautiful may please because of accuracy or novelty:

> And farther, to obtain comparative beauty alone, it is not necessary that there be any beauty in the original; the imitation of absolute beauty may in the whole make a more lovely piece, and yet an exact imitation shall still be beautiful, tho the original were entirely void of it: Thus the deformitys of old age in a picture, the rudest rocks or mountains in a landskip, if well represented, shall have abundant beauty, tho perhaps not so great as if the original were absolutely beautiful, and as well represented: Nay, perhaps the novelty may make us prefer the representation of irregularity. ("Beauty" IV.1)

This concession to the experience of the senses, if that is what it is, allows Hutcheson to vindicate certain formalist principles that we might have expected him to ignore. This occurs when he turns to poetry. Poets, he asserts, should attempt relative, rather than original beauty, for in depicting human character complete perfection is not credible. Absolute beauty in poetry applies only to the rhythmical qualities of artistic language, whereas figure (metaphor, simile, allegory) belongs to relative beauty ("Beauty" IV.2–3).

What one notices as Hutcheson's argument moves along is that although he has initially accepted the Lockean proposition that what we perceive are

9. Cf. Caroline Wilkes Korsmeyer, "Relativism and Hutcheson's Aesthetic Theory," *JHI* 36 (1975), 319–30.

ideas in the mind and that the word "beauty" and terms like it refer to perception rather than to qualities actually in objects, he writes continually as if both propositions were the case, and hence as if taste were both objective and subjective. This is evident in a passage in which he explains how we take pleasure in ugly objects: "but as to our sense of beauty, no composition of objects which give not unpleasant simple ideas, seems positively unpleasant or painful of itself, had we never observ'd any thing better of the kind. Deformity is only the absence of beauty, or deficiency in the beauty expected in any species: Thus bad musick pleases rusticks who never heard any better, and the finest ear is not offended with tuning of instruments if it be not too tedious, where no harmony is expected" ("Beauty" VI.1). It should be noted that the standard by which one can judge music bad ought to differ from that by which one prefers different kinds of music at different stages of experience. Hutcheson has entered difficult territory, but he is determined to maintain his theory of a separate aesthetic faculty, an internal sense that is a "natural" power of perception, "or determination of the mind to receive necessarily certain ideas from the presence of objects" ("Beauty" VI.10).

Hutcheson's effort to maintain an archetypal aesthetic experience reminds us of the desire in much eighteenth-century criticism to adhere to a timeless standard and to identify works that transcend fashion. Yet the later pages of the *Inquiry* (VI.11–12) acknowledge another eighteenth-century commonplace, the awareness that taste is a fluid process. Hutcheson notes that our experience of beauty may be modified by association of ideas, education, and custom, all of them influences that rock our aesthetic appreciation off-center. The actual experience of beauty might almost seem to be a matter of the degree to which the psychological makeup of the individual corrodes the function of the internal sense. We get a glimpse of the notion of human experience as decline from an original, though Hutcheson does not consciously take such a position.

Does this fairly represent Hutcheson's position? Aware that taste is various, he accounts for variation by arguing that the habit of association, not in itself a capacity to experience beauty, may influence us either to prefer one kind of beauty over another or even to believe that something is beautiful which is not. Hutcheson contends that the association of ideas, though it may temper or distort our sense of beauty, is not to be confused with it. It is the capacity of association that makes us think of groves or woods as solitary or melancholy, for example. Association also accounts for the imposition of certain ideas of feeling upon neutral matter: "And this is often the occasion both of great pleasure and pain, delight and aversion to many objects, which of themselves might have been perfectly indifferent to us: but these approbations, or distastes, are remote from the ideas of beauty, being plainly different ideas" (VI.11).

There are a number of ways to regard this distinction. One is to conclude that by a sense of beauty Hutcheson means a kind of intuition. Ideally that intuition is confined entirely to registering in the mind the fact that what one contemplates is beautiful (or deformed). This interpretation would also make room for Hutcheson's attention to the concept of disinterestedness. Aesthetic experience, he believes, is positively distinct from any motive or acquisition, or from the joy of discovering an advantage to ourselves ("Beauty" I.14). The self is involved merely to notice, not to use or desire to use. Here, of course, he anticipates Kant. But it is not at all clear how far such a discrimination can be pursued, especially if one is dealing with poetry. By the time Hutcheson comes to discuss the role of education and custom in assisting our appreciation of "the finest Objects that are presented to us" ("Beauty" VII.3), he has more or less tacitly confessed that the sense of beauty is bound up with other forms of psychic and mental experience but without revising his original concept of a separate aesthetic faculty. However, the problem is not just one of inadequate psychology, or of a concept of the beautiful that is overly dependent on special circumstances and conditions. Hutcheson sought to affirm our common relation to a natural order, to find something in the world of matter that offered a connection between it and human perception. But his definition of beauty is so abstract as to be elusive. "Unity amidst variety" is a phrase that seems to say everything and nothing.

An equally difficult problem is how to shift from forms of art that are essentially visual or aural to the verbal. As I have tried to show, Hutcheson's assignment of responses to special senses or faculties compels him to abandon the idea of integrated perception he theorizes for the sense of beauty. Though he admits degrees of beauty, and though he acknowledges subsidiary forms of pleasure (or pain) derived from education, custom, association, and the like, he believes that a single sense allows us to register relative beauty by means of "resemblance" (which includes metaphor, simile, and "likeness") as well as measures and cadence, which are instances of absolute beauty ("Beauty" IV.3). But it is not until he is well into the second treatise, "An Inquiry concerning Moral Good and Evil," that there is a sustained discussion of imaginative literature, and when he does embark on such a discussion, he divides what we might call the technical features of poetry from character and action. As a result, it is the "moral sense" (at a higher level than the sense of beauty, but like it in being spontaneous and instinctive) that is the "Foundation . . . of the chief pleasures of poetry" ("Moral" VI.7). Poetry is, moreover, more powerfully affective than visual beauty, though Hutcheson still seeks to establish very close analogues between our responses to the beautiful and the moral:

> But as the contemplation of moral objects, either of vice or virtue, affects us more strongly, and moves our passions in a quite different and more powerful manner than natural beauty, or what we commonly call deformity; so the most moving beautys bear a relation to our moral sense, and affect us more vehemently, than the representations of natural objects in the liveliest descriptions. Dramatic and epic poetry, are intirely addres'd to this sense, and raise our passions by the fortunes of characters, distinctly represented as morally good or evil. ("Moral" VI.7)

But of course the moral sense takes in much more than poetry, so what Hutcheson seems to be offering is a psychology of feeling that may be responsive to real as well as to fictional events. The emotion he chooses to discuss is compassion, a feeling basic to his theory that we are naturally benevolent. Compassion is spontaneous, antecedent to advantage or interest, and requires exercise. It explains our interest in the characters and destinies of others, and though Hutcheson does not in any way develop a theory of forms, he at least notes that we are drawn especially to tragedies because they depict "the moral beauty of the characters and actions which we love to behold." But moral objects have no obvious parallel to sensory objects: as Hutcheson confesses, the literary depiction of morally perfect characters is not very interesting. The one connection is the subject's need for a lively representation. So Hutcheson resorts to a mimetic explanation for our delight in literature:

> Where we are studying to raise any desire, or admiration of an object really beautiful, we are not content with a bare narration, but endeavour, if we can, to present the object it self, or the most lively image of it. And hence the epic poem, or tragedy, gives a far greater pleasure than the writings of philosophers, tho both aim at recommending virtue. The representing the actions themselves, if the representation be judicious, natural, and lively, will make us admire

the good, and detest the vitious, the inhuman, the treacherous, and cruel, by means of our moral sense, without any reflections of the poet to guide our sentiments. ("Moral" VI.7)

As we shall see, Hutcheson's conviction that the very image of character and action is the center of our interest is one of the most important points on which his theory differs from Lessing's: Lessing argues that both the visual and verbal forms are, as signs, merely the agencies or media for what the imagination fashions. For Hutcheson it is the material object or the narrated action that draws us; for Lessing it is what they represent.

Hutcheson would seem to say that by our very humanity we can decide the nature of the object before us. If the uncertain parallel between the aesthetic and moral senses still holds, then one would expect that the possibility of variation from spectator to spectator that Hutcheson has noticed in the judgment of relative beauty would obtain in the moral realm. But he fails to resolve or clarify the problem of subjectivity partly because he insists on faculties designed for special rather than general responses and partly because he understates the endless variety of actual response. For him "our Sentiments" would appear to be universal and very nearly automatic, and his confidence in these sentiments perhaps leads him to avoid asking precisely how feeling is communicated[10] or whether some passions aroused in the audience might be other than disinterested. At the same time, one can see a kind of advantage to Hutcheson's system: it allows him to retain concepts of objective form, uniformity in variety in material objects, and patterns of moral destiny in literary works. These formal qualities can then be matched in normative or theoretical responses that preserve the current of understanding and sympathy between the arts and their audience.

---

10. For an excellent account of eighteenth-century speculations about the process of representing and communicating feeling in words of literature, see P. W. K. Stone, *The Art of Poetry 1750–1820: Theories of Poetic Composition and Style in the Late Neo-Classic and Early Romantic Periods* (New York: Barnes and Noble, 1967), chapter 7, "The Role of Feeling in Composition," 64–76. Many of the speculations are, as one might expect, based in traditional rhetorical theory.

Burke

The antidote to this is to deny altogether that abstract qualities such as proportion or harmony or perfection can in themselves evoke disinterested responses. This is the position of Edmund Burke. Obviously responding to Hutcheson, Burke enumerates the ways in which beauty in nature varies proportion between and within species and argues that reducing beauty to quantitative measurement is merely arbitrary. "The patrons of proportion," he charges, "have transferred their artificial ideas to nature," and he adds that having outlived the fashion of gardens sliced into geometrical patterns, "we begin to feel that mathematical ideas are not the true measures of beauty" (*A Philosophical Enquiry* [1757], 101). Burke ultimately settles for an interesting version of the subjective. Because one of his concerns is to distinguish the beautiful from the sublime, he looks for the subjective perceptions that justify the two terms. He finds them first of all in the senses—beauty seems to him to involve what is soft, yielding, gradually varying, and delicate while the sublime involves hard sensory qualities and emotions associated with peril and violence (112–18)—but, more suggestively, they are distinguished by the impression of authority and power generating sublimity and something more maternal linked to feelings of beauty:

> The authority of a father, so useful to our well-being, and so justly venerable on all accounts, hinders us from having that entire love for him that we have for our mothers, where the parental authority is almost melted down into the mother's fondness and indulgence. (111)

The passage articulates and crystallizes Burke's insistence on beauty as a term that reflects a prerational liking for certain objects, a very personal relation of the self to something outside us. As he says, "we submit to what we admire, but we love what submits to us; in one case we are forced, in the other we are flattered into compliance" (113).[11] In one sense, this is

---

11. The passages from Burke just reviewed are central to W. J. T. Mitchell's important essay, "Eye and Ear: Edmund Burke and the Politics of Sensibility," in *Iconology: Image, Text, Ideology*, 116–49. Mitchell emphasizes Burke's argument that language is nonpictorial, that its images are visually confused and obscure, and that therefore it prompts the sublime (which is fearful) far more readily than the visual, which offers clear images. As Mitchell points out, Burke's terms evoke political values that "link sublimity and beauty with the stereotypes of

potentially utterly subjective, except that Burke would be inclined to say that, while aberrant preferences may occur, we generally admire and love similar things. The worlds of the beautiful and the sublime are thus an extension of the "natural" relationships to our parents, or to objects of affection and authority. On these terms we might expect Burke to emphasize taste as an emotional reaction, and although much earlier in the "Introduction on Taste" he appears to assign it more to the judgment than to the feelings, he eventually shows himself mainly interested in the power of language to affect the passions. Before considering this topic, however, it is important to note that for Burke the experience of the senses is essentially uniform and universal: "I believe no man thinks a goose to be more beautiful than a swan, or imagines that what they call a Friezland hen excels a peacock" (15). Nature may vary, but the organs of human aesthetic response are uniform in function and, in the absence of "unnatural habits and associations," uniform in choice of object.[12] Whatever their differences, Burke and Hutcheson alike guarantee more or less without argument a natural connection, or so it would seem.

But Part V of Burke's *Philosophical Enquiry*, his discussion of language, sets off in a different direction altogether, arguing that language functions quite differently from the senses and implying that as a result the power that language has to move us has nothing to do with any power to transmit into our minds the images of objects. Compound abstract words (terms such as "virtue," "honor," "persuasion," and "magistrate") may well have the power to move us but "they do not derive it from any representation raised in the mind of the things for which they stand" (164). And if we try to translate

---

gender" (129), and he adds, "The sensory enforcement of sublimity in these authority figures [the father, the state, the leader] . . . is consistently described by Burke as a strategy of visual deprivation" (130). Burke makes the point that "deprivation," or what he describes as relative distance, allows us to take delight in sublime representations: "for terror is a passion which always produces delight when it does not press too close, and pity is a passion accompanied with pleasure, because it arises from love and affection," *A Philosophical Enquiry*, 46. Burke's effort to discriminate the two forms of affect on the subjective level seems to work through the familial images to a sense of their relationship on a social level. There are further complications in his associating beauty with the visual and sublimity with the verbal, but when these opposites are carried to an extreme they result in the sublime. Burke is also in these speculations seeking a universal explanation in the "natural and mechanical causes of our passions" (140). See Mitchell's account on 128–29.

12. For a reading that emphasizes this aspect of Burke's concept of taste, see Frances Ferguson, "Legislating the Sublime," *Studies in Eighteenth-Century British Art and Aesthetics*, ed. Ralph Cohen (Berkeley and Los Angeles: University of California Press, 1985), 128–47, especially 131.

such words into concrete ideas, we find ourselves simply substituting other "general words," so that when a particular idea finally emerges its effect is lost. In other words, the emotional power of words has nothing to do with visual ideas in the mind, and Burke goes on to argue that even detailed descriptions like, say, the geography of the Danube fail to yield any exact picture in the mind. All of this bears on his belief that clear ideas, which appeal to the reason, are radically different from vague or obscure ideas whose very indefiniteness contributes to the power of affect.

Burke is all the while talking about poetry, and he quotes liberally from Virgil, Homer, Milton, and Lucretius to the effect that none of them conveys any exact or useful sensory information:

> In reality poetry and rhetoric do not succeed in exact description so well as painting does; their business is to affect rather by sympathy than imitation; to display rather the effect of things on the mind of the speaker, or of others, than to present a clear idea of the things themselves. (172)

Burke testifies repeatedly to the enormous emotional power of language: "we find by experience that eloquence and poetry are as capable, nay indeed much more capable of making deep and lively impressions than any other arts" (173); "it is in my power to raise a stronger *emotion* by the description [of a palace, a temple, or a landscape] than I could do by the best painting" (60); "poetry with all its obscurity, has a more general as well as a more powerful dominion over the passions than any other art" (61). How, then, does it manage this? Burke is inexact, but what he seems to be getting at is that such affective force derives first of all from our awareness that poetic or rhetorical language translates how the speaker feels about things: sympathy impels us to "enter into the concerns of others" (44); "we take an extraordinary part in the passions of others" (173). This would suggest also that somehow the detachment of language from sensed objects has something to do with its power, and this is what Burke goes on to argue: "Now, as there is a moving tone of voice, an impassioned countenance, an agitated gesture, which affects independently of the things about which they are exerted, so there are words, and certain dispositions of words, which being particularly devoted to passionate subjects, and always used by those who are under the influence of any passion; they touch and move us more than those which far more clearly and distinctly express the subject matter" (175). The circumstances of usage determine how we respond to language, and such circumstances in one way or another so condition us that we may listen to words that have no rational relation to the immediate occasion of their use and be moved as if we were in the presence of momentous events. Burke was notoriously reluctant to accept association psychology as an explanation of the reaction to words, though he comes close to it in this section of his essay. What he does is suggest that words cut loose from circumstance or referentiality nevertheless somehow have the power to stir us, a power perhaps conferred by our interest in the emotions of others. At this point, he echoes in part Hutcheson's identification of sympathy as something close to an innate idea, and more particularly, he anticipates the speculations of Diderot on the disjunction of language and its material referents, a concern to be addressed in my concluding chapter.

Mendelssohn

To recover an earlier point, one of Burke's more notable insights is his linking of affective language to obscurity. Hutcheson, as we have seen, had similar thoughts when he distinguished the descriptive precision of the scientist from the emotionalism of the poet, but Burke goes further in suggesting that a positive lack of cognitive clarity is involved in affective language. A more complete and systematic exploitation of this issue is to be found in the German aesthetic thinkers of the mid-eighteenth century. I have in mind especially Moses Mendelssohn and Gotthold Lessing and their attention to the psychology of representation as a serial process. Their arguments can be seen in part as a refinement of the theories of Hutcheson and Burke just discussed, but there are significant differences. For one thing, Mendelssohn and Lessing, together with others in the German Enlightenment, rely upon the rationalist psychology of the Cartesian, Christian Wolff.[13] Mendelssohn had read the English and Scottish empiricists of the first half of the century, and in his willingness to attempt to account for aesthetic pleasure in a detailed way, he is much like them. However, Wolff's psychological system is basically cognitive rather than emotive and submits aesthetic responses to the requirements of a semiotic system in which aesthetic perception is part of a sequence of psychic and

13. Wolff's psychology and semiotic theory are thoroughly and competently analyzed in David E. Wellbery, *Lessing's* Laocoon: *Semiotics and Aesthetics in the Age of Reason*, 9–42.

cognitive events, as David Wellbery demonstrates. The system itself arranges *ideas* or representations according to a series of alternatives following each other in a kind of chain, which Wellbery calls "a map of the progress of knowledge from crude sensations to refined conceptualizations."[14] First an idea may be clear or obscure, then if clear, either distinct or confused. A clear idea is one in which an object is identifiably represented in the mind. An example of a confused clear idea would be the recognition of a human being as such but without knowledge of details of appearance or identity. If the representation becomes distinct as well, then the object is evident in all its different components or details; in other words the mind contemplates it analytically. (This last is a stage that both Hutcheson and Burke excluded from aesthetic affect.) If we find the representation clear and confused, then we are at the stage of aesthetic perception: in other words we perceive the object as distinct from other objects and as a whole. Although Wellbery suggests that Mendelssohn and his colleagues ascribe a power of affect (that is, pleasure or pain) to this stage of perception, they basically see it as a mode of knowledge.

In addition, Wellbery proposes a broad classification for the type of theory he reviews, one that makes it almost exclusively representational and semiotic.[15] This means that unlike a performance-type theory, which supposes that a specific affective response is designed by the creator of the aesthetic object, the representational mode is instead a function of the way in which the subject reacts to the sign. The sign, in turn, is considered to be transparent, an instrument to be seen *through*, functional and arbitrary in the sense that it is a substitute: "Representations are surrogative, referential and neutral" (10). The sign is arbitrary in the sense that it is not understood as a social institution with established meanings but as a set of instruments "which rational beings use to mark, externalize, manipulate, and communicate their mental representations" (18). For Wolff the sign is a

14. Wellbery, *Lessing's* Laocoon, 13. Wellbery argues here that "the notion of representation governs and gives unity to what today would fall into entirely disparate realms: the obscure representations can be as subtle as the functioning of our bodily organs and completely distinct representations would have the look of a calculus, but nevertheless both qualify as representations. . . . We have here first of all a set of formal distinctions, second a map of the progress of knowledge from crude sensations to refined conceptualizations, and third a schema for progress in history. . . . Whether talking about psychology, language, history, or art, the early eighteenth century was usually retracing the branching paths of this schematization."

15. What Wellbery designates as a "representational" aesthetics belongs to a threefold set of "theory-types." The other two are the performance-type, which is associated with rhetoric, and the expressive-type, which relates to hermeneutics. See the table on p. 48 for Wellbery's elaborated analysis of the three types.

liberation from sensation, for by withdrawing the mind from its involvement with matter the sign frees it to select and concentrate. One of the more salient features of later German aestheticism is the belief that too powerful an engagement of the mind with material sensations stalls imaginative response. And one of the important differences between British and German aesthetic theory is that for the Germans the work of art is no longer the object of aesthetic perception; it is simply the medium.

If this conclusion was implicit in the thinking of Addison and Burke, it was not one they openly claimed. And if the work of art is a sign or an occasion for the spectator's imagination to function, then how can it be the object of a judgment of taste? The answer might be, only as it permits certain kinds of response, in which case we might be thought connoisseurs of our own aesthetic sentiments rather than of the representations that prompt them.

These preliminaries help place Mendelssohn's aesthetic thinking not only with respect to Lessing and Kant, but also with respect to French and British theorists. His interest centers decisively in the way in which the mind responds to images, and his explanation of such responses deserves some attention. In his *Rhapsody, or Postscript to the Letters concerning Emotion* (1761) he argues that affect is not just a simple single attitude toward an object or idea, but a mixture of perception and awareness of affect. For example, "when we pay attention to ourselves, we notice that our annoyance at the unpleasant feeling is not always aroused by the idea but many times by the object of the idea. We do not always want *not-to-have* [*Nichthaben*] the idea, as I had explained, but the *not-being* [*Nichtseyn*] of the object. We disapprove of an impending evil, we wish it not to happen, or that it lay in our power to correct it. But once the evil happens, and happens without our fault and without our being able to prevent it, then the idea of it has a much stronger attraction for us and we long to take it to ourselves."[16]

The consequence is that Mendelssohn associates desire and pleasure first of all with the kind of relationship established between the self and the object of perception. The possibility that the representation of an unpleasant object may be enjoyed is to be explained by our lack of responsibility, our noninvolvement. Citing the avidity with which tourists visited the devastation from the Lisbon earthquake of 1755, he adds that our negative feelings

16. Moses Mendelssohn, *Aesthetische Schriften in Auswahl*, ed. Otto F. Best (Darmstadt: Wissenschaftliche Buchgesellschaft, 1974), 127. Unless otherwise noted, my quotations are translated from this collection.

are directed more to the object than to its representation. Wellbery's phrase is: "Art presents its objects as present, but as *present at a distance*" (66). Distance is thus for Mendelssohn virtually the definition of the aesthetic, but the notion requires our attention to some close reasoning.

As Wellbery notes (63) Mendelssohn's aesthetic writings all tend to separate representation and object and to locate the source of pleasure in the representation, not in the object: "the perfection, which is the source of aesthetic pleasure, resides in the representation itself."[17] This would suggest, contrary to all expectation, that Mendelssohn might be proposing something close to baroque theories of ornament, though such does not appear to be the case. Nor does the statement make it plain how perfection, which for Mendelssohn is "sensate" perfection, is determined. *Rhapsody* attempts an explanation by proposing, first of all, that perfection is accurate representation and, second, that pleasure comes from the mind's self-conscious awareness of its own activity in apprehending the representation. As Wellbery says, "This additional source of pleasure, the enhancement of the soul's reality (*Realität*) through actualization of its representational-conative potential, is, according to Mendelssohn more universal (*weit allgemeiner*) than the perfection inhering in the object" (65).

Nevertheless, for Mendelssohn affect consists in the perception of beauty (or "perfection") in a representation accompanied by a reflexive consciousness of the mind's own act of aesthetic perception. Moreover, it is not entirely clear whether the work of art, as a representation of an object, has the same status as a representation in the mind, to which one may presumably respond in the same way, even though the representation in the mind may be an image, not of an object but of a representation of an object. Wellbery says that Mendelssohn's theory requires a sense of unreality in the object derived through its representation: "As an object of art (and not as an existent met in nature), the object is encountered in a field of security. The

17. At the same time, it is not easy to determine from Wellbery's account whether Mendelssohn's position represents a significant advance over Aristotle's claim in *Poetics* 4 that mimetic representation allows us to view normally disagreeable objects with pleasure. Here is Wellbery's statement: "Objects in themselves ugly or evil, that is, objects with predominantly negative value qualities, can nevertheless be objects of aesthetic cognition so long as the representation itself is a perfect sensate representation" (63). The problem here is that in eighteenth-century thinking what one views is an idea of an object, and presumably these "predominantly negative value qualities" are themselves already in the mind. What in fact Wellbery records in this section of his book is Mendelssohn's developing theory which in the 1750s proposed a direct intuition of the object without the mediation of signs, followed by another phase, that being described here, followed by yet a third, which *Rhapsody* presents and which I discuss in my text.

subject is in no way threatened or overwhelmed by the object because the object is distanced from him by art" (66). This means, of course, not total absence, since we must be conscious of the nonpresence of the object perhaps as a result of the representation itself. It also might cause us seriously to question the concept of the representation as transparent, at least for Mendelssohn, if its task is to be placed between the object and our clear or distinct idea of it. One may wonder whether Mendelssohn's theory depends quite so much on a doctrine of artistic illusion as Wellbery claims. Perhaps even more serious is the implication that when the work of art is the object of our perception our pleasure may indeed depend upon that object, especially if it is mimetic. If that is so, we are back to Aristotle's theory that it is the quality of the imitation on which affective pleasure depends. In other words, we may be returning once more through the subjective to a theory of objective form.

It is, of course, much less simple. In explaining our capacity to enjoy the representation of deformed objects Mendelssohn says that our feelings are mixed in such a way that we recognize a deformed object as unpleasant but are pleased that our response is correct:

> For even a representation of defect in the object, as well as an expression of displeasure because of it [the deformity], are not defects on the part of the thinking being, but rather much more affirmative and substantive determinants of it. We can perceive no good act without feeling approval, without an inner pleasure, and no evil act without disapproval of the act itself and an inner loathing of it. Even the recognition [*Erkennen*] that an act is evil and the disapproval of it are positive characteristics of the soul, they are expressions of the powers of the soul insofar as recognition and desire are concerned, and are elements of perfection that necessarily excite desire and pleasure in this connection. (*Aesthetische Schriften*, 129–30)

Nothing in this process distinguishes art or our responses to art from any other kind of affective perception. And the more serious problem still remains: the theory of aesthetic representation Wellbery claims for Mendelssohn and his colleagues is one in which the work of art, the medium, is transparent, and yet pleasure is somehow derived from the medium. But for the moment Mendelssohn considers only general perceptions of the pleasant and unpleasant, and what concerns him here is the nature of the perception itself.

The mixture of perceived deformity and perfection, Mendelssohn writes, may vary:

> In general . . . the perception of the imperfect, the bad, and the ugly always prompts a mixed feeling in which displeasure in the object and pleasure in the idea come together. Considered as a whole, that such an idea will be pleasant or unpleasant depends on whether perception of the object or perception of our idea predominates. . . . When the object approaches us too closely, when we look at it as part of us or wholly as ourselves, then the pleasure of the idea totally vanishes, the relation to the subject will become at the same time an unpleasant relation to us in which the subject and the object will blend [*fallen*] equally into one another: that is why the idea will be unpleasant." (130)

To put the matter in terms we have already noticed in the works of other Enlightenment critics, our pleasure depends upon our being spectators, though Mendelssohn specifies exceptions such as the thrill of experiencing imminent physical danger. But allowing for such exceptions, he maintains that even in representations where we might be moved to sympathize with the sufferings of others, our pleasure depends upon our marking a certain boundary, "to place them at a certain distance" (132). He invokes Lucretius to support the notion that perceived exemption allows us to take pleasure in the sufferings of others, and even makes a concession not unlike that of Hume to the formal properties of artistic imitation whose perception "softens the strength of our horror at the object and at the same time enhances the idea of the subjective" (134).

Taste is for Mendelssohn acquired through habit, and it involves the temporary acceptance of illusion which is in some way simultaneously known to be just that. In perhaps his most important assertion for my argument, he points out that when works of art are in question it is necessary that we be aware of the media before us. Marble and canvas remind us that we are at a distance from natural objects, and this is important: "A waxwork figure in lifesize and in natural garments makes a very adverse impression" (135). But our perception of the art object as a work of art is an acknowledgment of the perfection of genius, of the power of the artist to stop short of complete illusion and to compel the imaginative presence of an object through the artistic medium. Wellbery argues (68) that what is required is a medium deliberately unlike the original object; therefore, he contends, language is the ideal medium, if it is transparent language. Transparency is what makes the idea (not the object) existentially present.[18] However, it might be objected that taste is directed at the medium, at the *way* in which something is represented. But it would appear that for Mendelssohn we perceive and take pleasure in art as a process rather than as a thing. We are offered ultimately an aesthetic which, though it claims a great deal for affective experience, substantially privileges cognition, and by implication at least, makes taste a cognitive judgment first and foremost. At the same time, it is, I must emphasize, a judgment directed at a mode of representation.

Lessing

It should be evident by this time that if the theories reviewed so far in this chapter are representative, there are two broad categories of thought about the interplay between the work of art and the perceiving mind. One category, prominent in the work of Hutcheson, proposes a kind of balance between objective qualities in material or human nature and the aesthetic or sympathetic spectator. This is also Burke's view, except that his theory of artistic language borders on a concept of illusion and at the very least cancels any easy notion that language or the emotions it produces can duplicate or replace the experience of the sense. The second category, represented by Mendelssohn, sees the aesthetic and the responses that word includes as a matter of the perceived distance between the object and the spectator, but the significance of that distance rests in how it is perceived, in what the subject believes he or she knows. This brings us to Lessing.

18. Wellbery argues that the emphasis of Baumgarten, Meier, and Mendelssohn on the transparency of language—an emphasis that he acknowledges is general in Enlightenment aesthetics—indicates a widespread and fundamental theoretical shift away from traditional rhetoric, away from a doctrine of eloquence. Language—the sign—is necessary but secondary, an instrument of aesthetic perception, not its object. Therefore, language as practiced by baroque poets is ruled out: "such linguistic pyrotechnics, such virtuosity in the formation of the expression as was characteristic of courtly aristocratic art, is adamantly rejected by the aestheticians" (71). I would agree that this reflects a powerful and persistent intention in both later seventeenth-century and Enlightenment aesthetic theory. Whether this intention is as clean and clear-cut as this is another matter.

For Lessing, even more decisively than for Mendelssohn, works of art are not in themselves the ends of contemplation or emotion, but rather the media for the spectator's or reader's imagination: the aesthetic object is what is not present but is instead indicated by the visual or verbal image. The act of aesthetic appreciation is a drawing of inferences or a reading of implications. In the *Laocoon* (1766) there is little of the schematic psychologizing that pervades Mendelssohn's aesthetic speculations. What interests Lessing first of all is the difference between the ways in which we perceive the plastic arts and literature, a difference he uses to exalt poetry over painting and sculpture. Poetry is superior because it can be less palpable, less immediately concrete and sensory. The plastic arts are of necessity intensely material and therefore tend to inhibit the imagination. The mind retains material details from a painting because the whole is immediately present to it. In a poem such details are awkward because they require an act of memory to retain them; hence, the linearity of language forces the poet to address us differently:

> I do not deny to language altogether the power of depicting the corporeal whole according to its parts. It can do so because its signs, although consecutive, are still arbitrary. But I do deny it to language as the medium of poetry, because the illusion, which is the principal object of poetry, is wanting in such verbal descriptions of bodies. And this illusion, I say, must be wanting because the coexistent nature of a body comes into conflict with the consecutive nature of language, and although dissolving the former into the latter makes the division of the whole into its parts easier for us, the final resembling of the parts into a whole is made extremely difficult and often even impossible.[19]

According to Lessing, the poet's illusion works best in representing objects "other than those that are visible" (76), and it is for this reason that he gives preference to poetry.

It is the material immediacy of the plastic arts that is their disadvantage. Only the particular and the momentary are available to the painter or sculptor; to be successful they must capture just the right moment, that which suggests far more than itself:

19. Gotthold Ephraim Lessing, *Laocoon: An Essay on the Limits of Painting and Poetry*, trans. Edward Allen McCormick (Baltimore: Johns Hopkins University Press, 1984), 88.

> Only that which gives free rein to the imagination is effective. The more we see, the more we must be able to imagine. And the more we add in our imaginations, the more we must think we see. In the full course of an emotion, no point is less suitable for this than its climax. There is nothing beyond this, and to present the utmost to the eye is to bind the wings of the fancy and to compel it, since it cannot soar above the impression made upon the senses, to concern itself with weaker images, shunning the visible fullness already represented as a limit beyond which it cannot go. Thus, if Laocoon sighs, the imagination can hear him cry out; but if he cries out, it can neither go one step higher nor one step lower than this representation without seeing him in a more tolerable and less interesting condition. One either hears him merely moaning or else sees him dead. (19–20)

The moment, he adds, must "express nothing transitory"; it must be a synecdoche for the universal or significant. Lessing thus discredits the visual or tactile and unlike Mendelssohn does not allow sensible qualities even the privilege of giving pleasure. What we find beautiful, he remarks elsewhere, "is beautiful not to our eyes but to our imagination through our eyes" (41). The sign may be the occasion of our taking pleasure in an aesthetic object, but in itself it is not the source of pleasure. It is the indirection of poetry especially that allows us to react aesthetically or to react to what occurs in our imaginations as a consequence of being given the effect and not the cause: "Paint for us, you poets, the pleasure, the affection, the love and delight which beauty brings, and you have painted beauty itself" (111). Thus, the advantage that language has over the plastic arts is, in a sense, a negative one: it offers nothing to our sight. And imagination, the faculty by which we supply the reality at which the sign, visual or verbal, beckons, is little more than a power of logical inference. One might argue, a bit unkindly, that Lessing has rediscovered Aristotle's probability.[20]

"Beauty itself" is another problem. Throughout *Laocoon* Lessing has to

20. Though it only treats probability in relation to eighteenth-century English critical theory, Douglas Lane Patey's *Probability and Literary Form: Philosophic Theory and Literary Practice in the Augustan Age* (Cambridge: Cambridge University Press, 1984) deals carefully and elaborately with the ways in which logical inference was thought to be structured by the literary work. For the terms set down by Aristotle and their subsequent influence, see Part I, "Stages in the History of the Idea of Probability."

deal with the fact that the statuary group that gives its name to his title depicts an incident of painful emotion. Yet the expressions on the faces of Laocoon and his sons are far from the torment such a situation might be expected naturally to produce. Lessing's explanation is what we have already discussed: a realistic representation of physical pain would merely be that and would not lead the imagination beyond. Moreover, he argues that the Greeks depicted only beauty, and the ugliness produced by suffering would hardly give pleasure (chap. 2). Visual beauty, he seems to suggest, has little to do with emotion or the dynamics of emotion itself. It does involve spatial organization, wholeness, and coherence. He offers no worked out definition, but perhaps we can accept that something like Hutcheson's unity in the midst of variety is in his mind. In addition, however, in talking of beauty and ugliness he seems to be thinking largely of the human form and features. In other words, the plastic arts for him, however much they may differ from poetry and drama, are derived from the literary. The context of the Laocoon group, he argues at length, is narrative, and the values Lessing expects the viewer to be interested in are, broadly speaking, values best realized through action. The difference between the synchronic nature of visual perception and the diachrony of language and our reception of it which Lessing insists on so repeatedly might be seen as less an absolute contrast than two different and hierarchically disposed means of portrayal. The synchronic, then, is merely a moment seized from the diachronic.[21]

Thus, physical beauty and ugliness are not separate and isolated qualities to which we respond: or if they are, then our response to ugliness is disgust or ridicule and to beauty, pleasure and attraction. But, as Hutcheson discovered, the poet has to deal with the ugly in some fashion. Noting Homer's account of Thersites (*Iliad* 2, 211ff.), Lessing suggests that the usual reaction to physical ugliness, ridicule, is blocked under certain

21. Murray Krieger, in "Representation in Word and in Drama: The Illusion of the Natural Sign," *Aesthetics of Illusion: Theoretical and Historical Approaches*, ed. Frederick Burwick and Walter Pape (Berlin: de Gruyter, 1990), 200, notes that although Lessing is generally credited with helping dismantle the close association of poetry and painting, he "by no means releases poetry from its mimetic obligation, no less obligatory than painting's." For Lessing, poetry's task is to turn the arbitrary sign as much as possible into something that functions as a natural sign, and drama, as Lessing reports in his letter to Nicolai, through a series of what Krieger calls "*moving pictures*," most completely translates the synchronic into the diachronic. As Krieger remarks, "In this ultimate extension of natural-sign aesthetic to literature, dramatic poetry alone becomes the most perfectly realized representation of the consecutiveness of human experience, because the fact that it is a representation is most completely hidden, so that the illusion is most effective." W. J. T. Mitchell's rather different account of the differentiation shows Lessing turning genre into gender; *Iconology: Image, Text, Ideology*, 98–113.

circumstances, and instead we feel compassion. This is the result of a kind of harmonizing of the physical and spiritual: Thersites' miserable character matches his physical ugliness, and we find the result interesting given the surrounding circumstances Homer supplies. Ugliness, in other words, must have a narrative motive, and when it does, "it loses its repulsive effect almost entirely by the change from coexistence to the consecutive. From this point of view it ceases to be ugliness, as it were, and can therefore combine more intimately with other qualities to produce a new and special effect" (128).

Lessing hovers on the edge of what Diderot was to claim, that our responses to both the plastic and literary arts are themselves a verbal scenario. He does not, however, enter this territory, for to do so would be to go well beyond the terms of the tradition of aesthetic thought to which his work belongs. Mendelssohn and Lessing assume that our aesthetic perception involves an intuition of perfection (*Vollkommenheit*) or imperfection that is a natural and automatic function of consciousness. Varying degrees and mixtures of positive or negative perception are possible, but there is no question of our capacity to make such responses. And in spite of Lessing's adherence to the transparent or natural sign, the effect of his argument is to provide language with an unexpected virtue. Sensory experience and the plastic arts are limited because they can only minimally register the sequence of events, and sequence seems to be in Lessing's mind a central feature of what is natural and elemental in human experience. Only language successfully returns us through its prompting of the imagination to a vision of nature denied to ordinary perception. And for all his attention to the processes of perception and imagination, Lessing emerges, like many of the theorists we are considering, as a kind of formalist.

Hume

The German tradition in eighteenth-century aesthetic theory tended, as I have said, to treat our responses as modes of judgment. Ultimately that is Hume's conclusion in "Of the Standard of Taste" (1757), but some of his earlier remarks offer a different insight, one that seems to classify taste as a mode of passion. In his *Dissertation of the Passions*, which appeared in 1757 but was composed much earlier as the second book of *A Treatise of Human*

Nature (1739), entitled more simply "Of the Passions,"[22] the sense of beauty and deformity is one of a class of secondary impressions, parallel to but less intense than the passions. The division, Hume admits, is "vulgar and specious," but the "raptures of poetry and music," he classifies as emotions, to distinguish them from nonaesthetic impressions (276). But they are at this stage of his thinking parallel in their operation. A later distinction, in *An Enquiry concerning the Principles of Morals* (1751), divides sentiment from reason and reunites taste to moral preference. Reason offers the knowledge of the true and false. Taste gives us the sentiment or feeling of beauty and deformity and vice and virtue, and thereby Hume expresses the broad division between the analytical and the affective we have already noticed in Hutcheson and Burke:

> The one discovers objects as they really stand in nature, without addition or diminution: the other has a productive faculty, and gilding or staining all natural objects with the colours, borrowed from internal sentiment, raises in a manner a new creation. . . . Taste, as it gives pleasure or pain, and thereby constitutes happiness or misery, becomes a motive to action, and is the first spring or impulse to desire or volition.[23]

In concluding this passage Hume asserts that the standard of both reason and taste is fixed by divine will, of the one in the nature of things, the other in the individuality or "peculiar nature" of each being.

This suggests an opening to the main and most prominent issue Hume argues out in "Of the Standard of Taste," whether, given the evident variety and changeability of taste in actual practice, there can be any universal

22. References in the text are to the earlier work, *A Treatise of Human Nature*, ed. L. A. Selby-Bigge, 2d rev. ed., ed. P. H. Nidditch (Oxford: Clarendon Press, 1978).

23. David Hume, *Enquiries concerning Human Understanding and concerning the Principles of Morals*, ed. L. A. Selby-Bigge, 3d rev. ed., ed. P. H. Nidditch (Oxford: Clarendon Press, 1975), §246. This passage is cited by M. H. Abrams, *The Mirror and the Lamp: Romantic Thought and the Critical Tradition* (Oxford: Oxford University Press, 1953), 64; James Engell, "The Source, and End, and Test of Art: Hume's Critique," in *Johnson and His Age*, ed. James Engell, *Harvard Studies* 12 (1984), 239–40; and David Summers, *The Judgment of Sense: Renaissance Naturalism and the Rise of Aesthetics* (Cambridge: Cambridge University Press, 1987), 323. Summers notes that at the end of the Renaissance there was a radical split of point of view toward particulars between the "mathematical," which tended to geometrical abstraction and the subjective, which involved sentiment. Thus Hume "assumed a contrast between reason as a faculty that dealt with the mathematically describable physical particular, and another separate realm called "internal sentiment," which is thoroughly associated with the subjective." The same division has already been noted in Hutcheson.

standard. The result is a brilliant review of the main points, with Hume's position more or less in suspension until the latter paragraphs.[24] His method of opposing arguments for a universal standard to those for its impossibility deliberately creates a context of uncertainty for the question of taste, so that each on either side is subject to rebuttal or contradiction. The careful statement that "it is natural for us to seek a *Standard of Taste*" is confronted by the assertion that "beauty is no quality in things themselves."[25] As Engell points out, no standard is ever established.[26] Instead he shifts the location of a possible standard from objective nature or from works of art themselves to human perception, to the realm of what he calls sentiment. And his evocation of taste as variant and individual and driven by culture, temperament, upbringing, even momentary mood, is articulated with some force. In "The Sceptic," Hume once again argues for the separation of object and sentiment, insisting that the "epithet *beautiful or deformed, desirable or odious,*" which sentiment attaches to objects, "must depend upon the particular fabric or structure of the mind, which enables such particular forms to operate in such a particular manner, and produces a sympathy or conformity between the mind and its objects."[27] And in "Of the Standard of Taste" we find that "One person may even perceive deformity, where another is sensible of beauty; and every individual ought to acquiesce in his own sentiment, without pretending to regulate those of others. To seek real beauty, or real deformity, is as fruitless an inquiry, as to pretend to ascertain

---

24. Useful accounts of Hume's argument are James Engell, "The Source, and End, and Test of Art: Hume's Critique"; Peter Jones, "Hume's Aesthetics Reassessed," *Philosophical Quarterly* 26 (1976), 48–62; Peter Jones, "Cause, Reason, and Objectivity in Hume's Aesthetics," in *Hume: A Re-Evaluation*, ed. Donald W. Livingston and James T. King (New York: Fordham University Press, 1976); and Jeffrey Wieand, "Hume's Two Standards of Taste," *Philosophical Quarterly* 34 (1984), 129–42. A negative analysis that takes "Of the Standard of Taste" as an example of axiological argument is that of Barbara Herrnstein Smith, *Contingencies of Value: Alternative Perspectives for Critical Theory* (Cambridge, Mass.: Harvard University Press, 1988), 55–64. Smith generally disapproves of efforts to decide the value of works of literature or art independently of their cultural determinants: "the argument always either dissolves into infinite regresses, or is supported in circular or bootstrap fashion by unacknowledged self-privileging a priori norms, or amounts to an axiologically impotent restatement of the diversity and conditionality of all preferences and the contingency of all value." This drastic devaluing of Hume's dialectic is followed by the strange concession that "Hume's essay is, to my mind, more interesting and theoretically richer than any other text in the axiological tradition, not excepting Kant's *Critique of Judgment*—though this, of course, is a matter of taste" (64).

25. David Hume, *Of the Standard of Taste and Other Essays*, ed. John W. Lenz (Indianapolis: Bobbs-Merrill, 1965), 5–6.

26. Engell, "The Source, and End, and Test of Art: Hume's Critique," 247.

27. *Of the Standard of Taste and Other Essays*, 124.

the real sweet or real bitter" (6). Yet Hume contemplates the actual results of such subjectivity with discomfort. It might mean the preference for Ogilvy over Milton or Bunyan over Addison (the reversal of preference in the latter pair has of course happened). And the extravagances of negligent or irregular writers are not what allows them to continue to please: Hume, in spite of seeming to accept a mild chaos of taste, nevertheless chooses its order and seeks to place it in the embrace of experience. Raw taste is spontaneous, but a cultivated taste is just that, cultivated and developed through repeated comparison and revision, so that what emerges is neither a standard nor a uniformity of taste, but rather a process by which an ideal model of the critic is matched to a concept of form: "amidst all the variety and caprice of taste, there are certain general principles of approbation or blame, whose influence a careful eye may trace in all operations of the mind. Some particular forms or qualities, from the original structure of the internal fabric are calculated to please and others to displease." (9). Variety and caprice take on the eccentricity of illness: "If, in the sound state of the organ, there be an entire or a considerable uniformity of sentiment among men, we may thence derive an idea of the perfect beauty" (10). Hume's phrasing is carefully conditional, and he is scrupulous to add that the ideal conditions of connoisseurship are not easily achieved.[28] The spectacle of deviant or errant taste appears once again under the concept of defect in the perceiving organs or insufficient delicacy. The cure here is experience over time: in order to join "the perfection of the man, and the perfection of the sense of feeling" practice is required, but even so the ideal of the excellent critic—and it is the critic who epitomizes the proper exercise of taste—is what Hume sets in the path of variation. His account of the career of this critic includes the sharpening of judgment through practice, the habit of comparing works of art, the effort to free oneself from prejudice, to submit one's individuality to the function of being "a man in general," to attend to the teleology of each work of art, to consider the motives and manners of past ages, in short, to become a professional who combines experience and discrimination. The effort is severe: "It is almost impossible," says Hume, "not to feel a predilection for that which suits our particular turn and disposition" (20). As Ralph Cohen has pointed out, Hume's purpose "was to prove that some tastes are better than others and to provide a basis for this

---

28. James Engell, *Forming the Critical Mind: Dryden to Coleridge* (Cambridge, Mass.: Harvard University Press, 1989), analyzes the essay as a treatise on the problems of criticism, especially Hume's effort to show how taste can be more than untutored preference.

distinction."[29] Hume also demonstrates that there are really two kinds of taste, one of them a general sort of taste, relatively untutored, unskilled, and subject to change, variation, and error, the other delicate, rare, and requiring extraordinary patience and discipline to achieve.[30] It is the second sort that reaches what is permanent and definitive in determining the beauty or excellence in a work of art, but as Hume describes it, the achievement seems an especially painful process, one that mutes the spontaneous response to beauty in favor of reasoned discrimination and subordinates both the individual sensibility of the critic and the identity of the age and culture of the work of art to principles or rules that are distant in time or hidden from ordinary sights.

Hume's use of empirical reasoning to work through the issues he deals with is at some distance from Kant's procedure, but their concepts of a disinterested or objective judgment are not without similarity. In order to conceive of a disinterested judgment of taste, Kant insists that it be walled off from charm and emotion: "Taste that requires an added element of *charm* and *emotion* for its delight . . . has not yet emerged from barbarism. . . . A judgement of taste, therefore, is only pure so far as its determining ground is tainted with no merely empirical delight."[31] In similar fashion, Hume imagines a standard of taste exemplified in the rare delicacy of judgment achieved by a professional critic. Both, whatever their differences, arrive at concepts of aesthetic judgment which, if not in their terms precisely cognitive, have allowed a kind of conscious discrimination to supplant affective power.

29. Ralph Cohen, "David Hume's Experimental Method and the Theory of Taste," *ELH* 25 (1958), 272.

30. In this context it is interesting to note Condillac's later and historically broader account of differences in taste as in part the result over time of a pattern of initiation, growth, maturity, and decline. Moreover, he notes that as the role of the analytical mind develops, pleasure diminishes. See *Traité de l'art d'écrire* (1775), in *Œuvres complètes* (Geneva: Slatkine Reprints, 1970), V:475–76. Moreover, Condillac, answering the question of why we are pleased or displeased with any particular aesthetic object, says: "it is that each one of them is in our mind the result of different associations of ideas, according to which we make a judgment, even though it is difficult to say in what they consist" (477).

31. *Critique of Judgment*, 3d moment, §13–14. Kant, in isolating taste from kindred forms of response, makes it the free determination of value: "The *agreeable* is what GRATIFIES a man; the *beautiful* what simply PLEASES him; [and] the *good what is* ESTEEMED (approved), i.e. that on which he sets an objective worth" (1st moment, §5). This division of kinds of pleasure is reminiscent of Burke's less precise distinctions. Burke classifies the relief from privation or pain as *delight*, to distinguish it from positive pleasure, which comes from a mode of representation (*A Philosophical Enquiry*, 35–37). For a discussion of Kant's efforts to distinguish aesthetic pleasure, see Donald W. Crawford, *Kant's Aesthetic Theory* (Madison: University of Wisconsin Press, 1974), 32, 43–55.

It is important to repeat that the level at which the aesthetic theories of Hume and Kant function is one where the theorist seeks to understand the process, without attempting to decide whether any particular perception is good or bad.[32] It might be likened to a theory that explains the physiology of speech and even classifies the content of speech in a broad way but says nothing about any individual utterance. In making such a statement I am of course being unfair to that mode of aesthetic thinking because its nominal purpose is really not to reconcile universal and subjective judgments of beauty, goodness, or perfection. For Mendelssohn and Lessing taste, as most of the British empiricists understood it, is subordinate to an interest in the ways in which we decide whether an object will give pleasure or not, and especially in the case of Lessing, what, in the manner in which the work of art is executed, governs our affective responses. Lessing, for all his attention to the processes of perception and imagination, ends up being a kind of formalist, but as I have already suggested, so does Hume, and another side to his formalism will be evident in the next chapter's discussion of his essay "Of Tragedy."

Kames

The attempts of many Enlightenment thinkers to offer an intelligible or defensible account of aesthetic experience that accommodates its emotional, nonrational side and yet makes room for understanding are perhaps most completely realized in Kant's theory, but there is another school of thought that grows out of Addison's sense that the work of art is a convenience, an occasion or stimulus for a dynamic mental process. This line of thinking is perhaps more elaborately laid out in Lord Kames's *Elements of Criticism* (1762; enlarged 1763). It does not offer neat solutions to the problem of a

---

32. A possible exception is Hume's effort to show in the case of Ariosto that our delight is selective: "If some negligent or irregular writers have pleased, they have not pleased by their transgressions of rule or order, but in spite of these transgressions: they have possessed other beauties, which were conformable to just criticism; and the force of these beauties has been able to overpower censure, and to give the mind a satisfaction superior to the disgust arising from the blemishes. Ariosto pleases; but not by his monstrous and improbable fictions. . . . He charms by the force and clearness of his expression, by the readiness and variety of his inventions, and by his natural pictures of the passions, especially those of the gay and amorous kind." ("Of the Standard of Taste," 7–8). Even so, this judgment is exercised in terms of generalities.

universal standard; only at the end of his long treatise does he tackle that question, doing so by asserting that what is universal is our "conviction" that there is a universal standard: "This conviction of a common nature or standard and of its perfection, accounts clearly for that remarkable conception we have of a right and wrong sense or taste in morals."[33] As with Hume, the standard of taste becomes shifted to a common subjectivity, in which aesthetic and moral judgments are parallel and companion processes. Our inclination to assume and insist on a standard Kames attributes to our fear of finding ourselves isolated and alone: "every man, generally speaking, taking it for granted that his opinions agree with the common sense of mankind, is, therefore, disgusted with those who thinking differently, not as differing from him, but as differing from the common standard" (chap. 25).

One might expect Kames, on the basis of these remarks, to distance himself somewhat from common belief, but he regards such belief as an indication of the existence of a universal standard and of its value: its value is made evident in the availability of the arts fashioned according to this consent, and its actual existence, though more difficult to prove, is confirmed finally by reference to a small elite of the instructed, that is, those who neither must labor merely to eat nor whose wealth, voluptuousness, and pride incline them to the merely gaudy and ostentatious. Kames admits that such requirements are severe, and in fact he really has no answer other than to reassert the naturalness of broad antimonies as examples of the qualities on which a standard can be based: "high or low, plain or elegant, strong or weak" (chap. 25). If this were all Kames had to say, he could be dismissed as someone who at one moment appears close to the thinking of Kant, and at another ducks any serious effort to deal intellectually with the problem of a universal standard. But this final chapter from which I have just quoted seems almost an afterthought. What is worth attention is what goes before: Kames's system of aesthetic perception is crossed and conditioned by association psychology as a way of accommodating diversity of response and by his attempt through association to adjust questions of taste and aesthetic response to a theory of language.

To relate affect to language, Kames is interested initially in the connections between what he calls "trains of ideas" and emotion. These trains, of which we are aware, are the result neither of will nor chance, since they depend upon our personal experience in the past. Yet what concerns him is

33. Henry Home, Lord Kames, *Elements of Criticism* (New York, 1845), chap. 25. My quotations are all from this edition.

not their content, since nothing is exempt that comes into our minds, but their process and the fact that every idea exists in some relation to other ideas: the names given, probably derived from Hume, are "cause and effect, contiguity in time or in place, high and low, prior and posterior, resemblance, contrast, and a thousand other relations" (chap. 1). The process is automatic and governs the direction of thought, but we have the power to intervene and concentrate on one group of ideas while ignoring others.[34] Moreover, the possibility of an infinite number of connections does not argue either chaos or randomness in thought, but rather a natural principle of order that links nature and the human mind, for "we are framed by nature to worship order and connection. When an object is introduced by a proper connection we are conscious of a certain pleasure arising from that circumstance" (ibid.). The possibility of randomness is thus corrected or deflected into focused thought by our natural affective disposition.

This model of the structures of consciousness is a paradigm for the interplay between nature and art, between the continuous dynamic presence of natural event and the selective attention that finds or makes order. In addition there are levels of complexity in connections, ranging from "a multitude of objects connected by contiguity solely," to far less casual and more profound connections (chap. 1). Those connections important to human life have not only linkage but direction, and it is these more directed connections that involve the fine arts and enable them to raise passions and emotions (chap. 2). The passions in turn are derived from our fundamental disposition to be either pleased or displeased by the objects and connections that draw our attention. For Kames the coincidence between connections that produce pleasure or displeasure and our perceiving and judging faculty seems, in the description, almost automatic, to the point that the world of nature, or the world outside us, and our consciousness seem in perfect accord. Kames's way of putting his case is sometimes frustrating: for example, "Sensible beings affect us remarkably by their actions. Some actions raise pleasant emotions in the spectator, without the least reflection; such as *graceful* motion, and *genteel* [emphasis added] behavior" (chap 2). As

34. For a more complete account, see Gordon McKenzie, *Critical Responsiveness: A Study of the Psychological Current in Later Eighteenth-Century Criticism* (Berkeley and Los Angeles: University of California Press, 1949). McKenzie notes that Kames sidesteps any attempt to provide a taxonomy: "Association is to Kames a basic fact about human consciousness, yet he sees no value in trying to make a list of all possible associative connections or in arranging them in categories which would show their relation to one another. To him, each relation is to be understood and evaluated by an interpretation of the context in which it occurs" (138).

a footnote makes evident, he distances himself from Berkeley's subjective theories: "it is sufficient for the present purpose to answer, that the eye never abstracts; by that organ we perceive things as they really exist, and never perceive a quality as separated from the subject. Hence it must be evident, that emotions are raised, not by qualities abstractly considered, but by the substance or body so and so qualified. Thus, a spreading oak raises a pleasant emotion, by means of its color, figure, umbrage, &c." (ibid.). Kames thus distances himself from the thinking of Burke on the one hand and Hume on the other.[35] It can, of course, be objected that although we do indeed respond to objects, those attributes we respond to are either selected by us, or the names we give them are indicative of the nature of our response, rather than some quality in the object.

But this is not an issue Kames raises; rather, his mind is on the emotions produced by objects. He begins first by distinguishing passion from emotion, the former being the consequence of desire, the latter simply a motion of the internal senses unaccompanied by desire. Desire and passion precede and prompt action. What chiefly seems to interest Kames, as he discusses the passions in some detail, is their communicability, their infectiousness. Not only do objects and events quicken our appetites and desires, but when we perceive the actions and emotional states of others we in turn respond emotionally. We have certain dispositions, such as hunger or sex, which activate us independently of any specific external event, but otherwise, our emotions and passions are described as responsive and therefore, in a sense, dependent. These "secondary" passions are begotten by the perception of other people's passions and in their turn may give rise to further passions in ourselves or in others, so that Kames's fairly lengthy discussion of emotive life in his second chapter amounts to a dynamics of social existence in which circumstances constantly modify communicated and mirrored passions.

Perhaps because Kames's purpose is to establish a system for the criticism of the arts, and especially of literature, he gives most of his attention to the communication of emotions and passions. However much he wants to move his discussion toward an objective set of standards for valuation, he gives his energies primarily to an account of processes—in this he is certainly representative of his century—and central to this account is a consideration of the difference between fictive and real events as they give rise to emotions or passions. We are thus cast in the role of spectators

---

35. Cf. Burke, *A Philosophical Enquiry*, 164; Hume, *A Treatise of Human Nature*, 211, 216.

"The Irregular Fancy of the World" 123

rather than participants, and we tend to conflate real and fictional events precisely because our relationship to them is the same: we are observers. Observation in its turn involves time and memory. From here the argument proceeds as follows: (1) we believe in the reality of what we perceive through the senses; (2) this conditions us to believe in the reality of things recalled from the past, if they were sufficiently notable to prompt us in the present to dwell on them intently and in detail; (3) we tend, in the process of recollection, to try to translate our perceptions into words, though with difficulty:

> For it is not accurate to talk of incidents long past as passing in our sight, nor of hearing at present what we really heard yesterday, or at a more distant time. And yet the want of proper words to describe ideal presence [i.e., something present as an idea in the mind], and to distinguish it from real presence, makes this inaccuracy unavoidable. When I recall any thing to my mind in a manner so distinct as to form an idea or image of it as present, I have not words to describe that act, but that I perceive the things as a spectator, and as existing in my presence; which means not that I am really a spectator, but only that I conceive myself to be a spectator, and have a perception of the object similar to what a real spectator has. (chap. 2)

Kames invokes this sort of mental event in order to explain how it is words can create something like ideal presence in the mind. Because the mind can entertain the illusion or fiction that a past event can be recalled as if it were happening now, so events cast in the form of words can enter our minds and maintain there the status of a present occurrence to which we are spectators. Thus fiction is like remembrance, only more distinct and therefore closer to ideal presence. But there is one more consideration, the question of how the idea of something one has never before seen can be raised in the mind by speech, writing, or painting. What confers presence and makes one a spectator now is vividness of description:

> I believe that Scipio existed about 2000 years ago, and that he overcame Hannibal in the famous battle of Zama. When I reflect so slightly on that memorable event, I consider it as long past. But let it be spread out in a lively and beautiful description, I am insensibly transformed into a spectator: I perceive them brandishing their

swords, and cheering their troops; and in that manner I attend them through the battle, every incident of which appears to be happening in my sight. (Ibid.)

Mental spectating and actual spectating are parallel and nearly identical experiences: the task of remembrance or of literary description is to supply a substitute that is equivalent in sharpness and impact. And in sharp contrast to Lessing, the kind of impact Kames is interested in is emotive. Insofar as language can recover the presence of events it results in emotion, and emotion comes from the ideas of events in our mind. David Marshall has argued with reference to Du Bos, who proposes a similar equivalence of real and imaginary event, that this mode of criticism is saying that our minds structure reality as if it were theater.[36] This ingenuity does not seem to have occurred to Kames, but he belongs to the tradition of Du Bos, Burke, and others that seeks to minimize the distance between real and fictional events in order to emphasize the spectatorial context of literary and artistic affect.

This is perhaps one reason why Kames, like so many others in the eighteenth century, considers the theater the most thoroughly affective artistic medium: language combined with visible motion is more powerful than the written word or the painted scene separately considered. Affect is for Kames better produced by things in motion, or what he calls "a succession of impressions": ideal presence is not a static phenomenon; it requires both proximity and succession. Thus, however much he seeks to tie what he calls our sympathetic (i.e., spectatorial) emotions to language, what he ends up with are qualities he attributes to language but which really belong to sense perception, especially sight and sound. Only insofar as language becomes defined as distance and movement, or only insofar as a writer's skill allows him to achieve the impression of these properties, is he successful. Once these are achieved, language is capable of wondrous influence: "In appearance at least, what can be more slight than ideal presence; and yet from it is derived that extensive influence which language has over the heart; an influence which, more than any other means, strengthens the bond of society, and attracts individuals from their private system to perform acts of generosity or benevolence" (ibid.). But as I have sought to show, Kames's theory of the influence of language "over the

36. David Marshall, *The Surprising Effects of Sympathy: Marivaux, Diderot, Rousseau, and Mary Shelley* (Chicago: University of Chicago Press, 1988), 24–27.

heart," which he proposes as the bridge between the universal and the subjective, and hence between the social and the individual, is really a theory of presence.

Such large claims are not necessarily eccentric, but they ignore the problems posed by language considered as a medium that distances, and Kames's enthusiasm allows him to ignore the implications of his earlier attention to association and relation in determining the quality of our perceptions. Behind the theory of linguistic presence is the Enlightenment preoccupation with the dynamics of tragic emotion. This occupies the next chapter. A related concern is the origin of language, the point at which, according to many accounts, human beings moved from the universal communication of feeling to something more private and isolating. That process will be taken up in the final chapter.

5 "An Unaccountable Pleasure"

The Attractions of Tragedy

> *It seems an unaccountable pleasure which the spectators of a well-written tragedy receive from sorrow, terror, anxiety, and other passions that are in themselves disagreeable and uneasy. The more they are touched and affected, the more they are delighted with the spectacle; and as soon as the uneasy passions cease to operate, the piece is at an end. One scene of full joy and contentment and security is the utmost that any composition of this kind can bear; and it is sure always to be the concluding one. . . . The whole art of the poet is employed in rousing and supporting the compassion and indignation, the anxiety and resentment, of his audience. They are pleased in proportion as they are afflicted, and are never so happy as when they employ tears, sobs, and cries, to give vent to their sorrow, and relieve their heart, swoln with the tenderest sympathy and compassion.[1]*
>
> —David Hume, "Of Tragedy"

The epigraph, which opens David Hume's essay on tragedy, sharply emphasizes the paradox of tragedy, its ability to cater to our positive appetite for spectacles of torment and suffering. Even more astonishing is the suspicion that scenes of distress are far more appealing than those of happiness. Hume's explanation of the paradox, which I will deal with later in this chapter, is suggested in the last phrase in the passage above, "the tenderest sympathy and compassion," and this points toward the most common explanation of tragic pleasure held by the eighteenth century. Distress and suffering, it was believed, held positive values for those who

---

1. David Hume, "Of Tragedy" (1757), *Of the Standard of Taste and Other Essays*, ed. John W. Lenz (Indianapolis: Bobbs-Merrill, 1965), 29.

observed. Some form of emotional relief was available, and a sense of connection to others, of a ground of universal human alliance, a comprehension of one's identity with others through the medium of suffering, could provide artistic affect with a morally positive value. In different terms much of this was, of course, addressed by Aristotle himself, and the effort to understand concepts of tragic pleasure lies at the heart of any attempt to explore more generally the connections between the work of literature and its emotional impact, offering the severest test of any broad theory of audience pleasure. Despite their familiarity, I propose first to look at Aristotle's comments simply because the Renaissance and neoclassical attempts at explanation grew out of the tradition of commentary on the *Poetics*. Aristotle was either accepted, modified, or contradicted, but every subsequent account was offered in the context of his views. I will also provide some comments on Renaissance approaches to the question of tragic pleasure because what developed from Corneille on was so clearly designed to rethink and reformulate the issue. And if Hume seems at first to concentrate on a psychology of affect, he will be seen eventually to recover a sense of causation based in the structure of language.

The Aristotelian Tradition

Aristotle's theory of tragic form, and his theory of epic form as well, is everywhere and persistently directed to the habits and requirements of the audience. These in turn center in the emotions of pity and fear exercised by the experience of purgation, but accompanied also by the perception of a kind of logical order usually expressed as probability and necessity. No one has ever, to my knowledge, sought to identify Aristotle as the father of reader-response theory, but if we wish to discover his motives for preferring what he considers the most central features of tragic structure—recognition, reversal, the complex plot, the probable order of plot, and the protagonist of mixed moral character—we can reasonably conclude that in his system they derive their value from their capacity to produce pity and fear. Plot is more important than characterization because it caters to "the proper function of tragedy," and, he adds, "two of the most important elements in the emotional effect of tragedy, 'reversals' and 'discoveries,' are parts of the plot."² Chapters 13 and 14, which discuss in detail the best kind of tragic plot, identify it as that designed to communicate pity and fear; some kinds of plot are inappropriate because they prompt other emotional reactions. Tragedy is defined, in effect, as the kind of work that produces these emotions in the audience, and the fact that in chapter 6 Aristotle rather vaguely tacks on to them unspecified "similar emotions" does not in any way hamper his insistence that tragedy exists for the sake of the cathartic experience.

This experience is in some way pleasurable. It can be generated from the spectacle, but this is the resort of the inferior poet:

> The plot should be so constructed that even without seeing the play anyone hearing of the incidents happening thrills with fear and pity as a result of what occurs. So would anyone feel who heard the story of Oedipus. To produce this effect by means of an appeal to the eye is inartistic and needs adventitious aid,³ while those who by such means produce an effect which is not fearful but merely monstrous have nothing in common with tragedy. For one should not seek from tragedy all kinds of pleasure but that which is peculiar to tragedy, and since the poet must by "representation" produce the pleasure which comes from feeling pity and fear, obviously this quality must be embedded in the incidents. (14.2–5)

Aristotle is silently distinguishing between the visual effects of staging and verbal representation. What we "see" in a verbal report is, in spite of distancing, analogous to seeing an object, but the object is only figuratively such, for it is a story, not a material form or shape. Furthermore, the belief has been widely shared that tragic pleasure occurs because the audience is knowingly witness to an imitation, rather than actual events. It is a common reading of Aristotle in the twentieth century.⁴ There is reinforcement for

---

2. *The Poetics*, trans. W. Hamilton Fyfe (Loeb ed., 1973), 6.17–18. Unless otherwise noted my references are to this edition.

3. However, earlier there is the remark, "One essential part of tragedy is the spectacular effect" (6.7).

4. Such is the argument of G. F. Else in his exhaustive commentary, *Aristotle's* Poetics, *The Argument* (Cambridge, Mass.: Harvard University Press, 1957). Discussing 14.2–5, he says, "The answer, in general terms, must be that the pleasure is derived *from* (hapo) the pity and fear *by means of* (dia) the imitation" (411). See also 447–49. A detailed summary of Aristotle on aesthetic pleasure may be found in Stephen Halliwell, *Aristotle's* Poetics (London: Duckworth,

this reading in chapter 4, where Aristotle notes "the enjoyment people always get from representations," which he says is demonstrated by the fact that "we enjoy looking at accurate likenesses of things which are themselves painful to see, obscene beasts, for instance, and corpses" (4.2–4).

But this explanation is not so easy to accept as one might suppose. First of all, Aristotle goes on to point out that all men enjoy learning to some extent; thus, we enjoy likenesses because they teach us something, or if we do not know the original, then we take pleasure in the artistry. But if we attempt to reconcile this reasoning with what is said in chapter 14, there is a considerable problem. Chapter 4 describes our reaction to an imitation as one of judgment: "we learn and infer what each is, for instance, 'that is so and so.'" But we respond in tragedy by experiencing pity and fear, so either we must supply the added benefit of imitations—that they allow us to experience with delight emotions that otherwise would be distressing—or we must seek some further reason for the pleasure peculiar to tragedy.

Other statements of Aristotle's are tantalizing but by no means definitive. In chapter 13 he refers to "the true tragic pleasure," which he distinguishes from that occasioned by a happy ending, and in chapter 18 he remarks that efforts to dramatize entire stories (for instance, the entire sack of Troy) fail, where in reversals and simple stories dramatists "admirably achieve their end, which is a tragic effect that also satisfies your feelings" (18.17). This associates pleasure with the cathartic process, which brings us back to chapter 6. Here, at the conclusion of his central definition of tragedy, he says that "it represents men in action and does not use narrative, and through pity and fear it effects relief to these and similar emotions" (6.2). We have already seen that in the same chapter he links reversals and discoveries to "the emotional effect of tragedy." Up to a point one can put together a set of interlocking propositions. The aim of tragedy, as of all representations, is to please the audience. But tragedy admits of only a special kind of pleasure, that derived from experiencing pity and fear and their catharsis. Only certain combinations of plot and character type will produce this effect. A particular kind of dramatic form is required for a particular kind of affect, and it is also the case that other kinds of affect are specifically ruled out. This tight system still leaves open the question of how pity and fear can be said to give pleasure, for even if they are responses to fictitious events, they are nevertheless negative emotions. Else answers

---

1986), 62–81. Halliwell argues, unpersuasively for me, that Aristotle thinks tragic pleasure derived from the cognitive experience of tragedy.

that they are produced by representation, but this has the weaknesses of excluding what Aristotle quite clearly identifies as a pleasure *in* experiencing an emotion. Else also fails to make the distinction that pity and fear are not represented but are real emotions produced by means of representation, so the case is not at all parallel to Aristotle's more general ascription of pleasure to imitation.[5]

Other requirements may also have something to do with the kind of effect Aristotle prescribes. Magnitude, a factor in beauty, is what can be "grasped at once," that is, in a single performance (7.12); chapter 9 discusses the necessity of distancing the spectator from actual events, the use of actual (historically familiar) names for the sake of conviction, and the desirability of avoiding episodic plots (pity and terror are the consequence of perceiving a kind of logic in the outcome). Aristotle is arguing, I think, that what is perceived as consequential will seem to be embedded in the nature of things. This is the drift of his remarks on discoveries and reversals in chapter 11. If a discovery, for example, is an essential element in the plot, rather than being effected by such devices as rings or scars, then "such a discovery and reversal of fortune will involve either pity or fear, and it is actions such as these which, according to our hypothesis, tragedy represents; and, moreover, fortune and misfortune are likely to turn upon such incidents" (11.7).

In sum, what Aristotle describes is a rather special type of affective experience tightly and pretty well completely bound by the context of a dramatic form in which plot and characterization are closely bound to probability. To perfection of form he adds something else that has been perhaps less noticed, a disposition on the part of the audience to a sense of justice and to moral persuadability. How tragedy could please—or more to the point, Aristotle's explanation of its pleasing—was discussed by his Renaissance commentators in the context of an already well-seasoned conviction that the end of poetry was moral profit, and in the context of their awareness of the importance of formal elements in the poem, as well as their reaction to the idea of purgation.[6] One result was the disposition to see

---

5. Else does not accept catharsis as an emotional process undergone by the audience, but instead considers it a ritual purification of the protagonist witnessed by the audience (224–32).

6. The definitive account of later sixteenth-century theories of catharsis is Baxter Hathaway, *The Age of Criticism: The Late Renaissance in Italy* (Ithaca: Cornell University Press, 1962), 205–300. Hathaway divides critics roughly into two camps: those who think of catharsis as offering moral control and emotional apathy through the elimination of extreme or unworthy passions and those who see it as the cultivation of morally positive feelings, especially pity or

pleasure and profit caused by separate and different structures in the poem. Robortello, for example, interprets purgation as the avenue to the moral lesson of tragedy and insists that pleasure is entirely a function of imitation.[7] Aristotle's most independent and eccentric commentator, Ludovico Castelvetro, argues a different division. He accepts imitation as the source of pleasure only if it excludes those things that would cause distress if seen in reality, which of course makes nonsense of Aristotle's point.[8]

Though he interprets Aristotle as saying that the tragic emotions are pleasant, Castelvetro flatly asserts that Aristotle was wrong; it is mistaken to believe that pity and terror in themselves can produce any delight whatever:

> At this point someone may ask what kind of pleasure it is that we feel in seeing a good man falling unjustly from happiness to misery. A story of this kind, they say, should normally be the cause not of pleasure but of sorrow. Now there is not the shadow of a doubt that by "pleasure" Aristotle means the purgation and expulsion of pity and fear from human souls by the action . . . of these same emotions. But if this purgation and expulsion are effected, as he affirms, by the action of pity and fear, it is patently absurd to speak of it as a kind of pleasure. It is rightly to be designated, rather, as a moral benefit, for its effect is by nature health of soul produced by the action of very bitter medicine. The authentic pleasure which derives from the experience of pity and fear we ourselves have called "indirect pleasure." We call it indirect because it is not the *direct* result of the experience of a tragic event.[9]

Thus, what Aristotle labels a form of pleasure, Castelvetro insists is "utility," noting that Aristotle "does not seem to assign [tragedy] any other

---

commiseration. The latter group generated the line of thought stretching through Heinsius and Rapin to the sentimentalism of the eighteenth century.

7. Francesco Robortello, *In Librum Aristotelis de Arte Poetica Explicationes* (Florence, 1548), 146, 149–50. Cf. Bernard Weinberg, "Robortello on the *Poetics*," in R. S. Crane, ed., *Critics and Criticism, Ancient and Modern* (Chicago: University of Chicago Press, 1952), 324–32.

8. *Castelvetro on the Art of Poetry*, trans. Andrew Bongiorno (Binghamton, N.Y.: Medieval & Renaissance Texts and Studies, 1984), 44.

9. Ibid., 150. These remarks do not square with one of his more famous generalizations, that "since poetry was invented for the pleasure and recreation of the common people, its subjects must be things suited to their understanding" (20). See xviii and 362 for Bongiorno's discussion.

end than that of pleasure; and if he concedes to it a certain utility he regards it as an incidental thing, like the purgation of pity and fear through tragedy" (156). Castelvetro's indirect pleasure is derived from reflection, after the event, so to speak, and involves a mixture of detachment from and sympathy for the tragic figures and their sufferings. First, "the immediate effect upon us of such events, which depict the unjust sufferings of others, is, in fact, one of sadness; this sadness, however, being caused, as it is, by injustice, brings us to a recognition of our goodness, and it is this recognition that, thanks to the love we bear ourselves, becomes the cause of very great pleasure" (150). This point is near cousin to the "Lucretian return upon ourselves," an explanation of tragic pleasure favored by many neoclassical critics that identified pleasure from our recognition that what is happening to those we observe suffering is not happening to us.[10] It is a form of pleasure by exemption, if I understand Castelvetro correctly. There is also what he calls a "private and unarticulated discovery" that misfortunes can happen to anyone and that we should not count on the tranquility of earthly existence. This astringent lesson becomes a pleasure by virtue of the fact that in contemplating a tragic action we make this discovery for ourselves. No doubt Castelvetro has in mind Aristotle's explanation of our delight in metaphor (*Rhetoric* III.2). Whatever the case, his reading serves to attenuate the purgative experience into a typical Renaissance moral lesson, refusing to see in the carefully arranged artifice of the better tragic plot itself or in the emotions it generates any source of delight. Pleasure is not the result of our involvement in the tragic action but deferred to logical inference resulting from contemplation after the event. What Castelvetro offers is an entirely different sort of pleasure, removed from the heat of emotional involvement and mixed in with not a little self-satisfaction. He thus anticipates an issue that would appear in the eighteenth century: whether aesthetic pleasure was to be understood as immediate sensation only or sensation mixed with judgment and reflection.

Though others of Aristotle's commentators, such as Vincenzo Maggi and Bartolomeo Lombardi, Antonio Riccoboni, Pietro Vettori, and Alessandro Piccolomini, differ from Castelvetro in their reading of some details, and though none of them is so rude as to say that Aristotle did not know what

---

10. See Baxter Hathaway, "The Lucretian 'Return upon Ourselves' in Eighteenth-Century Theories of Tragedy," *PMLA* 62 (1947), 672–89. Hathaway says (673) that the first mention of the doctrine he has found is in a treatise by Lorenzo Giacomini, *Sopra la purgazione della tragedia* (1586), which may be seen in *Trattati di poetica e retorica del Cinquecento*, ed. Bernard Weinberg (Bari: Laterza, 1972), 3:345–71.

he was talking about; nevertheless, on the whole they are also prepared to understand the emotional experience of witnessing calamity as a form of moral benefit.[11] Nicolò Rossi is unusual in claiming that purgation is pleasurable, but does not explain in detail.[12] The most thorough effort to find a convincing psychological explanation for pleasure drawn from the process of tragic catharsis is a lecture in 1586 to the Academia degli Alterati by Lorenzo Giacomini, "De la purgazione de la tragedia."[13] Giacomini's account involves the interaction of body and mind, locating pleasure in the relief from "perturbation." Negative emotions, expressing themselves in all the organs of the body, are discharged in lamentations and tears and are thus exhausted, "whence to the afflicted there is a certain delight from lamenting, secretly discharging by means of tears that which grieves them" (359). He includes the interesting point that pity is not purged, an emendation of Aristotle symptomatic of the difficulties handed down to his Renaissance students.

Although a quasi-medical reading of the idea of purgation offers one solution to the difficulties of Aristotle's theory, it was not widely accepted as an explanation of how pity and fear can be pleasurable. Divided and uncertain as to whether those emotions should be understood as negative or positive (i.e., potentially useful, even if uncomfortable) emotions, Renaissance critics spent considerable effort trying to explain and accommodate the idea of purgation to already established tenets of Horatian utilitarianism and contented themselves with locating sources of pleasure either in mimetic form or harmony and meter, rather than in the emotional content of the poem.

We can put it another way by observing that the sixteenth-century

11. Vincenzo Maggi and Bartolomeo Lombardi's *In Aristotelis Librum de Poetica Communes Explicationes* (Venice, 1550), 112–13, offers a different reading, referring to Plato's *Philebus* in support of the notion that pleasure and pain can be mixed. For examples of the more common view that pleasure derives from the mimetic nature of the work, see Pietro Vettori, *Commentarii, in Primum Aristotelis de Arte Poetarum* (Florence, 1560), 133; and Antonio Riccoboni, *Poetica Aristotelis ab Antonio Riccoboni Latine Conversa* (Padua, 1587), 66. Alessandro Piccolomini, in his *Annotationi nel Libro della Poetica d'Aristotele* (Vinegia, 1571), 62–70, agrees that pleasure comes from mimetic likenesses, though he believes this to be the pleasure attendant on discovering something to be so. He also, however, disagrees with Castelvetro about indirect pleasure and maintains that pity can be a source of delight, but still a delight born of the consciousness of having learned something (210–12).

12. *Discorsi intorno alla Tragoedia* (1590), in *Trattati di poetica e retorica del Cinquecento*, ed. Weinberg, 4:86–87.

13. *Trattati di poetica e retorica del Cinquecento*, ed. Weinberg, 3:345–71. See Hathaway, *The Age of Criticism*, 253–75, and note 10 above.

Aristotelians, however they differ among themselves, remain tied to the assumption that affect is to be understood as a function of the formal properties of the poem. The weight of their primary attention falls on formal and didactic questions first, and they tend with some exceptions, to explain audience response according to the inherited rhetorical formulas of pleasing, moving, and instructing. One might argue in rebuttal that Aristotle's *Poetics* was bound to be understood in the light of the Renaissance version of classical rhetorical principles, which, roughly speaking, regards discourse as a transaction moving from speaker through the formal medium to the audience. This formula includes, of course, the assumption that the response of the audience has to be understood to be controlled and limited by the speaker's intention. If intention coordinates with response, the result is a rational, coherent, predictable, and normative system of the arts, in other words, a rhetorical program in which the significance of literature answers to design more than to psychology.

These remarks are appropriate to much of what seventeenth-century critics had to say about tragedy and tragic pleasure. Francesco Robortello's view of the usefulness of purgation, for example, was widely accepted. He initiated the interpretation that repeated exposure to situations prompting pity and fear would harden and condition spectators so that they would, like veteran warriors accustomed to carnage, gradually be weaned from emotional sensitivity and weakness. This view appealed to those inclined to the Stoic doctrine that tragedy should temper and moderate emotion, encouraging, according to Baxter Hathaway, a kind of apathy.[14] Yet it is in the midst of French formalist theories in the seventeenth century that, for all their interest in tragedy as the instrument and instructor in control and order, one discovers the beginnings of a shift toward what has been called the "emotionalism" of the eighteenth century. The more conventional neoclassical opinion is that of Jean-François Sarasin's "Discourse on Tragedy or Remarks on *Tyrannic Love* by Monsieur de Scudery" (1639), which interprets Aristotle as believing that the tragic action raised the passions of pity and terror in order to "repress them and reduce them to a reasonable level of intensity" and insists that "he [Sarasin] was not of the opinion of those who consider the final purpose of these sublime compositions to be the pleasure of the people."[15] Corneille breaks more definitively with

---

14. Cf. Baxter Hathaway, "John Dryden and the Function of Tragedy," *PMLA* 58 (1943), 665–73, and *The Age of Criticism*, 210–20.
15. Elledge and Schier, *The Continental Model*, 56–57.

Aristotle in doubting that catharsis happens at all, at least as Aristotle describes it, because he cannot accept Oedipus and Thyestes as the moral types Aristotle claims are necessary. According to Corneille's "Discours de la tragédie" (1660) Oedipus really has committed no crime, so his torment is gratuitous, not earned, whereas Thyestes is in one place a criminal and in another virtuous.[16] But Corneille's most significant departure from Aristotle is to establish a more inclusive list of passions to which all men are subject as the common bond between protagonist and spectator, and to doubt that purgation occurs according to Aristotle's formula:

> Those passions [pity and fear] are to be found in *The Cid* and have been responsible for its great success. In it the virtue of Rodrigue and Chimène is subjected to their passions, and those passions cause their misfortune, since they are only unfortunate to the extent that they desire one another. They fall into infelicity by means of that very human weakness of which we are just as capable: their misfortune produces pity. . . . That pity ought to make us fear to fall into a like misfortune and purge in us that excessive love which caused their adversity and makes us grieve for them, but I am not sure that it gives us this fear, nor that it purges it, and I am really afraid that on this point Aristotle's reasoning is only a fine idea that doesn't work out in reality. (145–46)

Quite apart from making the point that there is a difficulty in knowing whether tragedies, however well constructed, actually do affect the audience as Aristotle claims, Corneille shifts the immediate source of emotion away from the recognition and peripety, away from the movement toward misfortune and our (and the protagonists') awareness of it, to a condition in the characters. Aristotle's four types of recognition (*Poetics* 14.12–19) give priority to plots in which protagonists commit crimes in ignorance and then come to know what they have done or to whom. The least worthy kind of plot "involves the way in which the old dramatists made their characters act—consciously and knowing the facts, as Euripides also made his Medea kill her children" (14.12).

It is precisely this that Corneille considers the best type, flawed only when someone desists from killing another whom he knows through a

---

16. Pierre Corneille, "Discours de la tragédie," *Œuvres complètes*, ed. Georges Coutin, 3 vols. (Paris: Gallimard, Bibliothèque de la Pléiade, 1987), 145.

change of will, rather than circumstance. He argues further that the type Aristotle prefers—"it is better to act in ignorance and discover afterwards" (14.18)—"causes the audience to feel only a certain inner movement of trepidation" (154). Moreover, our pity for the feelings of the person who has killed another in ignorance "can have no great depth because it is deferred and is confined in the catastrophe. But when one acts openly, and knows whom one has a grudge against, the combat of passions contrary to nature, or duty against love, occupies the more important part of the poem; and from that are born great and powerful emotions, which renew themselves moment by moment and redouble the pity" (ibid.).

Corneille also hints that Aristotle's preferences may have been appropriate for his own time but not suited to the taste of a seventeenth-century French audience. The argument is not simply over which is to be the preferred type of plot but concerns a change in what is understood to be the source of affect, from a type of plot movement to the feelings of the characters. Furthermore, there seems to be some difference in the type of protagonist. Aristotle's view of characterization—which involves figures whose intentions are on the whole just and decent and who fail through error or mistake—is that it appeals to our sense of what is just and logical. That of Corneille turns on our recognition of and identification with the inner conflict between passion and obligation. And in Corneille's system the tragic passions need no longer be pity and fear and only these: again using his own work, he maintains that "Héraclius and Nicomède have pleased even though they impart only pity and give us nothing to fear, nor any passion to purge, since we see them oppressed and near death through no fault of their own from which we can by their example correct ourselves" (147). Hence, both martyred innocence and criminal behavior that results from powerful feelings have an honored place in Corneille's theory and practice. This drastic broadening of Aristotle's categories comes in part from Corneille's belief that he and his contemporaries possess a somewhat different pragmatic psychology (or sense of what is verisimilar and therefore credible) from that of Aristotle, and in part from a different view of purgation.

Corneille understands pity and fear to be the exclusive property of the audience, and in this he is of course consistent with Aristotle, who talks of incidents that are pitiable and fearful. But according to Corneille the purgative process uses these emotions as its instrument, not its object. What is to be eliminated or avoided in the audience is a whole variety of other unworthy and excessive passions—unholy desire, pride, stubbornness, indeed almost any powerful irrationality—and this is to be accomplished by our ability to apply what we witness in the theater by a kind of logic of proportion to ourselves. It is moreover, a lesson that may be learned from characters other than the protagonists. Pity alone will not do: "it does not always happen that those we pity are unfortunate from their own faults. When they are innocent, our pity for them inspires no fear, and if we conceive a situation which purges our passions, it is by the means of another person than the one whom we pity, and we owe it all to the force of the example" (8).[17] What enlivens this otherwise conventional view of purgation as moral medicine is the sense that the emotional involvement of the audience should be intense, especially as a kind of imaginative identification with those in the grip of an internal conflict between passion and will. And although obeisance to moral benefit as the ultimate end of poetry is still evident enough, what commands detailed attention is the process of delight, which is more and more a challenge to the orthodoxy of the utilitarian view of poetry.

Rapin, the most authoritative figure in late seventeenth-century French dramatic criticism, says, "It is not easily decided what the nature and what precisely is the end of this art; the interpreters of Aristotle differ. . . . Some will have the end to be delight, and that it is on this account it labors to move the passions, all whose motions are delightful, because nothing is more sweet to the soul than agitation; it pleases itself in changing the objects to satisfy the immensity of its desires."[18] Rapin's statement suggests that the belief that emotional agitation is by its nature pleasurable must have been reasonably common at the end of the third quarter of the century. Descartes nearly twenty years earlier had written that "in general the soul is pleased to find passions arise in itself, no matter what they are, provided that it remains in control of them," and this is in the context of remarks on the contentment in weeping at tragedy "which arises chiefly from [the] impression that [one] is performing a virtuous action in having compassion on the afflicted."[19] Rapin's interest in the passions redeems his theories

---

17. This was roughly Minturno's view, though he did not make the same specification for pity; cf. Bernard Weinberg, "The Poetic Theories of Minturno," *Studies in Honor of Frederick W. Shipley* (St. Louis: Washington University Studies, 1942), 109–10, and *A History of Literary Criticism in the Italian Renaissance*, 738–39. However, Weinberg (739) translates Minturno as follows: "For who is there so possessed by an unbridled desire to avenge, or rule, or own, who, if he is aroused to pity and terror by the calamities of others, does not have his soul purged and purified of the disorder which brought him that unhappiness."

18. René Rapin, *Reflections on Aristotle's Treatise of Poetry, Book I: In General* (1674), trans. Thomas Rymer, in Elledge and Schier, *The Continental Model*, 281.

19. *Descartes: Philosophical Letters*, trans. and ed. Anthony Kenny (Minneapolis: University

from a somewhat routine formalism and expresses the tension underlying seventeenth-century affection for order, clarity, and emotional control as aesthetic values. If, on the one hand, the spectator is pleased by harmony and balance or responds, as Boileau maintains, when "each thing is in its proper place" (*L'Art poétique*, I.177), or if tragedy "rectifies the passions by the passions themselves in calming by their emotion the troubles they excite in the heart" (Rapin, 300), on the other hand, tragedy's impact has to be understood in terms of the power and force it exerts:

> But it is not enough that tragedy be furnished with all the most moving and terrible adventures that history can afford, to stir in the heart those motions it pretends, to the end that it may cure the mind of those vain fears that may annoy it, and those childish compassions that may soften it. It is also necessary, says the philosopher, that every poet employ those great objects of terror and pity as the two most powerful springs in art to produce that pleasure which tragedy may yield. And this pleasure which is properly of the mind consists in the agitation of the soul moved by the passions. Tragedy cannot be delightful to the spectator unless he become sensible to all that is represented; he must enter into all the different thoughts of the actors, interest himself in their adventures, fear, hope, afflict himself, and rejoice with them. The theatre is dull and languid when it ceases to produce these motions in the soul of those that stand by. (301)

The critic moves restlessly between language expressing the values of moderating, calming, and regulating and language of tectonic disturbance, inviting the spectator to a drastic and complete empathy. Though the point is not made explicitly, Rapin seems to be arguing that catharsis is the curative medium and empathy the way to pleasure. Notice the diction as he continues the remarks just quoted:

> But as of all passions pity and fear are those that make the strongest impressions on the heart of man by the natural disposition he has of being afraid and of being mollified, Aristotle has chosen these among the rest, to move more powerfully the soul by the tender sentiments

---

of Minnesota Press, 1981), 177. The letter, dated 6 October 1645, was to Princess Elizabeth of Bohemia.

they cause when the heart admits and is pierced by them. In effect, when the soul is shaken by motions so natural and so humane, all the impressions it feels become delightful; its trouble pleases, and the emotion it finds is a kind of charm to it which does cast it into a sweet and profound meditation and which insensibly does engage it in all the interests that are managed on the theatre. It is then that the heart yields itself over to all the objects that are proposed, that all images strike it, that it espouses the sentiments of all those that speak, and becomes susceptible of all the passions that are presented because it is moved. And in this agitation consists all the pleasure that one is capable to receive from tragedy, for the spirit of man does please itself with the different situations caused by the different objects and the various passions that are represented. (301–2)

The warmth of Rapin's celebration of affect no doubt owes a good deal to the fact that he is defending ancient tragedy against what he considers its less powerful, even effeminate contemporary disposition, penetrated as it is by "gallantry" for the pleasure of a female audience. But this is less important than the evidence he gives of a view of affect that threatens to spread itself beyond the territory of didacticism. What remains to be understood, as well, are the possible connections between language and emotion.

Hume and the Augustan View of Tragedy

It is now time to return to Hume's essay, "Of Tragedy," with which this chapter began. The essay, it will be recalled, opens with the question of how and why the calamitous events in tragedies can give delight. It states the issue in the roundest and strongest terms, emphasizing the alarming nature of the events dramatized and depicting the pleased audience as "swoln with the tenderest sympathy and compassion." It is a measure of the distance European thinking about tragedy has traveled even since the later seventeenth century that Hume opens not with a question of form or genre but instead with a discussion centered in issues of affective response. The opening query apparently demands an answer drawn from psychology or moral philosophy or even simply one's own empirically registered experience, not from Aristotle or other critics or the authority of centuries of theoretical discourse. As one critic has argued,[20] Hume's thinking concludes in a concept of the transformation of passion through artistic form, but the pathway by which that conclusion is achieved leads through a study of the mental processes of the spectator. Although one can spot the vestiges of Aristotelian ideas in what Hume says, and although he returns finally to a mode of aesthetic formalism, he represents a generation of critics no longer bound by Aristotelian assumptions or procedures, no longer writing, however independently, yet another commentary on the *Poetics*.

Hume's point of view is in part a response to the work of moral philosophers such as Hutcheson and critics such as Dennis, Addison, and Akenside, as well as Du Bos and Fontenelle whom he specifically names. His views owe much also to his own broader investigations of the passions, in particular to his examination of the process of sympathy in the *Treatise of Human Nature* (1739). His concepts of tragedy and tragic pleasure, which are symptomatic of the larger issue of aesthetic pleasure, should also be understood against the background of views he did not share: first, the tendency of the sentimental school of tragic theory to make the spectator part of the drama and to argue for an emotional rather than reflective response; second, this school's minimizing of distinctions between dramatic event and ordinary, real events, thus discounting the fictive as a source of pleasure; and third, the ignoring or underestimating of fear as a mode of tragic affect. Hume's position was shared by no one, but its lack of popularity is less significant than the way in which it illuminates issues common to the thinking of his times. Before addressing "Of Tragedy" directly, I will discuss the issues and critics related to it and to some extent at odds with it.

The question of tragic pleasure turns on the way in which pity and terror are understood, and from the time of Dryden pity had become much the more prominent and central object of critical interest. How the tragic emotions are formulated defines and expresses our concept of the manner in which each individual in the audience relates himself or herself to the characters and events in tragic drama. The Aristotelian tradition conceives of this relationship as a moral equation; hence, the emotions generated by tragedy are seen to be determined by our perception of the moral likeness or difference between ourselves and the characters, as well as by the kind of events to which they are subject (e.g., the change from good to bad fortune) and the benefit to the audience. The sentimental school, beginning

20. Ralph Cohen, "The Transformation of Passion: A Study of Hume's Theories of Tragedy," *PQ* 41 (1962), 450–64. I discuss Cohen's views below.

with Dryden, construes these relationships more broadly and loosely, though it still recognizes a moral bond between audience and fictional character (it is difficult for us to sympathize with a figure we find evil or depraved). In the *Essay of Dramatic Poesy* (1668), Dryden believes compassion, occasioned by the representation of love, a more fitting emotion to raise in the audience than horror, the chief accomplishment of Senecan tragedy.[21] Elsewhere he maintains that moral benefit is to be gained through the process of emotional involvement: "To raise, and afterwards to calm the passions, to purge the soul from pride, by the examples of human miseries, which befall the greatest; in few words, to expel arrogance, and introduce compassion, are the great effects of tragedy," though he goes on to doubt that such effects are lasting.[22] Dennis is more emphatic but holds much the same view, and he adds that tragedy is the most pleasing of all the genres because there the passions are moved by "their true springs."[23]

These pronouncements indicate a social, as well as a moral, context for tragedy, but they lack the supporting argument that might turn bald assertion into some more careful analysis of the bases for our compassion, an analysis of the ways of thinking and perception that allow us to make connections and even identify with fictional characters. Addison is scarcely more thorough. He maintains that "Terror and commiseration always leave a pleasing anguish in the mind" (*Spectator* 40), but his papers on English tragedy are largely devoted to complaining about methods of producing emotions he considers inferior. It is Francis Hutcheson whose examination of the passions offers a beginning effort to explain more carefully why we are drawn to representations of distress.

Hutcheson, following Shaftesbury, proposes a view of human affect that allows for spontaneous, "natural," virtually automatic responses to objects of material or moral beauty, a view already treated in the previous chapter.

21. *Of Dramatic Poesy and Other Essays*, ed. George Watson, 2 vols. (London: Everyman, Dent, 1962), 1:41–42.

22. Ibid., 2:227 (Preface to *Aeneis*, 1699). In "Heads of an Answer to Rymer" (1:212–13), Dryden doubts also that pity and terror are "enough for tragedy to move; and I believe, upon a true definition of tragedy, it will be found . . . that it is to reform manners by delightful representation of human life in great persons, by way of dialogue." He also notes (219) that our pity is for the criminal, not for those, or him, whom he has murdered, or who have been the occasion of the tragedy." For further discussion of Dryden's views, see Eric Rothstein, "English Tragic Theory in the Late Seventeenth Century," *ELH* 29 (1962), 306–23, and Baxter Hathaway, "John Dryden and the Function of Tragedy," 665–73.

23. "The Usefulness of the Stage," in *The Critical Works of John Dennis*, ed. Edward Niles Hooker, 2 vols. (Baltimore: Johns Hopkins University Press, 1939, 1943), 2:150.

We are possessed of "internal" senses or faculties that allow us to distinguish aesthetic and moral experience from other kinds. He maintains that "the ideas of beauty and harmony, like other sensible ideas, are necessarily present to us, as well as immediately so."[24] Our sense of compassion is similarly natural and spontaneous: "Our misery or distress immediately appears in our countenance, if we do not study to prevent it, and propogates some pain to all spectators; who from observation, universally understand the meaning of these dismal airs. We mechanically send forth shrieks and groans upon any surprising apprehension of evil. . . . This is the voice of nature" ("Moral" V.viii). Du Bos argues that spectacles of violence attract us because we prefer being stirred to being bored, but for Hutcheson the attendance at public executions is an expression of our "natural, kind instinct to see objects of compassion," and the same motive draws us to tragedies, with the addition of our interest in "the moral beauty of the characters which we love to behold" (ibid.). And no audience would wish to view fictitious scenes of misery if they were given no indication of the moral qualities of the sufferers, "as in such a case, there would be no beauty to raise desire of seeing such representations" (ibid.). This last phrase may have suggested something to Hume.

Moreover, Hutcheson tries to explain how it is we can manage the proper moral recognition. Moral objects affect us more powerfully than natural beauty or deformity, and epic and drama "are entirely address'd to [our moral] sense, and raise our passions by the fortunes of characters, distinctly represented as good or evil" (VI.vii). However, this occurs not simply because we have a moral sense, but also because the poet makes an effort to persuade us through his mimetic powers: "The representing the actions themselves, if the representation be judicious, natural, and lively, will make us admire the good and detest the vitious, the treacherous and cruel, by means of our moral sense, without any reflections of the poet to guide our sentiments" (ibid.). The statement points rather obviously in two directions: on the one hand we require well-chosen and well-presented moral images, a suggestion that our moral sense requires considerable assistance, but on the other hand, perhaps not, for we do not need to be told overtly how to respond. Hutcheson's confidence in the automatic power of our faculties is perhaps less firm than might at first seem the case. Moreover, he is not talking about the sort of judgment involved in taste, but instead pointing to

---

24. Francis Hutcheson, *An Inquiry into the Original of Our Ideas of Beauty and Virtue*, 1:xii.

the conditions under which our moral sense may be reached by literary images, characters, and events.[25]

Hutcheson was convinced that a power of recognizing and being moved by certain forms of representation was as necessary as the forms themselves. In explaining "relative," as opposed to ideal or "original," beauty, he says that resemblance based on a kind of probability informs and gives beauty to metaphors and similes (IV.iii).[26] A poet such as Homer builds upon our knowledge of the likeness between ourselves and others: "And farther, thro' consciousness of our own state, we are more nearly touch'd and affected by the imperfect characters; since in them we see represented, in the persons of others, the contrasts of inclinations, and the struggles between the passions of self-love and those of honour and virtue, which we often feel in our own breast" (IV.ii).

As we have observed it so far, Hutcheson's argument assumes a great deal: it postulates two faculties on the unstated proposition that there must be separate and distinct human powers capable of responding properly to objective conditions whose quality is neither doubted nor even remotely demonstrated. And it remains to be shown exactly how these faculties work. We have already sampled his belief that "our misery or distress immediately appears in our countenance" and that this appearance can be universally understood. It is not language, but it functions as most thinkers in the later seventeenth century and in the eighteenth century wished language would function: to provide quick and unequivocal signals of meaning, to erase or prevent misunderstanding or confusion.

Facial expression and gesture declare themselves and are thus prior to language. According to Lord Kames a kind of emotional semiotics was the basis for all society: "The natural signs of emotions, voluntary and involuntary, being nearly the same in all men, form an universal language .... This is a wise appointment of Providence: for if these signs were, like words, arbitrary and variable, the thoughts and volitions of strangers would be entirely hid from us."[27] Not only does this sign system eliminate

25. Earl Wasserman, "The Pleasures of Tragedy," *ELH* 14 (1947), 283–307, provides a useful account of the sentimental theory in the eighteenth century.

26. As Patey observes in another context, resemblance is a widely held basis for probable conclusions in the eighteenth century, as it was earlier; *Probability and Literary Form*, 269, 333n. The noting of resemblances is, of course, one of the fundamental tasks of the imagination according to classical psychology. See Patey's discussion on p. 227.

27. Henry Home, Lord Kames, *Elements of Criticism*, 208. The fifteenth chapter, from which the quotation is taken, is a discussion of the external signs of passion. See Stephen K. Land, *From Signs to Propositions: The Concept of Form in Eighteenth-Century Semantic Theory* (London: Longman, 1974), 92.

language, and hence artifice, as a medium of emotional communication and mimesis, it also subtly corrupts the very motive Hutcheson and his successors professed: the demonstration of the natural moral benevolence of human creatures. For, if indeed spontaneous and unreflected responses to the distress of others amount to a positive moral condition, we are virtually robbed of choice and volition, and the artist becomes scarcely more than a purveyor of moral smoke signals. And at the outer reaches of this line of affective theory in an essay by George Walker (one of Hume's critics) there is the position that "the more the fiction is kept out of view, the more perfect is the art of the poet, and the more perfect the effect of the imitation upon the mind of the spectator; whose interest rises to its greatest height, when, by a kind of divine power, he is carried entirely out of the consideration of self, and contemplates the misery, as if it were real, and enters into it with all the glow of natural feeling."[28] Pleasure, evidently, is to be had by submitting to near-oblivion occasioned by the presence of misery. And the observance and enjoyment of emotional spectacles become the means of universal communication, the connection by which we understand and sympathize with one another.

Hume, building on Hutcheson's notion of resemblance and discarding his theory of special internal senses, moves in quite another direction toward a more precise account of how it is that the spectacle of emotion in others urges us to respond emotionally. He asks, in effect, very basic questions. How do we know when we see another human being that he or she is like us? How do we recognize correctly the emotions in others? The answer involves what he called "relation," or the power of constructing complex "ideas" out of simple sensations and perceptions, and this concept is the basis for his preliminary understanding of the sources of tragic affect.

Relation is the quality "by which two ideas are connected together in the imagination, and the one naturally introduces the other."[29] It works in four ways, by resemblance, identity (later omitted in the *Inquiry concerning Human Understanding* [1777]), contiguity in time or place, and cause and effect. The faculties that permit us to establish relation and continue to do so (so that every new sensation or perception can be connected to those previous and thus permit continuity and intelligibility of consciousness) are those common to all sentient experience, that is, imagination and memory.

28. George Walker, *Essays on Various Subjects* (London, 1809), 49–50.
29. David Hume, *A Treatise of Human Nature*, ed. P. H. Nidditch (Oxford, 1978), I.I.iv., p. 11. Further references will be in the text.

Imagination is the capacity to reproduce or refashion relations and is thus necessary to both repetition and change in our thinking (I.I.iv–v, pp. 12–13). But these operations are not exactly the same. The imagination easily copes with resemblance, but in dealing with contiguity it "must by long custom acquire the same method of thinking, and run along the parts of space and time in conceiving its objects" (I.I.iv, p.11). Experience and habit allow us to associate ideas with some regularity, while imagination makes ideas lively and intense, qualities that tend to compel our belief that what we perceive is true.[30] Hume is here on the very threshold of the proposition that subjective experience determines relation, especially the kind that is not dependent upon more or less obvious sensory likeness. If comparisons are made within the mind, not simply registered there, then we are nearing the borders of Kant's concept of judgment.

This theory of relation has to be kept clearly in view when we examine Hume's remarks on tragedy. Illustrating compassion or pity by tragic affect, he notes that "We have a lively idea of everything related to us. All human creatures are related to us by resemblance.[31] Their persons, therefore, their passions, their pains and pleasures must strike upon us in a lively

---

30. Cf. Harold Taylor, "Hume's Theory of Imagination," *UTQ* 12 (1942–43), 180–94; and the more detailed account in John W. Yolton, *Perceptual Acquaintance from Descartes to Reid*, 152–80. Yolton says Hume claims that no rational system can explain our belief that objects exist apart from our perceiving of them; hence, only experience and imagination (in this instance a form of supposition) are required (158–63). Imagination for Hume is both the conceiving of what is not present to the mind and part of the process of association, linking words to ideas, for example (169–70). The working of the imagination must also be accompanied by a reality principle that allows us to construct both the ordinary fictions of conscious life, such as inference or comparison, and those involved in the making of poetry; otherwise, madness might result (171). Yolton has much more to say than there is space to review; what is crucial is that Hume conceives of imagination as a part of the natural logic by which daily consciousness maintains coherence. It also allows us to conclude, whether rightly or wrongly, that the inner thoughts and emotions of others are what we take them to be. Hume's sense of the waywardness as well as the necessity of imagination is treated by James Engell, *The Creative Imagination: Enlightenment to Romanticism* (Cambridge, Mass.: Harvard University Press, 1981), 52–53.

31. Adam Smith's conjecture on this matter is more radical: "As we have no immediate experience of what other men feel, we can form no idea of the manner in which they are affected, but by conceiving what we ourselves should feel in the like situation. Though our brother is upon the rack, as long as we are at our ease, our senses will never inform us of what he suffers. They never did, and never can, carry us beyond our own person, and it is by the imagination only that we can form any conception of what are his sensations"; *The Theory of Moral Sentiments* (1759) (London, 1853), 3–4. It is not resemblance but the mental identification with another that is the connection: "we enter as it were into his body, and become in some measure the same person with him" (4).

manner, and produce an emotion similar to the original one; since a lively idea is easily converted into an impression" (II.II.vii, p. 369).[32] Hume then goes on to sketch tragic affect as a vicarious reproduction of the emotions experienced by characters in the drama: "A spectator of a tragedy passes thro' a long train of grief, terror, indignation, and other affections, which the poet represents in the persons he introduces. As many tragedies end happily, and no excellent one can be compos'd without some reverses of fortune, the spectator must sympathize with all these changes, and receive the fictitious joy as well as every other passion" (ibid.).

Hume has thus tied a version of tragic affect into his basic system of association. We respond emotionally to tragedy because we recognize through resemblance and contiguity the emotions of others, and the "idea" we have of their "impressions" generates similar feelings in us, or feelings we experience as similar. As the above passage continues, Hume's reasoning is important:

> Unless, therefore, it be asserted, that every distinct passion is communicated by a distinct original quality, and is not deriv'd from the general principle of sympathy above-explain'd, it must be allow'd, that all of them arise from that principle. . . . As they are all first present in the mind of one person, and afterwards appear in the mind of another; and as the manner of their appearance, first as an idea, then as an impression, is in every case the same, the transition must arise from the same principle. . . . Add to this, that pity depends, in a great measure, on the contiguity, and even sight of the object; which is a proof that 'tis deriv' from the imagination. (II.II.vii., pp. 369-70)

The communication of passion from its literary or dramatic expression to an audience is presumably no different from that between two or more human beings outside the theater.[33] The process of inference works in both

---

32. Impressions, Hume explains at the very beginning of the *Treatise*, are "all our sensations, passions, and emotions, as they make their first appearance in the soul." Ideas are "faint images of these in thinking and reasoning." They resemble each other, as the idea of red and the actual impression of it. Impressions or sensations leave ideas in the mind, and when these return or are recalled to consciousness they may in turn create new impressions (I.ii).

33. That connection is common. As P. W. K. Stone shows in his chapter, "The Role of Feeling in Composition," *The Art of Poetry 1750–1820*, 64–76, many eighteenth-century critics and theorists understood the communication of the passions as a function of traditional rhetorical figuring, and like Hume, considered sympathy to be the faculty of conveyance. But

cases and when in the next chapter we meet Diderot's argument in *Paradoxe sur le comédien* that in the theater there may be no valid inference of inner emotion to be drawn from the actor's language, we will see even more clearly just how uncertain such connections might be. Hume, perhaps because he is at this point discussing tragedy as an instance of the more general way in which sympathy works, establishes no difference in our being spectators to a drama and to an actual event, and he seems to consider tragic pleasure to be one of several other (unpleasant?) emotions stimulated by the drama and its characters. In the *Treatise* and later in *An Inquiry concerning Human Understanding* (1748) his attention remains instead chiefly on association, and in the *Inquiry* he uses the concept to explain the way in which we relate ideas to each other, as well as tying others' experiences to our own, and goes on to point out that in "compositions of genius" events and actions "must be related to each other in the imagination, and form a kind of *unity* which may bring them under one plan or view."[34]

Hume's notion of unity or coherence is complicated and not at all simply the resurrection of the dogma of Renaissance and seventeenth-century classicism. It amounts, in effect, to a unity of audience consciousness and "affection," derived not just from a principle of verisimilitude, but from the triad of resemblance, contiguity, and cause and effect:

> It is evident that in a just composition all the affections excited by the different events described and represented add mutual force to each other; and that, while the heroes are all engaged in one common scene, and each action is strongly connected with the whole, the concern is continually awake, and the passions make an easy transition from one object to another. The strong connection of the events, as it facilitates the passage of the thought or imagination from one to another, facilitates also the transfusion of the passions and preserves the affection still in the same channel and direction. Our sympathy and concern for Eve prepares the way for a like sympathy with Adam. (36)

---

sympathy in turn requires signs or "tokens" of passion in order to function. Patey argues that these signs must be interpreted probabilistically; that is, the audience supposes the cause from the presence of the effect or sign; *Probability and Literary Form*, 96. As I trust my discussion shows, it would be to misread Hume to conclude that he supposes that the rhetorical tradition of histrionic or impassioned speech can by itself explain this communication.

34. David Hume, *An Inquiry concerning Human Understanding*, ed. Charles W. Hendel (Indianapolis: Bobbs-Merrill, 1955), 33.

There is, in other words, something in a work of art more powerful than the logic of plot, setting, or character, a dynamism born of intensity and proximity that permits a current of "passion" to be maintained. The introduction of an unrelated person or event breaks the current and "prevents that communication of the several emotions by which one scene adds force to another, and transfuses the pity and terror which it excites upon each succeeding scene until the whole produces that rapidity of movement which is peculiar to the theater" (37).

We may sense in these remarks the rudiments of a concept of artistic form. At this point in his thinking about tragedy and the theater Hume is an illusionist. In a narrative poem we are dependent on the author's plan, and we are conscious of the artifice. But in the theater the author is absent and "the spectator supposes himself to be really present at the actions represented." The illusion of presence allows the author some license: "any dialogue or conversation may be introduced which, without improbability, might have passed in that determinate portion of space represented by the theater" (ibid.). The portions of the discussion quoted here are part of a much too condensed effort to argue for unity of plot and setting, and the account of dramatic illusion is simplistic. And it seems to collide with remarks elsewhere in the same chapter that emphasize the spectator's consciousness of unity as the avenue to effective continuity. Yet Hume's concept of structure is not one in which the poem is to be fashioned according to an idea of objective reality or conventional decorum. Instead, he requires artistic formality to arrange itself according to the ways in which our minds habitually tie perceptions together. If this is still a variation on the theme of verisimilitude—relation is, it will be remembered, Hume's notion of the way we perceive and fashion reality—it is a significant variation. A more conventional version would suppose that the general experience of the audience and reality—the way things happen, the way people in various walks of life speak and behave, the way we register time—fit together quite comfortably. Hume's system suggests a more radical theory about the way poetic form mirrors the process of audience perception. For Hume the content of perception is less important than its structure.

Hume also seems to make use in the *Inquiry* of the theory of Du Bos that stimulation of the emotions, whether pleasurable or not, is the fundamental motive of art. An epic poet who attempts too inclusive and broad a narration risks losing his grip on the reader's imagination, "and his passions, agitated by a continual sympathy with the actors, must flag long before the period of narration and must sink into lassitude and disgust from the repeated violence of the same movement." (35). Although we may infer that these matters are bound up in and responsible for the pleasure we take in epic or drama, Hume makes no effort to discuss pleasure directly and does not raise the issue at all with regard to the tragic emotions. Only one remark suggests that he has in mind the problem of whether poetry can have a special effect. This occurs when he notes "a particular situation of the imagination and of the passions which is supposed in that production. The imagination of both writer and reader is more enlivened and the passions more inflamed than in history, biography, or any species of narration that confine themselves to strict truth and reality" (35). "Enlivened" and "inflamed" are terms that recall his earlier favorites, "vivacity" and "intensity," which, as we have seen, are qualities implicated in our belief in the truth of any relation the imagination presents to our view. The question, then, is not one of objective truth being less interesting but, apparently, of poetry being more believable than nonfictional forms of narration.[35]

I want to return for a moment to the earlier *Treatise of Human Nature* where Hume gives more attention to this issue, because it bears upon his later and final view of the distinction between artistic and other kinds of affect.

In the *Treatise* Hume is more detailed in discussing fictionality. Poets, he says, are "liars by profession" but still try to give an "air of truth to their fictions," a point that distantly resembles Diderot's later and more emphatic distinction between the detachment of poet and actor and the credibility, even credulity, with which the audience soaks up their illusions. For Hume, we require that whatever is offered us seem logical, since we reason from cause and effect and our "entertainment" comes from our sense of the reality—what he calls "the solidity and force"—of ideas in the mind. However, he does not argue, as we might expect him to, that the audience reaction to poetic fictions is credulous. Rather, poetic fictions and poetic discourse enjoy a kind of courtesy reality, a temporary visitor's pass in the country of truth, simply because we are used to them. "We have been so much accustom'd to the names of MARS, JUPITER, VENUS, that in the same manner as education infixes any opinion, the constant repetition of these ideas makes them enter into the mind with facility, and prevail upon the fancy, without influencing the judgment" (121). These are convenient fictions, accepted by custom but normally understood for what they are.

---

35. Liveliness of representation can, for example, replace comparison of an imitation with reality as a source of credibility. Cf. Patey, *Probability and Literary Form*, 156–58.

For this basis of belief that is not really belief Hume next talks directly about tragedy. He wants to demonstrate a peculiarity of the mind, namely, its disposition to accept a fiction transparently robed in the garments of truth. The imagination, he asserts, "can be satisfy'd without any absolute belief or assurance," and "poets make use of this artifice of borrowing the names, and the chief events of their poems, from history, in order to procure a more easy reception for the whole, and cause it to make a deeper impression on the fancy and imagination" (122). The poet, like the audience, has a "counterfeit belief, and even a kind of vision of his objects" (123), but he is not, as one might suppose, launching into a discussion of the concept of the willing suspension of disbelief. Instead, what he is driving at is the way in which the mind of the spectator, with some encouragement from author or narrator, constructs relations if it is convinced that one item has authenticity. Hume makes an important statement of this phenomenon which argues that the effect of tragedy (as well as of other forms of fiction[36]) is to give the mind the opportunity to accept or infer associations:

> The several incidents of the piece acquire a kind of relation by being united into one poem or representation; and if any of these incidents be an object of belief, it bestows a force and vivacity on the others, which are related to it. The vividness of the first concept diffuses itself along the relations, and is convey'd, as by so many pipes or canals, to every idea that has any communication with the primary one. This, indeed, can never amount to a perfect assurance; and that because the union among the ideas is, in a manner, accidental: But still it approaches so near, in its influence, as may convince us, that they are deriv'd from the same origin. Belief must please the imagination by means of the force and vivacity which attends it; since every idea, which has force and vivacity, is found to be agreeable to that faculty. (122)

Hume is talking about judgment, but it is judgment influenced by vividness, not logic, or perhaps logic operating on the lifelike. Vividness is in turn a quality of language: "'Tis difficult for us to withold our assent from what is painted out to us in all the colours of eloquence; and the vivacity produc'd by the fancy is in many cases greater than that which arises from custom and experience" (123).

---

36. Comedy, he points out, does not need historical names because characters and events are more familiar and typical and therefore gain easy credibility.

Coherence, liveliness, and belief prompted by imagination may explain our sympathetic responses not just to tragedy but to all forms of representation, but they do not explain why these responses should be pleasurable even when distress, suffering, and melancholy are depicted. This omission undoubtedly accounts for the direct attack on the problem of tragic pleasure Hume mounts in "Of Tragedy." Here he argues that the pleasure given by tragedy is an aesthetic emotion caused by the artistic representation, which therefore must be understood by the audience for what it is and not confused with reality. Hume thus emerges as the lonely champion, in England at least, of a position that isolates and distinguishes aesthetic affect from any other kind.

Although Cohen argues that by the time he wrote "Of Tragedy" Hume had abandoned the idea that it is our recognition of the nonreality of a tragic event that permits us to respond to it with pleasure, that theory is sufficiently close to what he eventually arrives at to merit some attention.[37] In *A Treatise of Human Nature* he has, as we have noticed, proposed that certain ideas, such as poetic representations, have a surrogate reality. In the Appendix there is a passage that he directed "*To be inserted in* Book I, page 123." He is once more discussing "vivacity," and his insistent language reveals how anxious he was to clarify a difficult point:

> But how great soever the pitch may be, to which this vivacity rises, 'tis evident, that in poetry it never has the same *feeling* with that which arises in the mind, when we reason, tho' even upon the lowest species of probability. The mind can easily distinguish betwixt the one and the other; and whatever emotion the poetical enthusiasm may give to the spirits, 'tis still the mere phantom of belief or persuasion. The case is the same with the idea, as with the passion it occasions. There is no passion of the human mind but what may arise from poetry; tho' at the same time the *feelings* of the passions are very different when excited by poetical fictions, from what they are when they arise from belief and reality. A passion, which is disagreeable in real life, may afford the highest entertainment in a tragedy, or epic poem. (631)

This is the point to recall two previously noted accounts of tragic affect: Rapin's nearly automatic transfer of emotion from work to audience and

---

37. Cohen, "The Transformation of Passion," 450. Cohen's characterization of Renaissance theory might well be modified to include other possible sources, such as those suggested by Castelvetro.

Hutcheson's belief that the moral sense guarantees an unhesitating and appropriate response. In contrast to both these relatively naive formulations, Hume proposes a more active, chosen decision on the part of the spectator about the reality of the *source* of passion. By this path Hume has arrived at the point where "Of Tragedy" begins, and in the light of his statements here we may wish to think of the essay not so much as a reversal of an earlier position, as a modification, for what is incompletely worked out or simply neglected in the *Treatise* or the *Inquiry* is now ready to be directly addressed.

Hume's solution to the problem of tragic pleasure is twofold: first of all, language replaces the awareness of fictional event as the source of emotion; in the second place, the fact that the members of the audience are spectators to distressing events allows them to entertain mixed and contradictory feelings in themselves. Cohen's account, with which I largely agree, is this: "The solution which Hume proposed was not a theory of technique but of the conversion of passion. The underlying doctrine was not the Renaissance theory that artistry seized the interest of the spectator but that what one felt about incidents in real life was converted into aesthetic emotion. The work of art transformed experience, and artistry was one agent of the transformation."[38] We might note, by the way, that Hume makes statements hardly distinguishable from Aristotelian notions of the effects of eloquence and imitation: "And the soul being at the same time roused by passion and charmed by eloquence feels on the whole a strong movement, which is always delightful. The same principle takes place in tragedy; with this addition, that tragedy is an imitation, and imitation is always of itself agreeable" ("Of Tragedy," 32).

The second necessity is that the audience be detached or, in Cohen's terms, be in a position to experience "a disinterested involvement such that the emotional response of the spectator did not prevent him from enjoying the work as a complete unit." To be disinterested is to respond to "the passion pertinent to the work" (457). Hume's efforts to exemplify the detachment of the spectator are instructive. He notes that the oration of Cicero describing Verres' massacre of the Sicilian captains must have powerfully moved his auditors, "but I believe none will affirm, that being present at a melancholy scene of that nature would afford any entertainment" ("Of Tragedy," 31–32). A bit later he remarks that "The shame, confusion, and terror of Verres, no doubt, rose in proportion to the noble

38. Ibid., 454.

eloquence and vehemence of Cicero: so did his pain and uneasiness" (35). And lastly, in accounting for the predominance of one passion over another, he points out that in trying to comfort the parent bereaved of a favorite child one would not use eloquence to exaggerate the loss, for that would only increase the suffering. In other words, verbal artistry is powerfully capable of moving us, but the way in which it does so, the positive or negative nature of the affect, depends on whether we are spectators and thus not directly involved. Earlier in *A Treatise of Human Nature* Hume had proposed a related but slightly different theory of why the fictional is able to affect us: in effect it parallels the way in which the imagination absorbs our responses to an actual object and makes us believe in its actuality (120–21). This theory, however, does not account for the difference between affective responses to fiction and to real events, and those differences are essential to any reasonable explanation of tragic pleasure.

The theory of affect that emerges from "Of Tragedy" is complex. It is evident from the examples cited above that Hume considers artistic language capable of producing powerful distress or delight, though we should also remember that the elements of art, "the force of imagination, the energy of expression, the power of numbers, the charms of imitation," are "naturally, of themselves [i.e., without reference to the object], delightful to the mind" (35). But once an object is present, the audience is then subjected to two contrary and contesting "movements":

> And when the object presented lays also hold of some affection, the pleasure still rises upon us, by the conversion of this subordinate movement into that which is predominant. The passion, though perhaps naturally, and when excited by the simple appearance of a real object, may be painful; yet is so smoothed, and softened, and mollified, when raised by the finer arts, that it affords the highest entertainment. (Ibid.)

What Hume calls "sentiments of uneasiness" do not disappear, nor does the audience's awareness that they are, ordinarily, uneasy. The resulting affect, though delightful, nevertheless depends upon a sense of contrast:

> Objects of the greatest terror and distress please in painting, and please more than the most beautiful objects that appear calm and indifferent. The affection, rousing the mind, excites a large stock of spirit and vehemence; which is all transformed into pleasure by the

force of the prevailing movement. It is thus the fiction of tragedy softens the passion, by an infusion of a new feeling, not merely by weakening or diminishing the sorrow. (32–33)

It is perhaps unfortunate that Hume uses the word "fiction" here when he has early in his essay objected to Du Bos's theory that it is the fictionality of the work of art by itself that allows us to experience pleasure. What he seems to mean is that the artistic representation accomplishes this metamorphosis. He illustrates the point that "the subordinate [i.e., painful] movement is converted into the predominant [i.e., pleasurable], and gives force to it" first by suggesting that novelty can have this effect, as well as the use of delay or suspense. We have to remember, when to illustrate suspense he mentions "the artifice practised by Iago," that suffering may well be the consequence of art if what is treated too closely involves oneself. The fact that this seems to mark the difference between pain and pleasure does not eliminate another fact: that Hume is still talking about the medium of artifice. The fictionality of the object will not guarantee pleasure, but the sort of pleasure Hume is dealing with nevertheless commands it as part of the complex of circumstances he assembles.

Of the various points of view different from Hume's, two require some comment, one because it deals with the divided perception at the center of his theory of transformation, and the other because it brings in a concept of language quite different from that assumed in all the works in which he discusses tragedy.

The first is George Campbell's. Campbell accepts the power of eloquence to vivify the subject matter. In terms close to, but on one point crucially different from, those of Hume himself, he says, "it enlivens the ideas in the imagination to such a pitch as makes them strongly resemble the perceptions of the senses, or the transcripts of the memory."[39] But he will not accept that an audience could or should respond to the artifice of representation. He thus bases his objection not in a superior understanding of affective psychology but in a preference for the Horatian doctrine that art should conceal art, that the purpose of art, to echo one of Addison's favorite ideas, is to bring the mind into a lively perception of the object, analogous

---

39. George Campbell, *The Philosophy of Rhetoric* (1776), ed. Lloyd F. Bitzer (Carbondale: Southern Illinois University Press, 1963), 119. See Cohen's discussion of the objections of Campbell, as well as those of Hurd and Walker: "The Transformation of Passion," 455–56. Hume does not propose that words raise mimetic pictures in the mind, though his position on this is not easy to determine; cf. Yolton, *Perceptual Acquaintance*, 182–87.

to the clarity of visual experience. Walker's position, fairly common throughout the eighteenth century, serves to point up the significance of Hume's refusal to agree that our responses to a work of art are identical to our responses to objects in nature or social experience. Walker refuses the idea of a dynamic and mixed aesthetic response proposed by Hume. What Hume adds is a concept of ambiguous perception in which the mind and its affective powers respond to aesthetic experience without at the same time shutting out an awareness of its difference from the nonaesthetic.

The second view that differs from Hume's is that of Burke. Burke shares the understanding that the situation of the spectator is crucial to affective pleasure, but the agreement is limited, as his discussion of sympathy reveals:

> For sympathy must be considered as a sort of substitution, by which we are put into the place of another man, and affected in many respects as he is affected; so that this passion may either partake of the nature of those which regard self-preservation, and turning upon pain may be a source of the sublime; or it may turn upon ideas of pleasure. . . . It is by this principle chiefly that poetry, painting, and other affecting arts, transfuse their passions from one breast to another, and are often capable of grafting a delight on wretchedness, misery, and death itself. (*A Philosophical Enquiry*, 44)

Burke, however, denies that the difference between real and fictional events conditions affect; even real events attract us, mixing delight with uneasiness (46). Moreover, there is his notorious argument that terror is pleasurable "when it does not press too close" (ibid.). This brand of terror is equated with the sublime, associated with imminent but vague threat.

Distance is provided by spectatorship as well as by obscurity, though Burke strays from tragic to epic poetry to make this point, quoting Milton and then remarking: "the mind is hurried out of itself, by a croud of great and confused images; which affect because they are crouded and confused. . . . The images raised by poetry are always of this obscure kind; though in general the effects of poetry, are by no means to be attributed to the images it raises" (62).

The corollary to these statements is Section V of the *Philosophical Enquiry*, discussed in the previous chapter. Burke argues first of all that our normal reaction to the imagery in language is not to form a mental picture and secondly that we respond emotively to language because of the ways in our experience that words have been associated with objects and then repeated: "by having from use the same effect on being mentioned, that their original has when it is seen" (167).[40] Emotional value, not descriptive accuracy, is responsible for communication. In dissociating certain classes of words ("aggregate" words such as man or horse and "compound, abstract" words, such as virtue, honor, and the like) from pictures or ideas in the mind, Burke deprives them of their visual referent both as a source of understanding and of affect. Land notes that Burke "is very close to the assertion that what matters in semantics is not the mental or physical apparatus behind the word but the situation of its use."[41]

The importance of all this for the discussion of tragic affect is that Burke is trying to scuttle the notion that words may be emotionally powerful because of what they represent, because of visual clarity or liveliness:

> In reality poetry and rhetoric do not succeed in exact description so well as painting does; their business is to affect rather by sympathy than imitation; to display rather the effect of things on the mind of the speaker, or of others, than to present a clear idea of the things themselves. (172)

He concedes in the next page that in "merely *dramatic* poetry" words can represent emotions, but this limited mode of imitation is not offered as a cause of the affective power of words. Rather, Burke proposes that words, quite apart from their representational value, and especially in combination, draw their power from other causes, from the part we take in the passions of others (sympathy), from our opinions concerning things, from things that seldom occur in reality (though words for them do exist), and from metaphor. He concedes that it is difficult to understand how words can be affective without representing, because we do not in discussing language distinguish between "a clear expression, and a strong expression." The one "describes a thing as it is; the other describes it as it is felt" (175), and how it is felt is a matter of habit and repetition.

The critique of Hume's position should be obvious. Hume does not, as we have seen, accept the sentimental view that the difference between real and

---

40. Burke's editor, James T. Boulton, claims (lxxxi) that "The section on words provides . . . an organic and stimulating conclusion." A more searching analysis is that of Stephen K. Land, who examines Burke's dependence on and differences from Locke in some detail; see *From Signs to Propositions*, 36–50.
41. Stephen K. Land, *From Signs to Propositions*, 47.

imagined or mediated things is irrelevant. He requires artifice as part of the "transformation" of emotions, but Burke goes well beyond this to propose that all the affective experience we attribute to ourselves as spectators is based on our previous, and probably collective, experience of language quite independently of what it may represent. For Burke the word becomes the presence to which we respond:

> The truth is, all verbal description, merely as naked description, though never so exact, conveys so poor and insufficient an idea of the things described, that it could scarcely have the smallest effect, if the speaker did not call in to his aid those modes of speech that mark a strong and lively feeling in himself. Then by the contagion of our passions, we catch a fire already kindled in another, which probably might never have been struck out by the object described. (175–76)

What is interesting here is that the cause of affect is deferred not simply to previous experience but to previous *linguistic* experience. Words at some point in our conscious life have become firmly attached to emotions.

Only a few remarks are necessary to complete this discussion. We must observe, first of all, how easy it is for Hume and Burke to drift from the strict subject of tragic pleasure (Burke of course has a larger subject anyway) to the more general topic of verbal affect. Perhaps tragedy and the understanding of its conventions had begun to give way to what was called the pathetic and to the powerful interests of the doctrine of benevolence. What was at issue was not simply the question of whether real and imagined passions, as well as real or imagined suffering, should be distinguished or conflated. Also worth notice is the growing awareness that some combination of the peculiar ways in which language could represent things and the subjective situation of the audience might be more crucial than artistic form. Therefore, Hume's insight that tragic pleasure is a function of distancing rather than bringing close, and Burke's notions of the power of obscurity and the resonance of language independent of objects may suggest that potentially, at least, their theories are not so opposite as we might have supposed.

6   Connections and Discontinuities

Du Bos, Condillac, and Diderot

> *The language of the first men is represented to us as the tongues of geometers, but we see that they were the tongues of poets. . . . One does not begin by reasoning, but by feeling. It is suggested that men invented speech to express their needs: an opinion which seems to me untenable. The natural effect of the first needs was to separate men, and not to reunite them.*
> —Jean-Jacques Rousseau,
> On the Origin of Language

Underlying the question of tragic pleasure—or more broadly the question of how what may be initially painful can be enjoyed—is another topic, one not precisely describable in a phrase. What I have in mind is the way in which the emotional in the arts comes to be understood almost entirely as a function of language, even if initial perceptions are thought to be nonlinguistic. These developments are hinted at in Hume's writings on imagination and Burke's theory of the sublime: an act of supposition is required to believe that what is not seen exists. But the assumption in their thinking that there is a continuity between the intention of the artist and the quality of audience response is one that in France, at least, founders eventually on the line of thought moving from Du Bos through Condillac to Diderot, precisely because for Diderot language, at least in the theater, ceases to be a medium. That idea contradicts one of the fondest neoclassical beliefs, that however much language comes to alienate us from the direct and universally communicable contact with nature, it can be managed to correct that error and return us under the proper conditions to a direct apprehension of natural order and the feelings attendant upon it. I wish to address once again the manner of this communication and the issues clinging to it in the thinking of three major figures in the French Enlightenment.

Du Bos

It is with the Abbé Du Bos that we begin. His *Réflexions critiques sur la poésie et la peinture* (1719), sometimes regarded as the first systematic treatise in aesthetics, opens with the sweeping assertion that boredom is the cause of art. As Addison had done not long before, he grounds his entire account first in an audience psychology, in a need for "sensible" pleasure, but his notion of pleasure is not so much that it is a function of the imagination as that it is a craving to experience and reexperience emotions, especially those associated with tragedy and suffering. And he includes in the orbit of his discussion paintings that depict distressing circumstances:

> The pathetic representation of the sacrifice of *Jephtha*'s daughter, set in a frame, is one of the most elegant ornaments of a sumptuous cabinet. The several grotesque figures, and most smiling compositions of painters of the gayest fancies, pass unobserved, to attend to this tragical picture. A poem, the chief subject whereof is the violent death of a young princess, graces the most august solemnity; and the tragedy is marked out for one of the principal amusements of a company assembled for their diversion. 'Tis observable, that we feel in general a greater pleasure in weeping, than in laughing at a theatrical representation.[1]

For Du Bos the daily round of sentient existence lacks a great deal. Either nonaesthetic mental activity is a "fruitless" effort to possess the objects of

---

1. Jean-Baptiste Du Bos, *Critical Reflections on Poetry, Painting, and Music*, trans. Thomas Nugent (New York: AMS Press, 1978), I.1 (references are to book and section). Unless otherwise noted, all quotations of Du Bos are from this eighteenth-century translation.

attention, or the imagination becomes pestered by confused and unrelated impressions, or concentration worries the mind. "Every man must have experienced the weariness of that state, wherein he finds himself incapable of thinking; as well as the uneasiness of that situation, wherein he is forced into a tumultuous variety of thought, unable to fix his choice upon any one particular object" (I.1). The blessing of a single object of attention is Du Bos's version of the neoclassical reaction against the visually detailed complexities of baroque wit and "gothicism" in art, and perhaps his description of what he conceives to be common ennui provides a reasonable explanation of that reaction. In any case, he makes an argument not just for distraction as the purpose of art, but for a mode of attention and a context in which the mind can yield to external impression without confusion. These in turn would seem to demand something prepared and arranged both to substitute for "the disquiet arising from business," which is not a pleasurable release from boredom, and to avoid being reduced to "the common amusements of mankind," which are "idle and frivolous occupations" (ibid.). Hence, our taste for "scenes of affliction."

Such scenes keep us moving, keep the emotions warm, and prevent that positively physical "heaviness" and languor that Du Bos believes even more unwelcome "than the most frightful spectacles, that human nature can behold" (I.2). What he terms the "attractives" of suffering are explained in terms of the "Lucretian return," the sense of safety enjoyed by the spectator observing the perils of others to which he is immune. The examples Du Bos offers are for the most part scenes of danger, of imminent rather than accomplished disaster, though he mentions especially the gladiatorial games, which had the advantage both of suspense (who would triumph, the man with the offensive weapon or the defensive?) and closure.

With some justification a recent critic has categorized this psychology as voyeuristic.[2] The benefit is to the spectator, even when witnessing a real event. What Du Bos is dealing with, however, are events created and staged for amusement or distraction. The gladiatorial games, however mortal and sanguinary, were nevertheless staged events, made to occur for the sake of spectating. What interests Du Bos early on is the fact that such sports were the delight of Romans at their most "polite" and civilized. "The same," he adds, "may be said of other very polite nations, who make also

2. Marian Hobson, *The Object of Art*, 193. Hobson's comments on the eighteenth-century fondness for "vicarious suffering" are carried to the point of identifying the spectator as "the commiserating torturer," a label that partially obscures the point Du Bos is trying to make about suspense. See note 6 below.

profession of a religion averse to the effusion of human blood. . . . Our annals furnish us with a much stronger proof, that even the most cruel spectacles have a kind of allurement to captivate the affections of people of the greatest humanity" (ibid.). Gambling has a similar appeal, precisely because the outcome is not predictable, and because there is danger. Du Bos has no illusions about our bloodthirstiness, but his real point is not that we are vicious at heart. Rather, we crave intensity of sensation and emotion. As he remarks of a gambling game, "as every stroke is decisive, and each event attended with loss or profit, the soul is of course in a kind of extasy" (ibid).[3]

All this suggests a managed universe of art designed to enhance pleasure, short-circuit pain, and produce an effective response only so long as performance, reading, or viewing lasts. The similarity to the situations in which formal rhetoric is employed is almost too obvious to mention, but rhetoric usually implies an intentional relation between occasion, medium of communication, and predicted affective response. Also, Du Bos asks, "Might not art contrive to produce objects that would excite artificial passions, sufficient to occupy us while we are actually affected by them, and incapable of giving us afterwards any real pain or affliction?" But these passions are artificial only in that they are imitations of the real. "Painters and poets raise those artificial passions within us, by presenting us with the imitations of objects capable of exciting real passions" (I.3). The artificial object differs from the real only in "force." Here Du Bos runs into difficulties. A gladiatorial combat may in a sense be an imitation of a battle, but it is also a real battle, involving real blood, real wounds, real death. A similar point could be made about gambling. What Du Bos shifts to is the spectator's ability to register the difference between a real and an imitating event. He insists that "the impression of the imitation is not serious, inasmuch as it does not affect our reason, which is superior to the illusory attack of those sensations" (ibid.).

We can judge the nature of the object to which we are responding, at least to the extent that we can tell what is real and what is not, and he adds, astonishingly, that the impression of an imitation touches only the sensitive soul, by which he seems to mean that our reason is not unhinged by appearances or efforts at illusion. But Du Bos is here on rather slippery

3. David Marshall, *The Surprising Effects of Sympathy*, 22–23, comments that one aspect of Du Bos's theory is to render real suffering theatrical, in that our tendency is to treat all such events as spectacles.

ground and resorts to vague statements about the power of the *natural* object that somehow communicates itself to us. We could ask also whether, as he seems to be saying, the only difference between an object's filling us with horror and filling us with pleasure is our awareness of its status, our knowledge that the object is or is not real. But this does not deal with the pleasure attendant upon the gladiatorial games or gambling, which are, as I have suggested, real events, though of a special kind. However carefully arranged and staged, their outcome is uncertain; they are examples of risk and peril and so produce a special brand of emotion.

The course of Du Bos's argument to this point seems to be as follows: first of all, our need for mental and emotional activity is sufficiently great to make us prefer even vicious spectacles such as gladiatorial games to boredom or the ordinary business of life. Granted this much, if there is then a choice between unmixed pleasure in affective experience and that in which pleasure and pain are mingled, unmixed pleasure is obviously preferable and is to be gained from imitations, as opposed to real events. If we refer to the illustration used by Hutcheson and Burke, Du Bos would argue that death in a tragedy would be chosen over a public execution. (Burke, it will be recalled, argued the reverse.) For Du Bos what is of primary importance is that as spectators we be conscious of two things, the imaginary or artificial nature of what we are witnessing and the fact that we are witnesses, not participants. Here is his conclusion:

> The pleasure we feel in contemplating the imitations made by painters and poets, of objects which would have raised in us passions attended with real pain, is a pleasure free from all impurity of mixture. It is never attended with those disagreeable consequences, which arise from the serious emotions caused by the object itself. (Ibid.)

His illustrations are standard: Le Brun's painting of the slaughter of the innocents and Racine's *Phèdre*, both of them renderings of events that in reality would cause horror. Because they are represented, they do not distress us. Le Brun's painting "moves indeed our humanity but leaves no troublesome idea in our mind," and as for *Phèdre*, "We are pleased with the enjoyment of our emotion, without being under any apprehension of its too long continuance. This piece of Racine draws tears from us, though we are touched with no real sorrow; for the grief that appears is only, as it were, on the surface of our heart, and we are sensible, that our tears will finish with the representation of the ingenious fiction that gave it birth" (ibid.).

This is not a reassuring conclusion: it risks grounding our taste for art in our positive expectation that its power to move us is momentary and superficial, and it suggests that our compassion is pleasing to us precisely because we know that there is no need for action. And Du Bos goes so far as to claim that affect is in the control of the spectator: "The painter and poet afflict us only inasmuch as we desire it ourselves; they make us fall in love with their heroes and heroines only because it is thus agreeable to us" (ibid.). Yet, surprisingly, the following chapter seems to take back the discretion this passage allows the spectator and sets off in quite a different, almost opposite direction.

Having explained the distance from genuine emotions that imitations provide, he now begins to analyze their power, especially when the imitations are paintings or statues. This power is not simply that of momentary emotion, but a more enduring and persuasive control over behavior. Pictures have a distinctly political and moral purpose, to encourage a fear of punishment, for example. Here the effects derive from the closeness of the representation to the real thing. Du Bos cites Quintilian to the effect that pictures can enter the soul more profoundly than rhetoric. Thus, "When we give ourselves time to reflect on the natural sensibility of the heart of man, on his proclivity to be moved by the several objects, which poets and painters make the subjects of their imitations, we find it very far from being surprizing, that even verses and pictures have the power of moving him" (I.4). What is being developed here is a theory of our dependence upon and habit of responding to the outward signs of emotion. "We are moved," claims Du Bos, "by the tears of a stranger, even before we are apprized of the subject of his weeping" (ibid.). Emotion precedes knowledge, deriving merely from the sign. And the illustration, once again from the theater, points to an imitative theory of the passions. What Du Bos calls "the art of the complete actor" is the ability to appear to be moved by the emotions he seeks to reproduce in the audience.[4]

Du Bos seems not to notice at this point that he has previously developed a theory in which pleasure is the primary response to artificially represented emotions, so that while spectators may recognize, say, grief portrayed on stage, their own emotion is compassion. Now, however, Du Bos assumes that the spectators' emotions may be a replica of those represented, and

---

4. Quintilian, *Institutio Oratoria* VII.ii.35.

instead of underlining the relative weakness of "artificial" emotions, he reminds us of their strength and dwells on our instinct to draw close to what moves us. Responding to Plato's objections to the turbulence of literary representations and their consequent effects, Du Bos tries to confront the issue that poetry, and especially theatrical representations, have altogether too strong and too corrupting an influence. One answer is that the moving power of the poem ends when the fates of characters have been decided. He adds that poetry is more generally useful than Plato supposed and remarks with some irony that French poetry is unlikely in any case to gain ascendancy in men's minds. He concludes this part of his discussion rather lamely by saying that sometimes the imitator is more to be valued than the maker.

What we can rescue from these early confusions and contradictions of Du Bos's argument is his persistent belief that what moves us in art are representations of the very things that move us naturally. Art, he maintains, can never really compensate for a drab or dull subject matter, since the imitation is always less forceful than the original. Proximity, it is clear, has much to do with Du Bos's theory of affect, but most of all he requires, in paintings for example, canvases depicting scenes of emotion. Country feasts or soldiers lounging at a guard house are unlikely to command much interest, and a landscape without figures is even less compelling. The better painters "are not satisfied with giving a place in their landskips to the picture of a man going along the high road, or of a woman carrying fruit to market; they commonly present us with figures that think, in order to make us think; they paint men hurried with passions, to the end that ours may be also raised, and our attention fixed by this very agitation" (I.6).[5] For similar reasons tragedy affects us more than comedy. And even though comedy is more apt to present us with characters like ourselves with whom we can identify, the characters in tragedy are subject to stronger passions with greater consequences.

5. Du Bos was the first of the antirococo critics to insist that chief among the genres in painting should be history painting, a view grounded in the theory that the viewer would be most affected by the representation of the passions and that these in turn are best exhibited in action. Michael Fried sums it up well: "Du Bos argued on empirical grounds that a painting's power to move the beholder and thereby to command his attention (and ultimately to divert him from *ennui*) was a function of the power of its subject matter to do so in real life. The effect of this argument was inevitably to exalt the subject matter of history painting as traditionally conceived"; *Absorption and Theatricality: Painting and Beholder in the Age of Diderot* (Berkeley and Los Angeles: University of California Press, 1980), 73. It should also be noticed that the subject matter of history painting was not so much historical as literary in origin.

The representation of emotion is central to Du Bos's theory because "The mind has no repetition of pleasure in learning twice the same thing; but the heart has its pleasure repeated in feeling twice the same emotion. The pleasure of learning is exhausted by the pleasure of knowing" (I.8). One might add that because aesthetic affect ends when, for example, the play is over, that is another reason why emotion can be reexperienced without boredom. And like most of his contemporaries in England, as well as in France, Du Bos is unwilling to concede that artistic technique, or manner, is quite as compelling as subject matter. Thus, painting built around a human narrative is more interesting than still life or landscape, an opinion held without reference to the painter's style, power of arrangement, sense of color or any other aspect of the medium.

Du Bos's commitment to emotion as the central element in art involves attempts to explain how emotion is perceived and replicated, but these attempts are partially obscured by his profound conventionality when it comes to discussions of genre (I.14–23). He views the natural world and human society as organized into various expected contexts for the passions, and his accounts of both what is appropriate in various generic subjects and the responses they occasion are simply ordinary. What is perhaps not so ordinary is his sense of the ways in which audiences perceive and respond to art. It amounts to an effort to establish a kind of middle ground between encouraging a taste for the exotic or bizarre or darkly symbolic on the one hand and the ordinary or daily or overly familiar on the other. And at the same time he takes pains to insist that the quality of representation be carefully managed. If technique is not a source of pleasure by itself, controlled context is at least necessary to the system that would exclude pain or annoyance from the spectator's experience.

If the audience is to respond with emotions imitative of those in the representation, then the characters experiencing those emotions must embody both universal and national interests. These interests are rather vaguely described in terms of "a subject capable of touching all mankind, and of being particularly agreeable to the author's countrymen, by reason of its treating those matters, wherein they are chiefly concerned" (I.12). Because poems "are not read for instruction, but amusement," Du Bos would seem to be arguing that familiar and conventional subjects are the more compelling, again a deviation from his earlier point that the ordinary or too familiar subject is boring. Here at least he insists on a mode of art that seeks responses on grounds already prepared. The French reader will be disposed to an epic dealing with Henry IV rather than some ancient ruler, though he concedes that the *Aeneid* is still read with pleasure largely because of the artistry of Virgil. But on the whole he sees difficulties in poems "which draw all their pathetic from the invention of the artist." At a later stage Du Bos goes into considerable detail to demonstrate the effects of technique in both poetry and painting, but it is significant that he does so only after having repeatedly insisted on the primacy of a subject matter that would, even in the absence of artistic representation, be expected to move us. In attempting to locate the causes of mimetic or sympathetic emotion in the audience Du Bos, because he so thoroughly discounts the author's or painter's artistry in favor of our already existing interest in certain subjects over others, is forced then to try to establish what those subjects might be. He begins to do so first by arguing that some subjects are better suited to poetry than to painting and vice versa. But we should note that it is not so much the type of incident or character that makes the difference to him as it is the manner in which character and event are perceived. The poet, says Du Bos, is much better at rendering the inner thoughts of characters, whereas the painter is dependent upon physical gesture and facial expression to convey whatever they can plausibly represent. Passions generally show themselves outwardly, but the thoughts that attend them, the more detailed and secret workings of the mind are inaccessible to painters; in this sense their art is less subtle.

But there is a more fundamental and ultimately more interesting difference between poet and painter. The poet's work unfolds in a narrative, in a linear and diachronic sequence that allows concentration on a character or event as it passes through time. Indeed in Du Bos's theory the poet is almost bound by the terms of narrative. The painter can register several different and individual emotive responses to an event simultaneously in a fashion that, were it attempted in a poem, would make the work unreadable and digressive. Such detail would ultimately destroy interest in precisely those areas where poetic discourse cannot remain static. The poem has the power of establishing context, but because the picture, "which represents an action, shews only an instant of its duration, it is impossible for the painter to express the sublime, which those things, that are previous to its present situation, throw sometimes into an ordinary sentiment" (I.xiii). Poetry is more circumstantial, permitting each detail to take its force from those surrounding it. For this reason, Du Bos concludes, "The poet is much surer than the painter of attaining to the imitation of his object" (ibid.).

This is a matter of the concentration made possible by the linear accumulation of verbal detail. The painter's advantage is that he or she can display a variety of reactions to a single event simultaneously, for painting is spatial. It allows the artist to register passions almost instantaneously, and he or she can convey considerable factual information such as age, sex, profession, even nationality. In making this point Du Bos turns to a belief, widespread in the eighteenth century, that our capacity to read certain visual signs is automatic and instinctive, and that these signs in their turn are "natural," and therefore universal.

> Nature has implanted in us all an instinct, to discern the character of men; which instinct goes quicker and further than our reflections on the sensible marks of those characters are able to pervade. Now this diversity of expression is a wonderful mimic of nature, which, notwithstanding its uniformity, is always differenced in each subject by some particular characteristic. (Ibid.)

Du Bos's theory is thus controlled by two predominant models, the theatrical and the visual. The theatrical model is that which guarantees sufficient distance from ordinary existence to allow for cancellation of its random mixture of pleasure and annoyance and the substitution of a controlled and planned experience in which only pleasurable responses are to be had. However persistently Du Bos keeps insisting that poetry and painting must be "natural" and mimetically faithful to the world of human experience, he is nevertheless forced into an account of artifice in which a high degree of selectivity and contrivance are exercised to keep the affective atmosphere pure. As with Lessing, the natural is to be approached through the artificial, and the mode of response, even if it is understood as a reaction to subject matter, is shaped by a mode of artistic form.

He also demonstrates that the two arts imitate different things, or different aspects of the same object. Painting represents the outward expression of more or less crude states of emotion—astonishment, dismay, fear, anger, joy, disgust, and so on. All these are "natural" conditions stylized into facial expression, gesture, and bodily posture.[6] What the poet gets at is the interior condition, analyzed in greater depth and detail and presented as it changes and develops through time, both the time of the narrative and the time required to read it. The two sorts of imitation may overlap in that each can be said to imitate, for example, anger, but in most important respects what is represented is various. Or perhaps it would be

---

6. See Douglas Layne Patey, *Probability and Literary Form*, 90–92.

better to say that because the conditions of representation are different—the one visual, the other verbal, they overlap only in that each becomes a metaphor for the other. Verbal description and narration not only contain metaphors that turn thoughts into sensory images, they also themselves become a metaphor for visual perception, but without losing their linear, diachronic character. In a similar fashion, the elements of a painting can be read as if they were a text. We apply linguistic terms to what is expressed in the face or gesture of a painted figure, and we can see Du Bos's sense of the literariness of painting in his preference for canvases that depict important historical events, moments of human crisis. Such paintings have certain advantages over poems in seizing a moment in a narratable sequence of events. The two arts meet and part continually:

> 'Tis easy to infer from what has been hitherto set forth, that painting delights to treat of subjects, wherin it can introduce a great number of personages interested in the action. Such are the subjects above related [e.g., Raphael's *St. Paul* and Noël Coypel's *Susanna*], and such are also the murder of Caesar, the sacrifice of Iphigenia, and several others needless to be here mentioned. The emotion of the assistants fixes them sufficiently to an action, once this action has the power of moving them. This emotion renders them actors, as it were, in a picture; whereas they can only be spectators in a poem. . . . Those personages, who have not an essential concern in the action, in which they are to play their parts, are excessively frigid in poetry. The painter, on the contrary, can imbellish his action with as many spectators as he thinks proper. If they do but appear to be moved, there is no-body will ask what business they have there. (Ibid.)

This important statement offers a good deal more than the point about frigidity. For one thing, it combines the two central models of theater and visual image into a single hybrid. Both are dependent upon the fundamental assumption that the purpose of the two arts of poetry and painting is first of all to move the reader or spectator. But how precisely we are to be moved is not made clear at this point. In what ways is emotion communicable? Is the visual element in this kind of painting the medium of emotion, or is it the narrative implied by the visual? Du Bos is not exactly saying that the process of imitation does not require us to experience precisely the same emotions as the figures in the poem or on stage, but he may be thinking in this direction. In the picture, the secondary figures are spectators and are moved by the central incident, and presumably we register their emotion. On the other hand, just prior to this passage Du Bos has described Coypel's painting in such a way that the emotions of the two old men are noted rather than shared: "This is the natural character of men of that kind of complexion" (ibid.). Du Bos reads the emotions in the painting, but he is far less clear or certain about the ways in which spectators outside the work are supposed to be affected.

Moreover, it would seem that the distinction between actor and spectator is a central one: the secondary figures must be actors, for if we saw them merely as spectators in some way our interest would be diminished. If this is correct, then the action is of sufficient scope to include spectators, just as *Hamlet* includes the acting troupe and the courtly spectators, the latter providing a level of action in their reactions to the players and their play. Devices such as this measurably complicate the playgoer's response and our understanding of it: we are keyed to Hamlet's response, not to the play-within-the-play, but to Claudius's anticipated reaction to it, and we are also, like Hamlet, poised for that reaction.[7]

The visual model, if not exactly opposed, is at least quite different in its implications. It depends, as we have seen, on a notion of the universal significance of facial expression and gesture. Here again, what Du Bos considers natural and beyond the realm of contrivance may be read as extremely conventional—how can details of costume indicating nationality be natural?—and subject to more or less arbitrary sign systems. No doubt Du Bos would respond by saying that what is natural is our "instinct" for perceiving and understanding the meaning of nonverbal signs. But what is most evident in his treatise is the more or less continuous shifting between a claim for kinds of art that are as close as possible to the natural and requirements for careful management and control of audience perception.

Furthermore, there are places where Du Bos himself seems nearly to dismantle the distinctions between poetry and painting he has so patiently

---

7. Marian Hobson connects relationships of the spectator to theatrical works with kinds of illusion. Although she does not discuss plays or paintings that contain spectators within them, she does note that one form of illusion is the spectator's awareness of his own sensibility refracted through his view of others' emotion. Awareness here works against illusion and therefore against the emotional, unless it is internalized. But for many eighteenth-century French theorists this was what took place in the theater: intensity of emotion overrode disbelief. Cf. *The Object of Art*, 180–82. Du Bos, of course, refuses the theory of illusion that was to become common, according to Hobson, toward the middle of the eighteenth century in France. See note 12 below.

erected. The interplay of similarities and differences between the two arts, as he pursues them, seem to amount to this: poetry and painting imitate different elements of the same object, painting registering the outward signs of passion, and poetry concentrating on the narration of events that produce them as well as detailing their inner qualities; moreover, their means and the manner in which they cater to perception are quite different, painting achieving a synchronous vision of passionate event and its impact on witnesses; however, that stage of affect beyond perception approaches a kind of similarity. In other words, Du Bos seems to believe that our aesthetic experience, whether it is a response to poetry or to painting, should amount to a more or less equivalent kind of emotion, as if it were a destiny approached by different but parallel journeys. This, at least, is one of the inferences to be drawn from his effort to understand poetry as a kind of vision and painting as a mode of the historical or narrative, not to mention the theatrical.

At one point Du Bos notes that we register the defects and beauties of a painting in the same glance, and if the painting is sufficiently skilled we tend not to notice its weaker moments, and "we admire several poems that are far from being regular; but being sustained by invention, and a full style, they present us continually with affecting images which engage our attention. The sensible pleasure we receive from new beauties growing up at every period, prevents our perceiving part of the real defects of the piece" (I.xxxiii). Also, just as history paintings require a central event, an incident to generate the various emotions of the spectators situated within the painting, so a poem (and here Du Bos calls upon Corneille's *Cinna* to illustrate, continuing his bias for dramatic poetry) must distinguish in its treatment between language that directly renders emotion, which should be of the simplest kind, and that which expresses "all that is not properly sentiment," which can be more ornate, more figured, more complex (ibid.). And to observe even more closely the ways in which he tends to join the two arts together, we may notice how he supposes a painting can be judged by "reading" it. He paraphrases Pliny the Elder's account of a painting by Aristides of a woman stabbed as she nurses a child at her breast:

> One sees, says he, on this woman's dejected countenance, already seized with the symptoms of approaching death, the liveliest sentiments, and the most eager solicitude of maternal tenderness. Her apprehension lest the child should receive harm by sucking blood instead of milk, was so perfectly marked on the mother's visage, the

whole attitude of her body accompanied this expression in so accurate a manner, that it was easy to conceive what thought must have employed the dying parent.[8] (I.xxxviii)

Such a "reading" narrows the distance between poetry and painting, not in terms of technique, but in terms of the way each is supposed to be perceived and interpreted, for it assumes that the visual is narrative and the narrative is something to be seen. Generally Du Bos tends to give more attention to poetry than to painting and to make painting literary more than he makes poetry visual, as when he celebrates the superior power of a painting to show simultaneously a number of spectators and express their emotions. "The emotion of the assistants fixes them sufficiently to an action, once this action has the power of moving them. This emotion renders them actors, as it were, in a poem" (I.xiii). But the two arts, however he tries to distinguish them, emerge from his book thoroughly and deeply implicated in one another.

A major reason for Du Bos's importance in the history of aesthetics and critical theory is his attempt to discover in detail the ways in which both arts express and communicate feeling. I want to return for a moment to his comments on a passage from Corneille's *Cinna*. He is discussing what he calls "the poetic stile" and remarks that it "consists in giving interesting sentiments to those who are made to speak, and in expressing by figures and images capable of moving us, that which would have no effect upon us, were it related in the simplicity of a prose style." But there are in reality two elements to respond to and two modes of style. "The first ideas which rise in the soul, upon its receiving the impression of some lively affection, and are commonly called *sentiments*, have a power of affecting us, tho' expressed in the simplest terms, because they speak the language of the heart." The quotation from *Cinna* follows. Emilia says, "I Love my Cinna more than I detest Augustus," and Du Bos concludes: "A sentiment would cease to be so moving, were it expressed in magnificent terms, and with *pompous figures*" (I.xxxiii). The opposition between figured language, which Du Bos limits to bringing the inert to life, and simple speech is of course borrowed from that generated in Boileau's translation of Longinus and his many commentaries on it, but Du Bos employs it without any suggestion

---

8. This passage very neatly supports the thesis of W. J. T. Mitchell that among the French (as seen through the comments of Burke) there was a disposition to characterize visual representations as maternal, while the more remote and unseen verbal representations evoke paternal domination: *Iconology: Image, Text, Ideology*, 130.

that sublimity is the issue. The underlying argument is that emotion expressed in unfigured language appears more authentic, more probable, and is therefore more moving to us, though why this should be so, he does not say, any more than he explains why figured language dealing with other than emotional moments should also move us.[9] He is perhaps encouraged in his view by dealing largely with theatrical representation in which language and gesture are jointly the means of expression. Under such circumstances dialogue need not carry the weight of emotional expression by itself, and therefore should be simple. The emotion is, as it were, directly before us. But language recounting what is not happening directly before us requires figure to make the emotional vivid and hence present. I will touch on this point shortly. In the meantime, it is clear that for him emotion has direct means of showing itself and is, as we say, privileged.

That the "motions of the soul" could be "painted" (a technique that Du Bos calls poetic) was first demonstrated among the ancients. Pliny "relates as an important piece of history, that it was a Theban, by name Aristides, who first shewed it was possible to paint the motions of the soul, and to express the sentiments with strokes and colors in a mute figure; in short, that there was an art of speaking to the eyes" (I.38). The art, as Du Bos expands on it in borrowing Lucian's account of Zeuxis's painting of Alexander and Roxana,[10] is thoroughly narrative and "poetic," and he concludes that more quotation from the ancients is unnecessary. "Who can question," he adds, "after having seen the figures of the group of Laocoon but the ancients excelled in the art which infuses a soul into marble, and lends speech to colors?" (ibid.)

In other words, whereas poetry narrates painting animates. But there is more involved than this. In an odd way poetry and painting, by adopting something of each other's methods, imitate each other almost as much as they imitate nature. And the two central topoi of the theater and the painted image are combined by Du Bos into a single hybrid. Both are dependent upon the assumption that their purpose is to move the reader or spectator, and, we might add, it is really not a question of the reader, for Du Bos is

---

9. Those critics still bound to the rhetorical tradition, and perhaps others besides, take just the opposite view, that the pressure of emotion spontaneously generates figurative expression. See Brian Vickers, *In Defense of Rhetoric*, 294–305, P.W.K. Stone, *The Art of Poetry 1750–1820*, 64–66, and Stephen K. Land, *From Signs to Propositions*, 50–74.

10. The reference is to Lucian's dialogue "Herodotus or Aëtion," but Lucian assigns the painting to Aëtion, not Zeuxis.

comparing painting with dramatic poetry experienced in the theater.[11] But precisely how we are to be moved is not made clear at this point. Du Bos seems to be saying that the process of imitation does not require us to experience precisely the same emotion as the figures in the poem or on the stage, though he may be heading in this direction. In the picture, the secondary figures are at once spectators and figures who are moved (Fried's term for their state is "absorption"), and presumably in some way we register their emotion by witnessing the same central event as they do. On the other hand, as we have seen, just before this passage, Du Bos has described Coypel's painting in such a way that the emotions of the two old men are identified but not shared. Du Bos reads the emotions in the painting but is perhaps less clear about the ways in which spectators outside the work are supposed to be affected. Nevertheless, he makes an effort which we must attend to.

Painting alone, he believes, produces a more powerful effect on viewers than poetry, in part because the painter uses more "natural" signs. To underline the point he quotes Horace (*Ars Poetica*, lines 180–81): "Segnius irritant animos demissa per aurem, / Quam quae sunt oculis subiecta fidelibus." [The mind is stirred less vividly by what it hears / than by what is submitted to the trusty eyes.] The issue here is relative distance, and the belief that facial expression and bodily gesture are universal and hence untaught, uncalculated and unmodified by history, location, or particular culture:[12]

> Painting makes use of natural signs, the energy of which does not depend on education. They draw their force from the relation which nature herself has fixed between our organs and external objects, in order to attend to our preservation. Perhaps I do not express myself properly, in saying that the painter makes use of signs; 'tis nature herself which he exhibits to our sight. Tho' our mind be not imposed upon, our senses at least are deluded. The figure of the objects, their color, the reflection of light, the shades, in short, everything that can

---

11. Cf. Michael Fried, *Absorption and Theatricality*, 93, on the importance of Du Bos in establishing the complementarity of the two arts.

12. Monroe Beardsley notes that the seventeenth-century source of the later belief that the passions exhibit specific and identifiable facial expressions and bodily gestures is Descartes's *Traité des passions de l'âme* (1649), though there is an anticipation in Quintilian, *Institutio* XI; cf. *Aesthetics from Classical Greece to the Present: A Short History* (Tuscaloosa: University of Alabama Press, 1975; 1st pub. 1966), 151–52. The body as a sign system for emotions is common in Enlightenment discussions of acting and the theater.

be the object of sight, present themselves in a picture, just as we see them in nature. Even sometimes the eye is so dazzled by the performance of a great painter, as to fancy a movement in his figures.[13] (I.40)

Despite his conceding that the senses may be fooled, Du Bos is careful not to commit himself to illusion as an intellectual condition. Indeed, as we have seen, his whole theory of affect depends upon the argument for the spectator's awareness of the presence of a mimetic representation. However closely art may copy nature, it is never perceived as identical. Art is a substitution for the real thing, and we have already noted what Du Bos thinks are the affective benefits of that substitution in protecting us from ennui, annoyance, or actual suffering. "Illusion," therefore, is a term that refers to our sense of the authenticity of representation, and that sense of authenticity depends primarily on sight.[14]

The affective power of poetry works quite differently, but it still depends upon a perceptive process. The main difference for Du Bos is that between synchronic and diachronic processes of perception. Verse affects us only gradually. "Words must first excite those ideas, whereof they are only arbitrary signs. These ideas must be arranged afterward in the imagination, and form such pictures as move and engage us. All these operations are soon done; but it is an uncontestable principle in mechanics, that the multiplicity of springs always debilitates the movement, by reason that one spring never communicates to another all the motion it has received." The mechanical operation is entirely a matter of response to a different medium, but it eventuates in an object of attention that is perceived by the inner equivalent of sight. We turn words into pictures. And one operation, "that which is performed when the word excites the idea it signifies," is "purely artificial" (I.40). By artificial Du Bos means socially produced or arbitrary. There is no natural and universal connection between the word and the idea it prompts in our minds, whereas in the experience of purely visual perception sign and idea are virtually identical and automatic. Du Bos

13. Hobson contends that Du Bos's "whole aesthetic is designed to relate the work of art and the consumer without recourse to a theory of illusion" (*The Object of Art*, 38), but she maintains that at moments he reintroduces something close to illusion, as in the passage to which this note belongs. His motive apparently is that in low genre paintings the artist's skill substitutes for the lack of emotion generated by the object, so that we give a more intense scrutiny to the painted object than we would to the same thing in nature (41).

14. Cf. Hobson, *The Object of Art*, 40–42.

shares with virtually everyone in his time the belief that gesture, as opposed to verbal expression, is uncontaminated by time, convention, culture, or individual experience, whereas language and its use and reception are deeply modified by all these influences.

This widely accepted distinction does not seem to have been intended to disparage poetry, but it does serve in the system of Du Bos to place limitations on the power of language, to move his emphasis toward language as a more complex and partly artificial mode of seeing and, in order to preserve its distance from actual seeing, to try to account for the differences in our emotional responses to paintings and tragedies. Paintings, it may be objected, do not make us cry; tragedies do. Du Bos relies in his answers on an account of the circumstances under which we actually experience dramatic poetry:

> A tragedy represented on the stage, produces its effect by means of the eye; and is supported by foreign succours, whose power we shall presently explain. Tragedies that are read in private very seldom make us weep; especially when we read them without having seen them previously acted. For, as I apprehend, a private reading, which is incapable of itself of making such an impression as to draw tears, may be able nevertheless to renew this impression. . . . My second answer is, that a tragedy includes an infinite number of pictures. A painter who draws the sacrifice of Iphigenia, represents only one instant of the action. But Racine's tragedy exhibits to our sight several instants of this action; and the different incidents contribute to render one another reciprocally more pathetic. The poet presents us successively with fifty pictures as it were, which lead us gradually to that excessive emotion, which commands our tears. Forty scenes therefore of a tragedy ought naturally to move us more, than one single scene drawn in a picture. A picture does not even represent more than one instant of a scene. Wherefore tho' the latter would move us more than a single scene representing the same event, were it to be detached from the rest, and read without having seen any of the preceding scenes. (I.40)

What language interposes between object and the perceiving mind is not so much itself as the diachronous, almost cinematic, succession of pictures. Quantitatively these affect us more powerfully than a single picture, and Du Bos everywhere in his treatise indicates his belief that intensity of affect is a matter of the almost material closeness of the object to our senses. It does not seem to occur to him that one might view a painting more than once, but of course in that circumstance we are still confronted with a single unchanging scene. Yet the condition of the spectator might conceivably differ substantially from viewing to viewing, a consideration unreached by Du Bos's speculations.

The other important issue is the context in which we perceive, and for Du Bos that context is supremely exemplified by the theater in which aural and visual perception are joined. Here, the greater representational profundity of the poem can be seconded by the more powerful emotive energy of hearing and seeing: language and visual image are joined in such a way that the advantages of each may be used and we are afforded the closest possible approximation to the natural within the confines of artifice:

> The apparatus of the stage prepares us for being moved, and the theatrical action gives a surprising force to verse. As the eloquence of the body is no less persuasive than that of words, gestures are of great assistance to the voice in making an impression. This we learn even by instinct, which informs us, that those who hear us speak, without seeing us, are but half-hearers. (I.xli)

He then partially quotes Cicero: "For nature has assigned to every emotion a particular look and tone of voice and bearing of its own; and the whole of a person's frame and every look on his face and utterance of his voice are like the strings of a harp, and sound as they are struck by each successive emotion."[15] The artifice of the theater for Du Bos comes closest to nature, which suggests powerfully that he wants to have it both ways. We must remember that his treatise begins with the premise that ordinary human existence is boring and that art and artifice are called into being by such a "natural" condition. Yet real events, he has argued, have a greater power to move us than those of art, and the theater is more moving than other forms of art by themselves because it combines voice and gesture, sound and sight, language and the spectacle of human beings moving and being moved more completely than any other contrivance.

The theater approaches nature in the actors' capacity to appear to feel the very emotions they are representing on stage, the appearance of artlessness in the most artificial of circumstances. Du Bos cites Quintilian on this

---

15. Cicero, *De Oratore* III.lvii.216, Loeb trans.

commonplace, which includes the thought that actors must warm their own imagination with the images they create. (As we shall see, Diderot eventually dismantles this bit of theatrical criticism rather effectively.) Elsewhere Du Bos notes that tragedy should move us, though not in the exact way that the character in a play is rent by passion. Our passion responds to his or hers, variously depending upon the moral status of the emotion involved, and it is precisely this condition of spectatorship we noticed somewhat earlier that makes it plausible for Du Bos to confuse the distinctions between art and nature that appear to be so crucial to his argument. They are crucial, it seems to me, in a fashion he does not quite acknowledge: although real events might touch us more powerfully than those in a painting or a poem, ordinary life does not offer us much opportunity to witness them, for they are concealed within. Hence, the triumph of artifice is to lay bare the hidden, to bring us closer to the "nature" of the passions by transforming what is ordinarily concealed into appearance. Beyond this Du Bos does not venture.

Condillac

For the purposes of this study Condillac's *Essai sur l'origine des connaissances humaines* (1746)[16] forms a bridge between Du Bos's *Refléxions* and the various critical speculations of Diderot. It does so, not because Condillac was a literary theorist, which he was not, but because he offers a more complicated view of the way language relates, on the one hand, to nature or to prelinguistic perception and, on the other hand, to its audience. His theory of the origin of language is in effect a theory of the interruption and displacement of our perceptive contact with nature. This in turn lays a special burden on language in the sense that we are led to ask how it may be brought back to a kind of communication.

To return for a moment to Du Bos, his concept of the arts rests on the assumption that they supply the emotional excitement lacking in ordinary experience. They do so by a process of addition, by a kind of gratuitous but necessary embellishment in the form of imagined or contrived events plausible enough to command our feelings but not so realistic as to be

---

16. My text for quotation is the English translation, *An Essay on the Origins of Human Understanding*, trans. T. Nugent (London, 1756).

mistaken for the genuine article. Yet, however artificial they may be, the narrative painting we observe or the theatrical performance we both see and hear are for Du Bos mimetic of an absent and authentic original. The work of art carries the authority of its model and indeed stands in for it. Du Bos seems to be arguing that although there are real events that would move us even more powerfully than any painting or piece of poetry, they are unlikely to occur in such a way that we can enjoy them on a more or less regular basis. And of course, there is something else: the question of whether our emotions prompted by the work of art are the same emotions experienced by fictional characters in the work.

Perhaps Du Bos is approaching a concept of special aesthetic emotion, but my reading of his theory is that what is at issue is our situation as spectators whose affective reactions are both dependent upon our observing and even feeling the power of the emotions of others, whether or not those others are living beings (as in a gladiatorial contest) or invented persons. What this means is not so much that we experience vicariously, but that we experience emotions about emotions. As Du Bos points out, we do not at all share the vengeful feelings of Medea when she murders her children to pay back Theseus: the aim of tragedy "most frequently is to excite opposite sentiments to those, which it lends to the personages" (I.xliv). At the same time, as spectators we must recognize and respond to her emotions, and the theater with its synaesthetic representations offers the most complete opportunity to return our sentiments to some kind of vital contact with the natural.

The psychology Du Bos employs is relatively simple. He assumes a need for emotional stimulation and understands the arts as providing certain combinations of sensory data to cater to that need. The human faculties in this system (if it is not too crude to be called a system) are passive organs of reaction. Nor does he attempt to include the ways in which both our experience and our powers of attention may contribute to mental and emotional reactions. And finally he does not allow for much response beyond the emotive: reflection or judgment as aspects of aesthetic experience are not really addressed or accounted for.

Condillac is, of course, far more ambitious in seeking to establish a "metaphysics" to analyze the operations of the human mind, to discover the origins of our ideas, and to generally map the universal territory of human consciousness. Yet, as Jacques Derrida has observed, his intention was also to search the nature of language to find the universal nature that precedes all language, to discover the border between nature and artifice in the origins and limits of language.[17] This search for an origin, a common pursuit in the seventeenth and eighteenth centuries,[18] seems to derive from the sense that all meaningful human activity is what it is because of a process of development. Contemporary human beings and their society are seen as complex, a series of systems developed and complicated slowly over time through the accumulation of experience. Not a small part of this point of view is the desire of Locke and his followers, of whom Condillac is one, to refute the doctrine of innate ideas, which would seem to imply, among other things, a more or less static and uniform culture; observation and the historical record had already shown otherwise. At the same time, critics and philosophers who shared the belief that human society had moved people some distance from their early, original, and intimate contact with the natural, sought to recover some sense of what that condition was. And an almost universal assumption was that it involved the emotions, which were assumed to have preceded language. Therefore, the Enlightenment interest in the emotional and in that aspect of artistic affect.

In this context Condillac is important because of his proposal that while sensation and emotion may give rise to language, their communication in the absence of the object that prompted them is only possible after language has been established. His version of human development and especially how it relates to the arts is first of all evident in Part II of the *Essai*, which he titles "Of Language and Method" ("Du langage et de la méthode"). Language is preceded by responsive cries and gestures, the automatic reaction of the

17. *The Archaeology of the Frivolous: Reading Condillac*, trans. John P. Leavey, Jr. (Pittsburgh: Duquesne University Press, 1980), 37. In its original form, *L'Archéologie du frivole*, the essay is the introduction to Condillac's *Essai sur l'origine des connaissances humaines* (Paris: Galilée, 1973). Derrida notes the breadth of Condillac's claim and asks, "What particular name could one assign to a *general* science that ends nowhere, that brings into play an universal analysis that leads us back, through all the fields of knowledge, to the simplest, most elementary ideas, as well as defining their laws of relation, combination, complication, of substitution, of repetition? but also, *a principal difficulty (or difficulty of principle)*, their laws of generation?" Condillac's task, as Derrida interprets it, is to establish two sorts of metaphysic, one involving prelinguistic natural origins of instinct and feeling, the other a new language and a new form of reflection (38). It is Condillac's attention in this context to a theory of language that makes him of interest to my thesis.

18. Condillac's is the first and seminal effort to determine a nonbiblical account of the origins of language. Rousseau and Herder each produced influential essays on the topic; cf. *On the Origin of Language*, ed. and trans. John H. Moran and Alexander Gode (Chicago: University of Chicago Press, 1986). See also Hans Aarsleff, "The Tradition of Condillac: The Problem of the Origin of Language in the Eighteenth Century and the Debate in the Berlin Academy before Herder," in *Studies in the History of Linguistics: Traditions and Paradigms* (Bloomington: Indiana University Press, 1974), 93–136; and Stephen K. Land, *The Philosophy of Language in Britain* (New York: AMS Press, 1986), 131–92.

organism to outside impressions. At this stage responses are instinctive and unreflective. To illustrate his theory Condillac supposes two postdiluvian children living separately and thus capable only of rudimentary mental life:

> So long as the abovementioned children lived asunder, the operations of their minds were confined to perception and consciousness, which never cease to act whilst we are awake; to attention which must have taken place whenever any perceptions affected them in a particular manner; to reminiscence, which was when they recollected some circumstances that had struck them, before they had lost the connections formed by those circumstances; and to a very limited exercise of the imagination. (II.1.1.1)[19]

In other words, what Condillac describes is existence without language because language is communication and therefore a social function of thought and feeling, as well as the power within our own minds of storing up the relations between things we have perceived. In a state of total isolation the human being is dependent upon circumstance for whatever mental life he or she enjoys and is thus entirely a responsive or passive creature.

Isolation ends when the development of signs begins. As Condillac explains earlier in his treatise, signs are the manifestation of the connections our minds make between ideas and objects. There are three kinds of sign: accidental (objects fortuitously attached to our ideas); natural ("the cries which nature has established to express the passions of joy, of fear, or of grief, &c."); and instituted ("those which we have chosen for ourselves, and bear only an arbitrary relation to our ideas"). Signs are important because the capacity to remember experience without having to repeat it ceaselessly requires some kind of representation (I.1.4.35–36). Memory is the power to revive signs of our ideas or the circumstances that attended them. Present want may require us to call certain objects to mind. But we cannot call to mind something unless it has some relationship to something else in our power. This necessity of connection or liaison is for Condillac the source of the instituted or arbitrary sign. It allows us to revive sensations and perceptions at will whether or not we are driven by some need such as hunger. And this power of memory and imagination is the basis for social communication. What Condillac seems to be approaching is a theory that

---

19. The work is elaborately divided into parts, sections, chapters, and paragraphs; hence, there are four numbers in each reference.

affect is socially induced, even though he supposes that at first unmediated sensation creates language and language eventually creates emotion. Language, after being initiated, is essentially a social instrument and so may be responsible for the affect we believe is available from nonlinguistic sources.

What Condillac regards as a liberating power, the power to substitute signs for original perceptions or intuitions, shortly becomes regarded as a limitation, either because as language develops it stops well short of universal communication or because it stands between our sensibilities and the direct experience of nature. If language connects us to other human beings, it stands between our consciousness and its communion with nature. But the positive value of the sign is simply its greater efficiency. The instituted sign is the very thing that activates those mental functions (memory and imagination) that guarantee the continuity of thought, the freedom of the mind from dependence upon random event, perception, or experience. Signs are economical. They mean that experiences do not have to be endlessly repeated. "But as soon as a man comes to connect ideas with signs of his own chusing, we find his memory is formed. When this is done, he begins himself to dispose of his imagination, and to give it a new habit. For by means of the signs which he is able to recall at pleasure, he revives, or at least is often capable of reviving the ideas associated with them" (I.1.4.46).

Condillac illustrates this capacity by the example of a man viewing a painting. His mind moves between the ideas produced by the painting and those occasioned by his knowledge of natural objects that the painting imitates. This comparative process is called reflection. It too is voluntary, and though Condillac doesn't say so, his example implicates the arts solidly in his system, for they are a prime example of the instituted sign. Our experience of art is a model for our more general habit of reflection.

Now let us return to his discussion of language. Language develops out of the gradual and repeated association of certain cries and gestures with the occasions for them, and this development occurs, apparently, when two or more people are able to compare notes:

> When they came to live together, they had occasion to enlarge and improve those first operations; because their mutual converse made them connect with the cries of each passion, the perceptions which they naturally signified. They generally accompanied them with some motion, gesture or action, whose expression was yet of a more

sensible nature. . . . The more they grew familiar with those signs, the more they were in a capacity of reviving them at pleasure. . . . At first both of them acquired the habit of discerning by those signs the sensations which each other felt at that moment, and afterwards they made use of them in order to let each other know their past sensations. (II.1.1.2)

The "cries of passions" thus expand mental capacity. It is also called "a mode of speaking by action" (*le langage de l'action*). By experience and experiment "natural cries" grow into a pattern "to frame a new language" (II.1.1.3–6). Language thus develops from elemental need and feeling.[20]

As human society progresses, people gradually overcome their difficulties in fashioning precise verbal gestures to replace the simple cries and bodily gestures with which social intercourse was inaugurated. A sound such as "ah" had to make do to express admiration, pain, pleasure, sadness, and perhaps a host of other feelings. Context and variations in uttered sound would serve to particularize. The history of language according to Condillac is thus one of progressive refinement and complexity. But it is also important to note that he supposes that cry and gesture, which modern languages have tended to modify, both preceded language (oral and written) and for long stretches of time were necessary to supplement words in order to guarantee complete intelligibility. Hence, his chapters on gesture, music, metrics, and poetry. Gesture was an important and indeed necessary element in declamation among the ancients, and in their dramatic representations, lines were accompanied by music—the ancients saw it not as a separate art but as a means "of adding more energy or ornament to speech" (II.1.5.46). The general purpose of music is affective, to "move the passions," and by implication, this is one of the central purposes of language.

Condillac's motives for such a heavy reliance on affective arts in the course of his analysis of language requires some explanation, since he himself does not really provide one. And any such explanation will be necessarily speculative. We have noted that he believes that communication originates in the emotions or passions, in hunger, fear, joy, and the like, and not in any emotionally neutral

---

20. Rousseau's divergent view is well known. Language, he argues, develops not from need but desire, and he supposes the imagination as functioning entirely separately from verbal communication. Language becomes, in Rousseau's thinking, supplementary to what can be silently exhibited to sight; cf. *The First and Second Discourses together with the Replies to Critics and Essay on the Origin of Languages*, ed. and trans. Victor Gourevitch (New York: Harper and Row), 240–46.

expression of ideas. Emotion is prior to thought in the same way that perception is prior to judgment. Language thus has its roots in feeling and its primary function is to communicate or represent the passions. Ruminative, reflective, or logical uses of language come much later historically. Therefore, Condillac finds the affective arts useful because they exemplify this basic connection between perception and sign, the process of the human transaction with our surroundings. They preserve some vestige of the "language of action," and in effect offer evidence of stages of the process whereby the affective element has become muted. Moreover, however artful representation and communication have become, the effort we make in using language is to effect an accurate or true representation of what we perceive and feel. The arts are therefore an attempt to maintain an authentic connection of representation with the natural very much in the way the word order used in ancient languages follows, as he believes, the natural order from perception to judgment to expression (II.1.12.120).

If such is the case, how then did word order change, and why? Condillac's view is interesting. Poetry for him is not, as we might assume, necessarily an artificial construct that moves away from the natural. Rather it mimics a feature of the language of action. Natural word order doesn't really disturb the mind of the listener and hence it may not sufficiently catch his attention. Artfulness in manipulating word order can distance words that normally belong together and thus force the mind by imagination to supply the connection between them. He provides an example from Horace, *Odes* I.28.1:

> Nec quicquam tibi prodest
> Aerias tentasse domos, animoque rotundum
> Percurisse polum, morituro.
> (II.1.12.121)

> Nor is there any benefit
> In having explored the country of the air
> And traversed in mind the poles of the globe
> To you, destined to die.

Morituro, the reminder of death, is so positioned that it forces the imagination back over what separates it from the personal pronoun *tibi.* Paradoxically artifice practiced on language has the effect of reenacting an earlier stage of human communication: "This sort of transpositions [in which the whole weight of a sentence is brought to bear on a single word] partake of the character of the mode of speaking by action, where a single sign was oftentimes equivalent to an entire sentence" (II.1.12.121). Transpositions are also used to form a picture, to effect a change from a diachronic composite into a synchronic sequence and thus by emphasizing the sensible element in utterance to supply something of the emotive power diminished as cry and gesture gave way to more complex expressions. The importance of these notions in Diderot's aesthetic thinking will be evident before long.

The poetic and theatrical are then in Condillac's system survivals of an earlier stage of human representation and our means in effect of keeping in touch with the natural. He considers them fundamentally mimetic. The imagination, the faculty that allows us to use verbal signs in this way, is thus central, and we might note in passing that this concern for imagination as much as anything else distances Condillac from Locke, with whom he is otherwise consciously affiliated.

Language emerges in Condillac's formulation not only as a stage of human development but as a necessary substitute for repeated encounters with basic perceptions and passions. In one sense, it removes people from their primitive closeness to nature, but in another sense, it preserves that contact through substitution of the sign, and of course, as we have noted, it frees human beings through their exercise of imagination and memory to think, to communicate, and to represent at will rather than by necessity. Finally, and this is a complication, language as a function of the reconstituting power of the imagination gives the mind the power not simply to recover and repeat experience and communicate but also to transform it.[21] Language is an instrument of cognition, but had Condillac left it at that, he would hardly have devoted so much attention to poetic artifice, one of whose features, metaphor, allows us to connect the world of the mind and the world of nature by drawing all the terms developed to represent the movement and repose of objects into what is thought about the states of the soul. Metaphors such as this invaded abstractions and permitted us early opportunities to try to express events within the mind.

Diderot

Certain issues in the work of Du Bos and Condillac—the relations between poetry and painting, the process of perception, gesture, language, and

---

21. Derrida remarks (49) that "all the problematic of the *Essay* is deployed between the two senses of the word *imagination*, the reproductive imagination which retraces . . . and the productive imagination which, in order to substitute, adds more to it." It is through the function of both forms of imagination, according to Condillac, that language develops.

affect—Diderot handles in unconventional and often idiosyncratic ways. Du Bos's efforts to compare and divide painting and poetry are substantially extended and complicated by Diderot's attention, and Condillac's theory of a coherent system of perception and verbal sign endures serious questioning, though much of Diderot's thinking about language derives from his friendship with Condillac. Proceeding by a kind of dialectic Diderot does not so much discard the findings of his predecessors as rethink them skeptically so that the efforts of aestheticians and philosophers in his time to propose smooth and complete orders of consciousness in general and aesthetic consciousness in particular often seem less plausible. To the extent that the philosophic and aesthetic thought he was aware of confirmed an authentic bond between readers, viewers, and spectators and what the arts claimed to represent, Diderot's habit was to question and eventually reconstitute. The most obvious example is his handling of the works of Père André. According to Jacques Chouillet, he used them as a starting point and in most instances found his own way from there.[22] But his attention to Condillac concerns me especially, since it centers on connections between perception, language, affect, and judgment, those topics by which the experience of the audience or spectators was given theoretical coherence. Diderot's interests are by no means exclusively those of an affective theorist, but his aesthetic writings, and several of his other works, give vivid and original treatment to the experience of the spectator or audience. That experience, and the manner in which Diderot treats it, constitutes some of his most original thinking.

Like Condillac, Diderot in some of his earliest aesthetic writings centers on the nature of perception, especially on the way in which our responses might or might not accurately reflect the object. The general matter of perception is the first thing one looks at to approach Diderot's treatment of

22. Jacques Chouillet, *La Formation des idées esthétiques de Diderot, 1745–1763* (Paris: Colin, 1973); see, for instance, 29–30, 48 (on André), 33–49 (on Shaftesbury), 238–41 (on Du Bos); 172–76 (on Batteux), and 158–62 (on Condillac). Of the many other general studies of Diderot's effort in criticism and aesthetics, the following seem to me most useful: Herbert Dieckmann, *Cinq leçons sur Diderot* (Paris: Droz; Paris: Minard, 1959); Yvon Belaval, *L'Esthétique sans paradoxe de Diderot* (Paris: Gallimard, 1950); Michael Fried, *Absorption and Theatricality*; David Funt, *Diderot and the Aesthetics of the Enlightenment, Diderot Studies* 11 (Geneva: Droz, 1968). More recent studies addressing particular topics are D. J. Adams, *Diderot, Dialogue and Debate* (Liverpool: Francis Cairns, 1986); James Creech, *Diderot: Thresholds of Representation* (Columbus: Ohio State University Press, 1986); and Jay Caplan, *Framed Narratives: Diderot's Genealogy of the Beholder* (Minneapolis: University of Minnesota Press, 1985). Caplan's interests are closest to my own, though his conception of Diderot's transactions with audiences or theories of such transactions is centered in theories of dialogue.

more strictly literary and artistic questions, especially since he relates most of those questions, and certainly those involving audience response, to what he conceives to be their origins in sensation and perception. The habit of guessing at how perception, knowledge, and communication first began rests on the assumption that there was once a primary unmediated experience of the objective world and that the direct quality of this experience has since become altered and obscured by the artifices and conventions of social existence.

If eighteenth-century thinkers did not exactly seek a way to recover such originary contact with nature, they at least sought to explain it and sometimes to approximate its quality as unmediated sensation by supposition or by trying to test the first responses to sensory experience of children or the blind and deaf. In addition, those who like Condillac draw heavily upon Locke's theories, start by rejecting the concept of innate ideas. They are thus compelled to imagine a state of the human mind just at the point before conscious memory and thought begin, a point at which it registers nothing more than the sensory impressions of objects. This is a state to which no thinking being can return to report on what it is like but which is nevertheless critical in explaining the interaction of sensation, language, and emotion.

As we have seen, in Condillac's theory all thought has its beginnings in sensation and develops through experience; the faculties of memory, imagination, and judgment or reflection are born in the repetition of experience and in the gradually more efficient use of signs. Human beings move from solitude to society and at the same time from raw perception and the prison house of affect to the capacity to deploy signs and ideas at will.[23] Such a theory proposes not only the harmony and unity of the faculties, but also the identity of mental and material sensations. In broad terms, this is the account Diderot inherits and conditionally accepts.

---

23. Chouillet notes (158–59) that Locke and Condillac differ significantly on the relationship of thought to language. Condillac believed language necessarily preceded ideas, that until language had developed from sensations, cries, and gestures, the mind could not entertain an idea. The reasoning here is that our perceptions must be translated into signs before they can be lodged in memory and imagination *as* ideas. Locke on the other hand believed that ideas were formed before the invention of signs and were therefore independent of the means to communicate them (cf. *Essay* III.ii.1). Condillac's argument is that human beings' original sensations were simply that, and until they could put them together and remember them, they were more or less isolated and helpless. Language developed through the repetition of sensations and the habit of associating a cry or gesture with the sensation. Only then are ideas possible. (cf. *Essai* I.ii.4).

In the relatively early *Lettre sur les aveugles* (1749) Diderot seeks to demonstrate by reference to the blind and especially by an account of the blind mathematician, Nicholas Saunderson, our dependence for conceptual life on our senses. He notes that a blind acquaintance is a good judge of symmetry because of his highly developed sense of touch, "but when he says, *that is beautiful,* he is not judging, he is only reporting the judgment of those who can see."[24] The point is obvious enough, perhaps, except that a concept such as beauty is not necessarily derived only from sense experience: it is secondhand, an abstraction, in part, for those who see as well as for the blind, and Diderot seems aware of this point, for he adds to the words just quoted, "and what else do three quarters of those who judge a theatrical piece do after having seen it? For a blind man beauty, when it is separated from utility, is only a word; and minus one organ, how many things are there whose utility escapes him." Saunderson is used to illustrate those "who see, therefore, with their skin" (838). Toward the end of his life Saunderson was discussing immortality and God with a clergyman. The clergyman had cited the beauty of nature as an argument for God, to which Saunderson replied that for someone in his condition this was not a very convincing argument (839).

In other words, language by itself offers only hearsay evidence. According to William R. Paulson, "The problem with the blind man is his facility with discursive language, a facility which is deceptive in that it masks the figurative, subjective, and perhaps totally nonreferential character of that discourse."[25] Such language offers at best "the illusion of truth," and Diderot's analysis in the *Lettre sur les aveugles* raises the possibility that language might be peculiar to the individual and hence not transparent or universal. Communication might be an illusion, and at the least, Diderot destroys the notion that the origins of perceptions or ideas can be discovered by experiment (Paulson, 40–41 and 47).

The *Lettre sur les aveulges* suggests we are considerably distanced from such essential knowledge by our reliance on language, and as the comment about the judgment of theater audiences indicates, we may often be quite wrong in our judgment about what we do see and hear for ourselves. Thus one way in which Diderot appears to be deepening Condillac's system is in his making the blind man's lack of direct knowledge a paradigm for the

---

24. *Œuvres* (Paris: Gallimard, Pléiade ed.), 813.
25. William R. Paulson, *Enlightenment, Romanticism, and the Blind in France* (Princeton: Princeton University Press, 1987), 39.

general human distance from immediate contact with the natural. A similar problem bothered Hume, whose resource was to argue that belief prompted by imagination bridges the gap of unlikeness between perceptions and qualities in the thing perceived. For Diderot the possibility that language may only possess an imaginary referent is much less readily solved.

His preoccupation with distancing continues in the more complex *Lettre sur les sourds et les muets à l'usage de ceux qui entendent et qui parlent* (1751). This essay is generally understood to be Diderot's first major aesthetic speculation, though it is nearly contemporaneous with his encyclopedia article *Beau*. The piece is nominally addressed to the Abbé Batteux, whose *Beaux arts réduits à un même principe* (1749?) sought the unity of all the fine arts in an abstract notion of beauty. Through much of his essay Diderot seems to move in a different and opposite direction, toward a sense of the diversity of the arts, especially painting and poetry, arguing much as Du Bos had done that they demand radically different modes of mental reception. But no single problem dominates the discussion; rather, Diderot works his way through various topics involving language and perception that seem to him to underly the familiar issue of the relationships among the arts. For the most part, he is concerned with the arts as they are perceived, rather than as they are conceived.

Believing that our mental processes in response to objects are simultaneous, not sequential, Diderot concentrates his attention on the problem of turning perception into the linearity of linguistic representation, or what Chouillet terms the problem of translation.[26] He dwells at some length in the *Lettre sur les sourds et muets* on the belief that our mental processes in response to objects are simultaneous, not sequential, a point that underlines the discrepancy between language and perception: "The structure of language requires de-composition, but to *see* an object, to *experience* a pleasant sensation, to *want* to possess, these are instantaneous states of the soul."[27] In quoting a line and a half from Racine's *Phèdre* to exemplify the closest that poetry can come to the unified and simultaneous quality of visual impression, Diderot seems to be referring to *enargeia*, but clearly he has in mind a concept of the nature of perception not contained in the older rhetorical notion of a serial progression of thought mimetically echoed and represented by language.

---

26. *La Formation des idées esthétiques de Diderot*, 212–13.
27. *Œuvres complètes*, ed. Assézat and Tourneux (Paris: Garnier, 1875), 4:162. References in the text to this essay are from this edition, hereafter identified as *OC*.

190 Terms of Response

Language, Diderot argues, *analyzes* thought and by doing so necessarily rearranges it into a sequential order quite different from the way in which it occurs in our minds. Thought then follows and sorts out the cluster of initial impressions by means of the order of language, but it cannot recover the initial impression as it first occurred in all its synchrony and innocence. Language normally comes later and when it becomes discourse is at its best an attempt at clarity and precision. If language is not in some way at odds with thought, it must at least be charged with reshaping it from its original form. But there are two classes of language, and one of them is poetry:

> There is at work in the discourse of the poet a spirit that animates and enlivens all the syllables. What is that spirit? I have sometimes felt its presence; but all that I know about it is that it is what allows things to be uttered and represented all at the same time, that at that same time that the understanding grasps them the soul is moved by them, the imagination sees them, and the ear hears them; and that discourse is no longer only a chain of vigorous terms that expose thought with force and nobility [Diderot is here surely attempting to dispense with rhetoric], but that it is also a tissue of hieroglyphs heaped one upon the others which depict it. I would say that in this sense all poetry is emblematic. (*OC* IV.169)

But poetry, Diderot concedes, is a rather special case. Few of us are poets; ordinary discourse lacks the capacity to transform the seriality of words, and, as he demonstrates in the next few pages, the example of poetry only underlines the problem of the distance between the unity and simultaneity of impression and the linear and analytical nature of any attempt to talk or write about it. Poetic discourse is an effort to approximate visual experience, but it cannot be preserved in translation or critical discussion in its original state. Or rather, once we translate or discuss, once we turn the visual or the visualized into our own language, we fall short of and fall away from the original. (From the perspective of Diderot's reservations, Du Bos's repeated analogies between painting and poetry seem all too facile.) Nevertheless, Diderot analyzes a passage from Virgil (*OC* IV.172) attempting to demonstrate that poet's compressed emblematic character, almost as if to exhibit in his own account the very discontinuity he has been arguing.

There is another very important discontinuity also brought to mind by the question of natural and artificial word order. Quite apart from attempting to decide, as Batteux and a host of others had, what was "natural" (that is, original) word order and what artificial, Diderot points out that a quite different set of considerations may be in control, namely, that there is a natural order of ideas in the mind (as Condillac had proposed) that is repeatedly and unconsciously overridden by the "order of institution," which is the same thing as the scientific or grammatical order of language. He illustrates the point by discussing the opening period in Cicero's oration *Pro Marcello*, "Diuturni, silentii, patres conscripti, quo eram his temporibus usus non timore aliquo sed partim dolore, partim verecundia finem hodiernus dies attulit." (Of my long silence, conscript fathers, which has lately been my habit, not because of any fear but because of grief and reticence, this day has brought the end [*OC* IV.154–55].)

Diderot maintains that the grammatical features of the period reflect a habit of instituted orders of speech that are contrary to the actual order of idea in the mind. (He appears to distinguish between this mode of conscious thought and the sort he has just previously discussed as involved in visual perception.) But Cicero like the rest of us believed his speech reflected the actual order of ideas in his mind: "In effect, what is it in the preceding period that prompts Cicero to write 'Of my long silence' in the genitive but an order of ideas preexisting in his mind, quite contrary to that of his expressions, an order to which he conforms without being aware of it, constrained by the long habit of transposing" (*OC* IV.154–55). Moreover, if we confuse the structure of our utterance with the order in our mind, it is also the case that different minds have different orders of thought or perception and thus one man's inversion is another man's natural order. Finally, in communication the order of language is frequently determined by consideration of the audience:

> The second thing I wish to notice is that in a sequence of ideas we present to others, every time that the principal idea intended to affect them is not the same as the one affecting us, considering the different frames of mind of ourselves and our auditors, it is that idea we must first present to them; and in this case inversion is nothing other than oratory. . . . I picture for myself Cicero mounting to the speaker's platform, and I see that the first thing that must strike his auditors is that he has waited a long time to mount it; hence *diuturni silentii*, the long silence he has kept, is the first idea he should offer them, even though the first idea for him is not that, but *hodiernus dies finem attulit;* for what most strikes an orator who mounts the platform is that he is going to speak and not that he has long kept silent. (*OC* IV.156)

These two considerations, the conventions of grammar and the motive of affecting an audience in a certain way, guarantee that utterance will differ from the original structure of thought. One might suppose that such a disparity would condemn the mind to inner isolation and make it difficult to gain an accurate notion of what goes on within it. From a post-Saussurian point of view one might see Diderot as having approached the belief that thought and language are identical, that language refers to and expresses nothing other than language, but in fact his interest moves in another direction, toward underlining the discrepancy between the synchrony of thought and the diachrony of utterance that we have already considered (*OC* IV.156–57). And if, as Chouillet insists, he is pursuing at this point in his discussion the concept of the unity of mind (*OC* IV.116, 157 n. 69), he is also establishing a whole series of skepticisms about another set of conventionally believed-in coherences: those between poet and reader, speaker and audience, the intention of the artist and the affective consequences of his work, as well as the implications of differences between languages.[28]

Diderot's skepticism moves in several directions. In the *Entretiens sur Le Fils naturel* (1757) one of his voices, Dorval, asserts, "He who acts and he who looks on are two very different beings."[29] Dorval's voice has been characterized as that of the Romantic, but this pronouncement climaxes an argument for the unities, for a line of action and scene that appears logical and coherent to the spectator. The actor must not judge the nature of the play by reference to himself; the unities exist entirely to relieve the spectator of difficulty and to make everything that happens interesting and clear, a kind of nearly absolute verisimilitude.

It is also evident that Dorval's notion of verisimilitude is firmly based in perception as visualization. No scene should change, he argues, until the stage is empty. Every scene is a unit, and as spectators we must not be put in the position of believing that the scenery gets up and moves away by itself. Dorval's view would risk dramatic stasis, for he prefers scenes that have a minimum of dialogue and no events that appear gratuitous (the term for this is *coups de théâtre*). The scene should be a tableau in which

---

28. He accepts, for example, the belief that French is more cerebral than other languages: "we can make the mind speak better than other languages, and good sense chooses the French tongue; but imagination and the passions give preference to the ancient languages. . . . French is fashioned to instruct, to clarify, and to convince; Greek, Latin, Italian are made for persuading, moving, deceiving. Speak Greek, Latin, Italian to the public, but speak French to the sage" (165).

29. My text is *Œuvres esthétiques*, ed. P. Vernière (Paris: Garnier, 1968), 81. Further citations are incorporated in the text as *OE*.

everything is as natural as possible. The *coup de théâtre* is thus alien, a kind of movement suggestive of linear composition rather than synchronous arrangement. To Dorval the two seem incompatible, the one natural, the other artificial; he appears therefore to be arguing the limitations of theatrical representation precisely because it must organize its action artificially. Both Dorval and "Moi," who represents the dramatic author, agree that representation is most natural when it resembles a painting, and Moi notes that in the fourth scene of the second act "there is not a word that rings true. It annoyed me in the hall, but it gave me infinite pleasure to read it" (*OE* 89). This section discusses an ancient topic, that what is inappropriate to show on the stage may be narrated, but Diderot gives it added point by underlining the effective difference between visual and verbal representation. Dorval obviously prefers the former and repeatedly laments that stage representation cannot reach the still and emotionally moving perfection of a painting.

Dorval's emphasis on the visual in theater thus appears to be a reduction of the textual or verbal, an argument that texts are less authentic, that is, less moving, than tableaux: "'Theatrical action is still necessarily imperfect, because we almost never see on stage any situation that one would be able to make into a composition tolerable in a painting'" (*OE* 89). A bit later Dorval launches into an impassioned account (*OE* 97–98) of the manner in which nature may be encountered directly, that is, when a person of genius retreats from the city and society completely and submits to all the influences of the landscape. Under such circumstances genuine poetic enthusiasm may be generated, but for the moment at least, this direct rendering of the natural is at opposite poles from the kind of experience possible in the theater. We are confronted here with Diderot's habit of stating a topic first of all in terms of strong contrasts and apparent paradox: the first *Entretien* concludes with the point that however artificial dramatic representation may be, it is nevertheless capable of generating powerful emotions.

But even so the source of passion in the drama ought to lie in circumstances, not in language. Great moments, Dorval argues in terms reminiscent of Boileau's view of the sublime, produce great passions. The contemporary drama relies too much on language and too little on pantomimic gesture: "It is the actor who gives the discourse all its energy. It is he who conveys to our ears the power and truth of the tone of voice or expression" (*OE* 102). The rest of the piece discusses the ways in which various circumstances such as the size of the audience and the modes of performance of the actors produce powerful emotional effects. The consequence of all this is to reduce the place of language to only one among several elements necessary to dramatic affect, and language continues to be treated as secondary in the third *Entretien*, where the discussion turns for a moment to the question of what may be narrated and what represented in pantomime.

If we can discern Diderot behind the two voices in the *Entretiens*, we can perhaps see him as having inherited the idea that the task of drama (as well as painting) is to bring audiences and viewers as close as possible to the natural sources of emotion. As spectators we are to observe close at hand people being moved by what appear to be authentic representations of real, that is, natural, events. This is a proposition we have seen before in English neoclassical criticism, and it should be no surprise to be able to trace its footprints in Diderot's work. But in his hands this proposition, this dogma that literature and art must have the power to translate and convey the natural, is quite unstable. As with his *Lettre sur les aveugles*, his speculations question the easy transitions from the expressions of one sense to another, and so from one medium to another. The perceived world is seen as fragmented, its parts uncertainly related among themselves and to the viewer. Affect, possibly, is not a consequence of the perception of real things.

We have already noticed that there is the suspicion that language, which in its development has moved away from the natural, may lack the power on its own to convey emotion powerfully. There is also in dramatic representation the added fact of a nearly total artificiality. And even more unsettling is the fact that despite these handicaps drama nevertheless strongly affects its audience. Dorval at the outset of the second *Entretien* is seated beneath oak trees gazing at a mountainous and sublime landscape, and he maintains, as we have seen, that the poetic genius may himself draw sublimity from his direct contemplation of that landscape. Yet puzzlingly the drama is affective either because of or in spite of its nearly total artificiality. It is dependent less on the language of the dramatic poet than on the interpretive skill of the actors, on their capacity to add gesture, expression, and movement to words and this in a setting where the spectators are disposed mechanically and evenly in a semicircle, viewing the action on stage from a carefully arranged distance.

Diderot is also preoccupied by historical differences. The ancient drama, Dorval says, had an easier time generating emotion because it had large audiences seated out-of-doors and was able to exploit pantomime as well as grandiloquent oratory to give force to the text of the plays. The smaller modern audience confined indoors requires apparently a rather different set of techniques to be convincing, even more visual communication and less flamboyant language, perhaps because (though this is not said) language itself is the very instrument and measure of the human movement away from the natural and the spontaneously emotional. Artifice on the modern stage becomes both the index of our alienation from the natural and the means by which we try to return toward it in works of art.

A revealing interchange in the third *Entretien* bears on this point. Dorval describes his death scene as a character in the play. Although there is some broken and partial utterance, the burden of communication is pantomimic: "So there remain only cries, weeping, silence, and cries" (*OE* 147). In moving away from the reliance on language of classical French drama, the playwright will bring his work closer to the "real" and natural. The result will be serious comedy and domestic tragedy, two modes of a neglected genre intermediate between tragedy and comedy, and Dorval counsels, "'Above all forget the theatrical; look for tableaux; get close to real life and first of all preserve a space to allow the exercise of pantomime to its full extent'" (*OE* 148).

The notion is that an emphasis on the visual and a corresponding diminishment of the verbal will bring the audience closer to the conditions of its own existence: "'It is the picture of misery that surrounds us'" (*OE* 148–49), a phrase that recalls, however different the context, the belief of Hutcheson and Burke that tragedy must represent events and circumstances as close as possible to what the audience knows. However, restraining the verbal does not eliminate it by any means. If an action is simple, then representation is to be preferred, and representation involves making as much as possible evident to the spectator's sight. If, however, incidents multiply and action becomes complex, then narrative is the more powerful and moving medium: "'The dialogue . . . will carry me beyond the stage; I will track all its circumstances. My imagination will realize them just as if I saw them in nature'" (*OE* 150). We may wonder whether most playwrights would agree with this notion, since one of the attractions of the theater is that it draws the audience into the action and absorbs them in it. But Diderot's mind at this point is on another matter: the escape from the stage is an escape from language, or perhaps more exactly an escape from conventions in which language is deeply implicated in a theater that undervalues its visual environment.

From the examples Dorval cites we can see that he is talking about events on a grand scale, involving battles and the like that must be imagined rather than seen in the narrow compass of the stage. Language, then, should bring close to inner vision that which if it were experienced in reality might seem flat or banal. Poetic language, according to Dorval, actually distorts and enhances in order to stir the imagination: "'The mind's exaggeration avoids that and lavishes itself on everything close to the object. The actual event would have been small, weak, paltry, false, or defective; in narration it becomes large, strong, true, and even enormous. In the theatre it would have been quite inferior to nature; I imagine it a bit larger than nature. So it is in the epic that poetic characters become a bit more grand than actual characters'" (*OE* 151). Language has the power to transform, but not to render common experience as it is. As Dorval puts it, "'There's quite a difference between painting for my imagination and setting in action before my eyes. One can adapt whatever one wishes to my imagination; it is only a question of taking hold of it. It is not the same thing with my senses'" (*OE* 157). Diderot seeks here to articulate a view that divides poetic narration and theatrical language, to emphasize the power of the visual by attempting to minimize the evocative power of language.

Dorval's distinction between sense and imagination, reminiscent of Lessing's, is also a distinction between the familiar and near, on the one hand, and the distant and exotic, on the other. The epic belongs, according to Dorval, to the "genre merveilleux," and if its events were known to us they could no longer be represented in strong and exotic colors, a reminder of Du Bos's distinction between the plain style of dramatic dialogue and the figurative style of what is elsewhere and subject to report. Representing people as they ought to be—that is, at a distance—doesn't suit a mimetic art, and with quite startling suddenness Dorval inflates his account of a realistic art into a much more sweeping judgment. If, he maintains, we conceive of all being as in a state of rapid change ("vicissitude rapide"), then all painting would be merely the arresting of a fleeting moment and imitation would be superfluous. But beauty in the arts has the same foundation as truth in philosophy. Truth is the conformity of judgment with actuality, and the beauty of imitation is the conformity of the image with the thing (*OE* 160), a line of reasoning that reminds us of convictions we noticed in the criticism of Boileau and Addison. Dorval's verisimilar beauty is, in effect, totally dependent on visual experience. What cannot be verified in this fashion seems to him to be absurd, and he devoutly wishes that lyric poetry could be dragged back to, reduced to, conformity with an exact sense of ordered intelligible being. What this amounts to is not allowing the arts the free exercise of their own natures, confining them precisely to the limits of ordinary human situations: "'If the singer of sentimental airs subjects himself to imitating in his cadence only the inarticulate accent of passion or, in songs that paint a scene, the principal phenomena of nature, and if the poet understood that his melody as the peroration of the scene, then reform would be on the way'" (*OE* 162). Melody becomes the reiteration of something visible, and thus superfluous—a peroration.[30]

Diderot is nevertheless quite willing to acknowledge the powerfully affective nature of many different types of art, as he makes clear in *De la poésie dramatique* (1758). In this essay he is more openly concerned with the audience's emotion and with poetic drama as an instrument for representing virtuous characters. He asserts, on behalf of this concern, a belief in man's fundamental goodness and in the power of the theater to affect the audience emotionally for the better: in the theater even the evil man will react against the injustices practiced by characters like himself and will leave the hall less disposed to behave badly. Yet what one retains, according to Diderot, are impressions rather than words: "O dramatic poets! the true applause you should set yourself to obtain is not that beating of hands that makes itself heard immediately following a magnificent verse, but that profound sigh from the soul following the constraint of a long silence which is its solace" (*OE* 197). In some fashion that Diderot does not quite identify emotion is not the product of language but of its absence, "and your spectators are like those who, when a part of the earth shakes, see the walls of their houses waver and feel the earth give way under their feet" (*OE* 198).

In this essay Diderot introduces the paradox that if the playwright ignores what have traditionally been understood as the interests of the spectators, such as concerns for suspense, surprise, and recognition (in other words, all the obvious features of a theatricality openly designed for affective purposes), then spectators will be all the more powerfully affected. The structure of the play should no longer be designed to replace ignorance with knowledge at a studied and calculated pace. Rather spectators should be informed of relationships and circumstances, which in turn suggest that there would be an entirely different basis for their response, their "interest." Or yet again, the play would be so ordered and so presented as to

---

30. Chouillet understands Dorval's comments on the kind of theatrical style he would like to see as an even blending of gesture and discourse, but this reading neglects to observe the extent to which Dorval's system, and Diderot's, makes language distinctly secondary to the pantomimic essence of his ideal of theatrical representation; cf. *La Formation des idées esthétiques de Diderot*, 441–42.

convey the fiction that there are no spectators. Diderot's rupture with tradition as he sees it is deliberate and pointed:

> Moreover, the more I reflect on the dramatic art, the more I begin to be out of sorts with those who have practiced it. It is a tissue of particular laws from which they have made general precepts. Certain incidents have been seen to produce great effects; and straightway the necessity of using the same means to produce the same effects has been imposed on the poet, whereas had they looked at the matter more closely, they would have perceived that even greater effects could be produced by totally contrary means. (*OE* 230)

Diderot's answer to this tangle of rules is that the author and the actor must concentrate on the interests of the characters and their impact on one another, ignoring the effect on the spectator of what is written. That effect will take care of itself, as the inevitable by-product of an art that is essentially seen as a closed system. Diderot is obviously thinking of the classical theater in his time as a platform for declamation, as something not too far distant from a lecture hall or public square in which the audience is as much the deliberate centerpiece of the representation as the actors on the stage. He proposes a shift from the dramatic consciousness of the audience to a situation where one imagines a large wall separating stage action from audience. But at the same time, information, traditionally concealed from the audience until it may be sprung upon them for maximum emotional impact or events normally happening offstage and reported, would now be readily clear and available.

What I have just surveyed is a theory that Diderot pursues vigorously in the 1760s in his *Salons*, with the result that the discontinuity between artist, work, and spectator comes to seem even more drastic. At its best, the art of painting for Diderot involves human and dramatic subjects painted and arranged as naturally as possible. Within the painting itself there should be no hint, either in the arrangement of figures or in painterly technique, that the artist has a viewer in mind. The work is to appear totally self-enclosed, and just as the theatrical representation is to be something almost accidently overheard, so the painting is of a human situation accidently viewed.

This aspect of Diderot's critical thought is the subject of Michael J. Fried's *Absorption and Theatricality*, which deserves some comment here. Fried's thesis, based largely on Diderot's *Salons* and the paintings he reviewed, is that in reaction against the rococo paintings dominant in the 1740s, genre artists such as Chardin, Greuze, Vien, and Van Loo created works in which the figures were engaged in "quintessentially absorptive activities" (15). The intensity with which figures are bent to absorptive tasks, such as reading or listening or playing, indicates that the painting exhibits no awareness of spectators (as might be the case with certain kinds of portrait or with a still life in which the arrangement of objects and the use of light are openly managed for the eye of the beholder). The apparent self-enclosure of the work has a good many consequences. In the case of Chardin's paintings of games, which constitute an attempt to convey a moment seized from the stream of action, "paradoxically . . . stability and unchangingness are endowed to an astonishing degree with the power to conjure an illusion of imminent or gradual or even fairly abrupt change" (50–51).

Another and more important paradox is that by being deliberately excluded from the painting, the beholder is more surely and completely drawn into it, moved to imagine himself within its world, a development encouraging a shift from representations of absorption to the primacy of action and passion as the subject matter of the painting, which in turn leads to a greater emphasis on the value of pictorial unity so that the casual relationship of individual units becomes a dominant structural principle. Fried's theory gains support from Diderot's writings as critic and spectator. As in the *Entretiens sur le fils naturel* and similar pieces, Diderot fictionalizes himself as spectator or audience and even goes so far as to engage in conversations with some of the figures depicted in the paintings.

At this point Fried's argument may seem at odds with another proposition, that is, that there is an alienating barrier between the spectator and the action in the painting: "In Diderot's writings on painting and drama the object-beholder relationship as such, the very condition of spectatordom, stands indicted as theatrical, a medium of dislocation and arrangement rather than absorption, sympathy, self-transcendence. . . . What is called for, in other words, is at one and the same time the creation of a new sort of object—the fully realized *tableau*—and the constitution of a new sort of beholder—a new 'subject'—whose innermost nature would consist precisely in the conviction of his absence from the scene of representation" (104). This new breed of spectator is released from his or her fixed position in front of the picture and encouraged imaginatively to enter into the work (131).

Both in genre paintings of the 1750s and later and in Diderot's *Salons*, Fried discovers an attempt to abolish a rhetorical relationship between the work of art (and its creator as well) and the spectator or audience. This is the relationship we originally noticed in the Italian baroque theories of the mid-seventeenth century; despite efforts to dismiss baroque aesthetic values, it dominates the theoretical treatises of much of the British and French Enlightenment up to Diderot. It is a system in which author or artist, the work, and the audience or spectators more or less consciously participate. The author's aim, which is evident in the work, is to affect the audience in certain widely understood and accepted ways. The audience is assumed to be agreeable and to cooperate in the arrangement, so that there is a clear line of intention and consequence moving from the creator to the perceiving subject. Increasingly, eighteenth-century thinkers found the paradigm for this system in what they conceived to be the origins of communication, in a pattern of cries and gestures refined into signs connecting the mental processes and emotions of one person with another. Diderot's earlier dramatic theories appear to declare his agreement with this system.

But his persistent and restless questioning results finally in reservations that seem to be more and more central to his aesthetic thought and eventually quite disruptive to the rhetorical system. When Fried notes that Diderot insists that the beholder enter the picture if he is to be moved, he suggests that what is wanted is "a profound experience of nature . . . , one of existential reverie or *repos délicieux*," in which one apprehends "the fundamental beneficence of the natural world" (129–30). This may do for certain kinds of landscape painting: Fried accepts that there are really two theories of the role of the spectator, the dramatic which removes the beholder and the pastoral which compels his presence within the picture. But the emphasis on the pictorial needs to be supplemented with an acknowledgment of how important for Diderot is the distance between creator and spectator, that distance he had begun to notice in the *Entretiens sur Le Fils naturel*, and which he dwelt on increasingly in the *Essai sur la poésie dramatique*. It is most thoroughly aired in *Paradoxe sur le comédien* (1773).[31] The conventional view of the continuity linking artist, work, and spectator is consciously acknowledged; in other words, spectators know

31. My text for *Paradoxe sur le comédien* is *The Paradox of Acting by Denis Diderot and Masks or Faces by William Archer* (New York: Hill and Wang: 1957). Diderot's essay is translated by Walter Herries Pollock. Different sorts of background to this treatise are supplied by Joseph R. Roach, Jr., "Diderot and the Actor's Machine," *Theatre Survey* 22 (1981), 51–68 (Diderot's interest in physiology), and Allison Grear, "A Background to Diderot's *Paradoxe sur le comédien*: The Role of Imagination in Spoken Expression of Emotion, 1600–1750," *Forum for Modern Language Studies*, 21 (1985), 225–38 (the development of styles of declamation in the seventeenth and early eighteenth centuries).

their place. In the more important *Salons* and especially in the *Paradoxe*, Diderot imagines that this consciousness can be erased.

Diderot employs his familiar device of dialogue, giving most of the discussion to the "first speaker." What initially preoccupies him is the question of whether the actor ought to enter into the emotion of the piece he is acting. On the whole, the first speaker thinks the actor who is a person of feeling (*sensibilité*) will be the less effective: "The actor who goes by Nature alone is often detestable, sometimes excellent" (12). On the whole, the better actor is detached from the emotions he or she seeks to embody: "In my view he must have a deal of judgment. He must have in himself an unmoved and disinterested onlooker. He must have, consequently, penetration and no sensibility" (14). In similar fashion the poet, somewhat in the manner of the Modernist notion of the detached writer, must be a cold-blooded observer. However, Diderot's first speaker expresses this notion in a puzzling analogy. He takes Shakespeare's likening of the world at large to a stage, and says, "In the great play, the play of the world, the play to which I am constantly recurring, the stage is held by the fiery souls, and the pit is filled with men of genius . . . and it is they who discern with a ready eye the absurdity of the motley crowd" (18).

But the condition of the actual spectator is different. If poet and actor are totally without emotion, the spectator is for Diderot a person of sensibility who "obeys the impulse of Nature, and gives nothing more nor less than the cry of his very heart; the moment he moderates or strengthens this cry he is no longer himself, he is an actor" (37). The smallest degree of self-consciousness or reflection distances us from emotion genuinely experienced, and if we extend this perception a bit, we can see all mimetic feeling, that is, all feeling that is a response to the emotions of others as having a certain speciousness, a certain coldness. The distance between poet or actor and audience, or to put it more precisely, the difference between immediate response and calculated response, is interestingly parallel to the difference between the original human reaction to outside events (cries and gestures) and language (instituted signs) that we have noted in Condillac's theory of the origin of language and that caught the attention of a substantial number of Enlightenment thinkers. Diderot's earlier attention to the problem of language involved the relationship of grammar to the sequence of perception. Here in the *Paradoxe* his interest is different. At one point, he lets the first speaker launch into an unbridled negative characterization of *sensibilité*:

> Sensibility, according to the only acceptation yet given the term, is, as it seems to me, that disposition which accompanies organic weakness, which follows on easy affection of the diaphragm, on vivacity of imagination, on delicacy of nerves, which inclines one to being compassionate, to being horrified, to admiration, to fear, to being upset, to tears, to faintings, to rescues, to flights, to exclamations, to loss of self-control, to being contemptuous, disdainful, to having no clear notion of what is true, good, and fine, to being unjust, to going mad. (43)

Conversely, he seems persistently to approve the rationality and lack of emotional involvement in the poet or artist and the actor. But this is a heavily qualified approval: the actor, more or less, is in himself a much diminished being. Apart from his acting, whose genius is to create the illusion of passions he does not feel, he is nothing. Mme. Riccoboni, according to the first speaker, "one of the most sensitive [women] that nature ever made, was one of the worst actresses that ever appeared on the stage" (59). The great actor, on the other hand, is "everything and nothing." This is stated ironically by the second speaker, and the first speaker replies, "Perhaps it is just because he is nothing that he is before all everything. His own special shape never interferes with the shapes he assumes" (41).

So it is that Diderot appears to value art precisely for its distance from real existence or experience. Poems, he remarks in a passage that might have been written by Wordsworth, are written in a state of reflection: "It is when the storm of sorrow is over, when the extreme of sensibility is dulled, when the event is far behind us, when the soul is calm, that one remembers one's eclipsed happiness, that one is capable of appreciating one's loss, that memory and imagination unite, one to retrace, the other to accentuate, the delights of a past time: then it is that one regains self-possession and expression" (36).

"Expression" does not quite fully render Diderot's *parle bien* (speak eloquently), which indicates together with many other details in this piece that more than the distance between stage emotion and real emotion is his concern. The repeated emphasis on the particular kind of unreality or artificiality of acted emotion, the insistence that the most effective actor is the one who simulates but does not experience the passions he or she articulates, indicate a wider significance. David Marshall cites these points to argue that Diderot, in emphasizing the difficulty of finding anything real in the theater, is reminding us of the difficulty of distinguishing between the real and the fictive outside it.[32] Perhaps just as central to Diderot's view is his understanding of the way in which language positions itself between genuine feeling and the spectator.

The Wordsworth-like passage just quoted maintains that only when an emotional experience slips into the past can we render it into words, a notion close to, though not exactly the same as, that of Condillac that originally language followed perception and feeling and thus created memory and imagination. But for Diderot language does not provide a mimetic bridge between experience and our review of it. Poetic representation no longer comes to embody something in nature that has been recovered and copied, because it is not clear that such language represents emotions that either the poet or the actor have actually felt or emotions in any way like those one might observe in ordinary existence. Diderot more than once notes that acted emotions on stage seem exaggerated both in scale and authenticity. The sculptor or playwright may at one time have begun with a model in nature, but arts as they are practiced and refined draw increasingly apart from nature, depending more and more upon an ideal model, a model in the mind that with time loses any resemblance to daily experienced life. Hence, Molière's Tartuffe is drawn according to general traits; he is the portrait of no single individual (39). Diderot makes the obvious point that Tartuffe is a general type, but he suggests that it is a generality invented in the play and that its reality derives from the play.

The second speaker asks if the ideal model is not a chimera (40). The first replies, no, because well back in time at the origin of any art there was once a real model, but the second speaker's point is well taken. Unlike Pope's approach to this issue, Diderot's does not identify any original genius; he offers no Homer whose proximity to nature is enough for his successors. But he does maintain that all art has become conventionalized. As he remarks of classical and neoclassical tragedy, there is no relationship between their language and real conversations: "As old a writer as Aeschylus laid this down as a formula—it is a protocol three thousand years old" (22).

Yet the audience responds to an idealized and conventionalized art as if the language spoken by the characters on the stage and the emotions it represents were real, as if they were authentic imitations drawn straight from actual events and people. This is the heart of the paradox: there is no object of representation. The spectator, supposing he is responding with

---

32. Marshall, *The Surprising Effects of Sympathy*, 131.

feeling to the image of real events and real passions, is in fact reacting only to an appearance at an immense and unbridgeable distance from anything actual. The illusion is not an illusion in the sense that it represents or mimics a reality known to the spectators—though when he wrote the *Entretiens sur Le Fils naturel* (1757), Diderot seemed to be arguing for a kind of drama that might well function in such a way. Instead, in the *Paradoxe* he now proposes the theater is an illusion in the sense that it deceives the audience into believing it represents some kind of reality when, in fact, it does not. The audience believes that the language it hears is the genuine language of genuine passions, not perhaps that it is not in the theater at all but that the theater has re-created authentic human experience. But if one accepts Diderot's formulation, this is not so. In semiological terms, the theater is a signifier without a signified.[33] Actors who do attempt to play themselves or to identify with, rather than artistically represent, the feelings of the characters they portray, are mediocre and unsuccessful. The audience comes not to see tears but "to hear speeches that draw tears; because this truth of nature is out of tune with the truth of convention" (68).

The oddity of this insight is not that in the process of representation art departs from nature or improves on it but that Diderot portrays it as utterly at odds with the natural at the same time that the audience, composed of *hommes de sensibilité*, believes implicitly in its own responses as natural and authentic. And as we have seen, he states that a genuine person of sensibility would be mad, a great collection of emotions within which he was an unthinking prisoner. Sensibility in the theater, perhaps, is only temporary. Yet for all his championing of the cerebral poet and the clinically detached actor, and for all his apparent contempt for the unthinking responses of the audience, Diderot has effectively made the audience the center of attention, and what the audience responds to is language, which is the only thing available to respond to.

This system of illusion is not quite the same as the situation fashioned by Diderot in his *Salons* or, for example, in his *Eloge à Richardson*. There, Diderot as spectator or reader turns the work of art not simply into the

33. For a somewhat different view, see Susan Gearhart, *The Open Boundary of History and Fiction: A Critical View of the French Enlightenment* (Princeton: Princeton University Press, 1984), 190–97: the theatrical paradigm, used by both Condillac and Diderot, is seen as an image for life at large, especially as it is a place where the spectator selects among several possibilities for perceptual attention. However, I would argue that in *Paradoxe sur le comédien* Diderot underlines the radical discontinuity between art and life so as to argue that we cannot experience the real in the theater, only the conventional or artificial posing as the real.

occasion for his own emotions, but also into words, into a language by means of which he may fictionally and with great feeling enter into an imaginary world, not quite of his own creation but approaching that.

According to the *Paradoxe sur le comédien* the audience is totally defined, even consumed by its affective responses, perhaps because, unlike the critic, it can't talk back or fabricate dialogues that turn drama into stories. Diderot exaggerates the contrast between the cool deliberation of creator and actor and the oblivious emotionalism of the theatrical audience in order to emphasize the discontinuity between nature and art, in order, perhaps, to distance his own thinking from that of someone like Du Bos, or even Burke, both of whom maintain that our responses to plays are not primarily responses to art. To repeat the assertion of Du Bos, "Painters and poets raise those artificial passions within us, by presenting us with the imitations of objects capable of exciting real passions" (I.iii). Diderot's audience may believe this to be the case, but he does not. Instead, he says that the audience's tears are occasioned by language and gestures that are the very opposite of real, either because the language is that of imagined figures quite different from anything members of the audience might know from their own experience or because the emotions portrayed by the actor are not his or her emotions. As audience, then, we respond to nothing but words, or to words and gestures that are literally empty, entirely made up. In the *Salons* Diderot's position is otherwise. Here he assumes for himself, at least in the more striking and original of his commentaries, the role of the audience, inventing encounters with the figures in the paintings and turning them into narrative or dramatic works, and thus emphasizing the ways in which these works of art are in harmony with nature. Or is this really the case? By playing the spectator perhaps Diderot instead underlines the ways in which the successful work gives us the occasion in our own minds to fashion the illusion of the real.

Index

Aarsleff, Hans, 74 n. 9, 180 n. 18
Abrams, M. H., 115 n. 23
absorption, 199–200
acting, 174 n. 12
action, 199; dramatic, 195, 196
actor, 8, 9, 41 n. 31, 139, 149, 150, 164, 169, 170, 172, 177, 178, 192, 193, 194, 198, 201–5; as everything and nothing, 202
actuality, 16, 20, 196
acutezza, 29, 31
Adams, D. J., 186 n. 22
Addison, Joseph, 3–7, 46, 47, 64, 65, 69–87, 94, 106, 117, 119, 141, 142, 155, 160, 196; *Spectator* papers on: ballads, 75–76, 85; *Paradise Lost*, 70, 73, 77, 83, 84–85; "Pleasures of the Imagination," 65 n. 24, 69–70, 71–72, 77–87; taste, 70, 87, 89; wit, 70–75, 84, 85
Ad Herrenium, 20
admiration, 183
Aeschylus, 203
aesthetic, aesthetics, 6 n. 8, 23, 80 n. 16, 86 n. 24, 91, 94, 107, 110, 114, 139, 143, 175 n. 3, 179, 186, 189; appreciation, 111; cognition, 107 n. 17; experience, 44, 96, 97–98, 119, 171; faculty, 98; judgment, 34; object, 112; perception, 37; representation, 108; response, 42, 102; sense, 95, 96, 97, 100; theory, 2, 5, 119
baroque, 12, 71, 200; British, 106; Enlightenment, 27 n. 23, 110 n. 18; German, 5, 37, 70, 104, 106, 114; neoclassical, 4, 5, 29
affect, affective, 3–5, 7, 8, 12, 22, 24, 25–29, 33, 35–39, 41–44, 47, 50, 55, 57, 61, 63, 65, 70–71, 75–77, 79, 82, 83, 84, 84 n. 21, 85, 86, 91, 92, 93, 99, 102 n. 11, 103, 106, 107, 108, 110, 115, 118, 120, 121, 124, 127, 128, 130, 131, 137, 140, 142, 144, 146, 146 n. 31, 150, 154, 157, 158, 163, 164, 165, 165 n. 5, 168, 170, 171, 172, 175, 179, 180, 182, 186, 187, 191–92, 194, 197; aesthetic, 105, 152, 166; affective pleasure, 87; affective power, 156; affective power of language, 3, 7; affective response, 74 n. 8; affective theory, 12, 145; dramatic, 194; intensity of, 176; musical, 183; tragic, 141, 147, 157; verbal, 158
agreeable, 118 n. 31
Akenside, Mark, 141
Alexander, 27

allegory, 72, 83, 85, 96
allusion, 72–73, 73 n. 7, 84, 85
ambiguity, 54, 55, 57, 58 n. 10, 59, 66
amplification, 20, 41, 43
amusement, 160, 166
anagrams, 71
analogue, analogy, 13, 28, 81
André, Père, 186, 186 n. 22
antithesis, 17 n. 14, 45
Apelles, 27
aphorism, 23
Apollo, 46 n. 35
appearance, 21, 22–23, 31, 34, 37, 40, 56 n. 7, 178, 204
appetite, 24–26, 38, 44–45, 122
apprehension, 39–42, 46, 86, 107. See also first apprehension
architecture, 79, 86
argutezza, 16–17, 24, 26, 28, 29
Ariosto, Ludovico, 54, 119 n. 32
Aristides, 171, 173
Aristotle, 4, 11, 12, 17, 30, 44, 45, 54, 55, 64 n. 21, 77, 153; and metaphor, 13–16; *De Anima*, 79 n. 14, 80 n. 15; *Poetics*, 4, 13, 18, 25 n. 20, 43, 59, 107 n. 17, 112, 112 n. 20, 128–40, 141; *Rhetoric*, 4, 13, 19–20, 22, 23, 25 n. 20, 43, 55 n. 5, 77, 80 n. 15, 82, 133
Arnauld, Antoine, 72 n. 6; and Pierre Nicole, 58 n. 10, 63 n. 20
art, 2, 9, 14, 17, 25, 36, 37, 39, 42, 44, 50, 51, 57, 58, 59, 62, 66, 77, 79, 80, 82, 83, 83 n. 20, 85, 86, 87, 90, 91, 92, 93, 94, 98, 103, 105 n. 14, 106, 107, 108, 109, 110, 111, 114, 116, 116 n. 24, 117, 118, 120, 135, 139, 145, 149, 155, 160, 162, 164, 165, 166, 177, 179, 182, 194, 195, 197, 199, 202, 204; affective arts, 183, 184; and nature, 69, 79, 80 n. 16, 82, 175, 178; and religion, 83 n. 20; and transformation of emotion, 153; as distraction, 161; as substitution for reality, 175; fine arts, 189; mimetic and realistic, 196; plastic arts, 36
artifice, 1, 9, 12, 13, 14, 16, 22, 24, 25, 26, 27–31, 34, 44, 45, 46, 47, 49, 50, 61, 62, 73, 80, 81, 101, 145, 151, 155, 158, 164, 168, 177, 178, 179, 184, 185, 187, 195
artificial, 72, 73, 193, 194, 204 n. 33
artist, 3 n. 6, 8, 17, 18, 49, 51, 82, 109, 167, 198, 200, 202

Index

association, 40, 97
asteia, 17. *See* urbanity
audience, 2, 4, 5, 7–9, 12, 13, 14, 15, 19, 22, 23, 25, 28, 29, 30–31, 33, 35, 38, 39, 40, 41 n. 31, 42, 43, 45, 47, 49, 50, 51, 53, 54, 58, 59, 63, 64, 66, 81, 85, 87, 90, 94, 95, 100, 130, 131, 131 n. 5, 137, 142, 148 n. 33, 149, 151, 153, 155, 164, 166, 167, 178, 186, 188, 191, 193, 194, 195, 197, 198, 199, 200, 201, 203, 204, 205; emotion, 138; response, 57, 135; psychology, 4; female, 140: psychology, 4; response, 57. *See also* pleasure, delight
auditor, 65. *See* listener, reader, spectator
aural, 37
author, 7, 13, 15, 31, 47, 50, 63, 75

Bacon, Francis, 5–6, 28, 30, 59, 74 n. 9, 75
ballad, 3, 75–76, 76–77 n. 12
Balzac, Guez de, 50, 51; 51 n. 1
baroque, 3, 4, 9, 47, 49, 50, 51, 52, 55, 107; aesthetics, 12, 52, 84; poets, 110 n. 18; rhetoric, 32; style, 42; theory, 11–47, 200; wit, 5
Batteux, Charles, Abbé, 186 n. 22, 189, 190
Baumgarten, Alexander Gottlieb, 8, 110 n. 18
Beardsley, Monroe, 174 n. 12
beauty, 8, 15, 22, 29, 30, 31, 33, 42, 43, 46, 53, 56, 72–73 n. 7, 78, 82, 83, 83 n. 20, 86, 90, 93, 94, 95, 97, 101, 102 n. 11, 102, 107, 112, 116, 117, 118, 118 n. 31, 119, 119 n. 32, 131, 142, 143, 154, 188, 189, 196; ideal, 94, 95, 96, 144; ideas of, 98; moral, 99; natural, 99, 101; relative, 95, 96, 100, 144; sense of, 8, 115; standard of, 8; visual, 99
beholder, 24, 199, 200
Belaval, Yvonne, 186 n. 27
belief, 42, 151, 152, 154, 159; willing suspension of disbelief, 170
beneficence, 200
benevolence, 99, 145, 158
Berkeley, George, 122
bienséance, 51
biography, 150
blindness, 188–89
Boileau-Despreaux, Nicolas, 3, 4, 5, 56, 58–67, 71, 76, 77, 85, 87, 172, 193, 196; *Art poétique*, 50, 58, 65, 76–77 n. 12, 139; *Reflexions critiques*, 50, 64, 65
Bonarelli, 62
boredom, 22–23, 49, 160, 161, 163, 166, 177
Bouhours, Dominique, 3, 4, 5, 47, 50–58, 61, 66, 76, 77, 87; *Doutes sur la langue françoise*, 55 n. 5, 85; *Les Entretiens d'Ariste et d'Eugène*, 50, 52 n. 3, 55–57; *La Manière de bien penser dans les ouvrages de l'esprit*, 52–58
Briggs, John C., 6 n. 7
Brody, Jules, 60, 60 n. 16
Bunyan, John, 117
Burke, Edmund, 5, 8, 57, 90, 91, 106, 110, 115, 124, 159, 163, 172 n. 8, 195, 205; *A Philosophical Enquiry into Our Ideas of the Sublime and the Beautiful*, 7, 8, 89, 101–4, 118 n. 31, 122, 156–58

Campbell, George, 2, 155
Caplan, Jay, 186 n. 22
Castelvetro, Ludovico, 132–33, 134 n. 11, 152 n. 37
catachresis, 14
catharsis, 128–40, 131 n. 5
cause and effect, 145, 150
Chapelain, Jean, 50
character, 12, 36–37, 60, 147, 149, 167, 195, 196, 197, 198, 203, 204; dramatic, 148, 178; fictional, 179; literary, 143–44
characterization, 137
Chardin, Jean-Baptiste Siméon, 199
charm, 118, 140
Chouillet, Jacques, 186, 187 n. 23, 189, 197 n. 30
Cicero, 17, 153; *De Oratore*, 20, 177; *Pro Marcello*, 191
clarity, 7, 57, 59, 73, 103, 104, 139, 157, 190
classicism, English, 70 n. 4; French, 49–67, 70, 70 n. 4
cleverness, 29, 30–31, 32, 33, 34
cognition, 4, 8, 14 n. 10, 21, 38, 44, 70 n. 4, 110, 118, 185; taste as, 4
Cohen, Ralph, 91, 117–18, 141, 152, 152 n. 37, 153, 155
comedy, 41 n. 31, 59, 151 n. 36, 165, 195
communication, 182, 183, 183 n. 20, 184, 185, 187, 187 n. 23, 191, 195, 200
compassion, 75, 99, 114, 127, 138, 139, 142, 143, 146, 164, 202
conceit, 12, 17, 25, 40, 43, 44, 45, 46, 46 n. 35, 47, 49, 69
concreteness, 15, 21
Condillac, Etienne Bonnot de, 4, 5, 8, 159, 186, 186 n. 22, 187, 188, 201, 203, 204 n. 33; *Essai sur l'origine des connaissances humaines*, 178–85, 187 n. 23; *Traité de l'art d'écrire*, 118 n. 30
congruity, 72
connections, 121, 121 n. 34, 128
consciousness, 181, 182, 186; aesthetic, 186
Conte, Giuseppe, 12, 24 n. 19, 42 n. 32
contiguity, 145, 146, 147
convention, 51, 204 n. 33
Corneille, Pierre, 50, 128; *Cinna*, 171, 172; "Discours de la tragédie," 135–38
coups de théâtre, 192–93
Cowley, Abraham, 71
Coypel, Noël, 170, 174; "Suzanna," 169
Crawford, Donald W., 118 n. 31
credibility, 42 n. 32, 137, 150, 150 n. 35, 151 n. 36
credulity, 150
Creech, James, 186 n. 22
cries, 180, 181, 182, 183, 185, 187 n. 23, 195, 200, 201

Index   209

critic, 117, 118, 205; Diderot as, 199
Croce, Franco, 29n. 24, 35n. 29
Crousaz, Jean Pierre de, 63n. 20; *Traité du beau*, 92–95
custom, 97, 98

deception, 17n. 14
decorum, 24, 61, 149. *See* fitness
deformity, 94, 96, 98, 99, 108, 109, 115, 116, 143
delight, 1, 12, 13n. 3, 15, 19, 22–23, 25, 26, 29, 31, 33, 34, 38, 41, 43, 44, 45, 46, 47, 59, 60, 62, 73, 75, 81, 82, 82n. 15, 83n. 20, 94, 98, 99, 102n. 11, 112, 118, 118n. 31, 127, 130, 134, 138, 140, 153, 154, 156. *See also* enjoyment, pleasure
De Man, Paul, 3, 74n. 8
Demosthenes, 60
Dennis, John, 91, 141, 142
denotation, 27
Derrida, Jacques, 179; *L'Archéologie du frivole*, 180, 180n. 17, 185n. 21
Descartes, René, 6, 58, 59, 75; *Philosophical Letters*, 138; *Traité des passions de l'âme*, 174n. 12
description, 7, 77, 79, 80, 81, 82, 82n. 19, 83, 99, 103, 104, 111, 123, 158
desire, 59, 106, 108, 115, 116, 122, 138, 183n. 20
detachment, 5
diachronic, 113, 167, 169, 176, 185, 192. *See also* synchronic
dialectic, 28, 30
didacticism, 4, 135, 140
Diderot, Denis, 3, 4, 5, 8, 9, 41n. 31, 114, 150, 159, 160, 178, 185–205; *Beau*, 189; *De la poésie dramatique*, 197–98, 200; *Eloge à Richardson*, 204; *Entretiens sur Le Fils naturel*, 192–97, 199, 200, 204; *Lettre sur les aveugles*, 188–89, 194; *Lettre sur les sourds et les muets à l'usage des ceux qui entendent et qui parlent*, 189–92; *Paradoxe sur le comédien*, 8, 148, 200–205; *Salons*, 198, 199, 201, 204, 205
Diekmann, Herbert, 186n. 22
distance, 109, 110, 129, 131, 156, 158
disinterestedness, 98, 100, 101, 118, 153, 201
diversion, 4, 49
diversity, 93, 116n. 24
doctrine, 12, 13n. 3
Donato, Eugenio, 27, 27n. 23
drama, 11, 70, 113, 113n. 21, 141, 143, 147, 148, 150, 193, 194, 197, 199, 204, 205; ancient, 194; classical French, 195; moral benefit of, 142
dramatic poetry, 157
dream, dreamer, 42
Dryden, John, 47, 71, 141, 142, 142n. 22
Du Bos, Jean-Baptiste, Abbé, 4, 5, 8, 87, 91, 124, 141, 143, 149, 155, 159, 179, 185, 186, 186n. 22, 189, 190, 196; *Réflexions*

critiques sur la poésie et la peinture, 160–78, 205

education, 97, 98
eloquence, 1, 2, 29, 43, 62, 74, 103, 110n. 18, 151, 153, 154, 155, 177, 202
Else, G. F., 129n. 4, 130–31, 131n. 5
emblem, 55n. 6, 77
emotion, 2, 3, 4, 5, 6, 8, 9, 21, 24, 25, 25n. 20, 26, 32, 34, 35, 38, 41, 41n. 31, 43, 44, 60, 61, 61n. 16, 62, 63, 64, 64nn. 21, 22, 66, 67, 86n. 24, 90, 91, 92, 94, 99, 101, 102, 103, 104, 110, 111, 112, 113, 115, 118, 119, 120, 121, 124, 128, 129, 130, 131, 132, 133, 134, 135, 137, 138, 139, 140, 142, 144, 146, 146n. 30, 147, 147n. 32, 148, 153, 157, 159, 161, 162, 163, 164, 166, 168, 169, 170, 170n. 7, 171, 172, 173, 173n. 9, 174, 174n. 12, 175n. 13, 176, 177, 178, 179, 180, 182–85, 187, 193, 194, 195, 197, 198, 200, 201, 202, 203, 204, 205; aesthetic, 152, 153, 179; artificial, 164, 165; audience, 64n. 21; communication of, 145, 149, 169; emotional response, 8, 141, 145; mimetic, 167; stage vs. real, 202; sympathetic, 167; taste as, 4; tragic, 125; transformation of, 158. *See also* feeling, passion
empiricism, 74, 118
enargeia, 7, 40, 41, 41n. 31, 42n. 32, 55n. 5, 76, 77, 85
energeia, 18, 40. *See also* liveliness, vividness
Engell, James, 115n. 23, 116, 116n. 24, 117n. 28, 146n. 30
enigma, 14
enjoyment, 22, 36, 78, 79, 84, 91, 92, 130, 163
Enlightenment, 2, 4, 9, 73, 91, 94, 109, 174n. 12, 180, 201; aesthetics of, 110n. 18; British, 200; French, 160, 200; German, 104
ennui, 175. *See also* boredom
entertainment, 3, 4, 49, 72–73n. 7, 78, 81, 87, 150, 152, 154
enthymeme, 23, 28, 30, 31, 32, 33, 55
epic, 2, 59, 60, 66, 67, 71, 75, 76, 76–77n. 12, 85, 99, 143, 149, 150, 152, 156, 166, 196
epigram, 33, 51, 53, 71, 75
epistemology, 5, 21
equivoques, 51. *See* puns
ethos, 17
Euripides, *Orestes*, 76, 76–77n. 12
experience, 189
expression, 168, 172, 173, 184, 202; clear, 157; facial, 168, 170, 174; figurative, 173n. 9; strong, 157; verbal, 176
expressive theory, 105n. 15

fables, 36, 37, 38, 39, 53, 58
faculty psychology, 12, 30, 32, 39, 57, 79, 80n. 15, 92, 98, 144, 179; aesthetic, 42, 95, 98. *See also* aesthetic sense

false, falsehood, 33, 34, 35, 53, 55, 115
fancy, 2, 6, 30, 46, 54, 67, 71, 72, 72–73 n. 7, 73, 74 n. 8, 78, 79–80 n. 15, 82 n. 19, 84, 87, 90, 112, 150, 160
fear, 139, 141, 202. See pity and fear, catharsis
feeling(s), 3, 4, 5, 6, 9, 14 n. 10, 19, 24, 26, 38, 39, 40, 43, 44, 50, 57, 63, 64, 67, 81, 90, 92, 92 n. 6, 99, 102, 106, 108, 117, 125, 130, 137, 146 n. 31, 147, 152, 155, 158, 159, 160, 178, 181, 183, 184, 203, 204, 205; of beauty, 101; communication of, 100, 100 n. 10, 145, 172; mixed, 109, 153; natural origins of instinct and, 180 n. 17; representation of, 100 n. 10; as *sensibilité*, 201. See also emotion, passion
Ferguson, Frances, 102 n. 12
fiction, 11, 15, 31, 34, 37, 41, 53, 55, 56, 73, 75, 119 n. 32, 123, 124, 141, 142, 143, 145, 150, 151, 152, 153, 154, 155, 156, 164, 198, 203, 205
figurae, 23
figurative, 30–31, 55, 55 n. 6, 85; language, 70, 84, 85, 93; propriety, 64; writing, 84
figures, 23, 24, 27, 33–34, 41, 56 n. 7, 60, 61, 63, 64 n. 21, 77, 82, 96, 172; pathetic, 24, 26, 27. See rhetorical figures
first apprehension, 35–37; second and third, 35–36
fitness, 30
Fontenelle, Bernard Le Bovier de, 141
form, 4, 7, 9, 15, 18, 21, 22, 23, 26, 27, 28, 31, 40, 42, 43, 56, 65, 66, 67, 84 n. 21, 91, 100, 108, 135, 140, 149; artistic, 168; dramatic, 130; epic, 128; tragic, 128
formalism, 96, 114, 119; aesthetic, 141; French, 135
Foucault, Michel, 14, 70 n. 4
Fried, Michael, 165 n. 5, 174 n. 11, 186 n. 22, 198–200
Funt, David, 186 n. 22

gambling, 162
Gearhart, Susan, 204 n. 33
gender, 102 n. 11
Genesis, 64, 65
genre, 4, 50, 60, 70, 140, 165 n. 5, 166, 195, 196
Gerard, Alexander, 7
gesture, 8, 103, 144, 167, 168, 169, 170, 173, 176, 180, 182, 183, 185, 193, 194, 197 n. 30, 200, 201, 205; as universal, 174; verbal, 183
Giacomini, Lorenzo, 134
Golden, Leon, 13
Gothic, Gothicism, 161; poetry, 71; taste, 89; wit, 72, 75, 80 n. 15
Gracian, Balthazar, 11, 22
grammar, 192, 201
grandeur, 93
Gravina, Gian Vincenzo, 12
Grear, Allison, 200 n. 31

Greuze, Jean-Baptiste, 199
Guarini, Battista, 62

Hagstrum, Jean, 6, 7, 76, 85
Hamlet, 170
Halliwell, Stephen, 129–30 n. 4
Hansen, David A., 84 n. 21
harmony, 22, 24, 31, 93, 97, 101, 134, 139, 143; of faculties, 187
Hathaway, Baxter, 13 n. 3; 131 n. 6, 133, 133 n. 10, 135, 142 n. 22, 161
hearing, 43
Heinsius, Daniel, 132 n. 6
Helen of Troy, 32
Hercules, 95
Herder, Johann Gottfried, 180 n. 18
heroic poems, 85
hieroglyphs, 190
historian, 43
history, 37, 41, 43, 58, 105 n. 14, 150, 151
Hobbes, Thomas, 74 n. 99, 79 n. 15, 80, 80 n. 18, 85
Hobson, Marian, 61 n. 17, 161 n. 2, 170 n. 7, 175 nn. 13, 14
Homer, 19, 35, 76, 103, 144, 203; *The Iliad*, 113–14
Horace, 22, 24, 41 n. 31, 59, 76, 134, 155; *Ars Poetica*, 174; *Odes*, 184
horror, 142, 163, 202
Huet, Pierre Daniel, 65
Hume, David, 4, 5, 90, 109, 120, 121, 159, 189; *A Treatise of Human Nature*, 114–15, 122; *An Enquiry concerning the Principles of Morals*, 115; *Dissertation of the Passions*, 114–15; "Of the Standard of Taste," 89, 114–19, 119 n. 32; "Of Tragedy," 92, 119, 127, 140–58; "The Sceptic," 116
Hutcheson, Francis, 8, 90, 92–100, 101, 102, 104, 105, 110, 113, 115, 115 n. 23, 141, 153, 163, 195; *An Inquiry into the Original of Our Ideas of Beauty and Virtue*, 93–100, 142–45
hyperbole, 17 n. 14, 53, 54
hypotyposis, 17 n. 14, 20–21

idea(s), 53, 55, 56 n. 7, 57, 62, 63, 64, 65, 77, 78, 80, 80 n. 17, 81, 82, 84, 86, 93, 96, 97, 106, 107 n. 17, 109, 121, 123, 124, 143, 145, 146 n. 30, 147, 147 n. 32, 150, 152, 155, 157, 163, 172, 175, 180 n. 17, 181, 182, 184, 187, 187 n. 23; association of, 97; of beauty, 92, 92 n. 6, 94; clear, 105; clear and distinct, 37, 108; communication of, 151; complex, 78 n. 13; confused, 105; distinct, 105; as image, 95; innate, 104, 180, 187; mathematical, 101; natural order of, 191; obscure, 105; origin of, 179, 188; presence of, 110; as representation, 105; resemblance of, 71; simple, 36, 74 n. 8, 78 n. 13, 97; "trains of," 120; visual, 103. See also clarity, obscurity
ideal model, 203

Index   211

identity, 145
illusion, 8, 9, 22, 31, 42, 60, 61 n. 17, 64 n. 22, 74 n. 9, 108, 109, 110, 111, 113 n. 21, 123, 149, 150, 162, 170 n. 7, 175, 175 n. 13, 188, 199, 202, 204, 205
image, 1, 12, 21–22, 25, 26, 32, 34, 37, 38, 39, 53, 55, 77, 78, 79, 79 n. 15, 82, 82 n. 19, 83, 84 n. 21, 85, 86, 87, 95, 100, 102, 106, 111, 112, 123, 140, 147 n. 32, 156, 169, 171, 172, 178, 196, 204, 204 n. 33; clear, 101 n. 11; literary, 144; moral, 143; obscure, 101 n. 11; painted, 173; sensory, 77, 169; verbal, 11; visual, 76, 111, 177
imagination, 2, 6–7, 14 n. 10, 21, 25, 26, 28, 32, 35, 38, 41, 41 n. 31, 46, 50, 53, 58, 63, 64, 65, 66, 69, 71, 72–73 n. 7, 74, 77, 78, 79, 79 n. 14, 81, 82, 83, 85, 86, 87, 90, 100, 106, 111, 112, 113, 114, 119, 138, 144 n. 26, 145, 146, 146 nn. 30, 31, 151, 152, 154, 155, 160, 161, 175, 178, 181, 182, 183 n. 20, 184, 185, 190, 192 n. 28, 195, 196, 199, 202, 203; audience, 75; and color, 80 n. 17; imaginary world, 205; imaginative presence, 109; imaginative response, 4; pleasures of, 78; primary pleasures of, 80 n. 16; productive, 185 n. 21; reader's, 70, 77, 149, 150; reproductive, 185 n. 21; secondary pleasures of, 79, 80 n. 16, 81; writer's, 150
imitation, 27, 28, 34, 37, 38, 39, 40, 46, 47, 82, 95, 96, 103, 108, 129, 129 n. 4, 130, 131, 132, 145, 150 n. 35, 153, 154, 157, 162, 163, 164, 165, 166, 167, 168, 169, 171, 173, 174, 196, 197, 203, 205
imitatione, 34
imprese, 21
impression, 140, 147, 147 n. 32, 161, 181, 197; unity and simultaneity of, 190; visual, 189
instruction, 12, 13 n. 3, 35 n. 29, 46, 135, 166
intellect, 17, 24, 25, 26, 30, 34, 36, 40, 44, 46, 92, 93
intensity, 2, 39, 40, 66–67, 146, 149, 150, 162, 170, 199
intention, 135, 159, 162, 200
interest, 90
intuition, 54, 70 n. 4, 98, 107 n. 17, 182
inversion (*hyperbaton*), 64 n. 22
invention, 167, 171
inventor, 47
irony, 34
Italian poetry, 54
Italian Renaissance poets, 12

"je ne sais quoi," 56, 57, 65
Johnson, Samuel, 18
Jones, Peter, 116 n. 24
Jones, Richard Foster, 74 n. 9
jokes, 33, 55 n. 5. *See also* puns
judgment, 4, 31, 35, 36, 37, 38, 40, 42, 43, 44, 46, 47, 51, 60, 63, 64, 65, 67, 72, 72 n. 7, 73, 74, 75, 80 n. 15, 87, 90, 94, 102, 110, 114, 117, 118, 118 n. 30, 119, 121, 130, 133, 143, 146, 150, 151, 179, 184, 186, 187, 188, 196, 201

Kames, Henry Home, Lord, 8, 91, 144; *Elements of Criticism*, 119–25
Kant, Immanuel, 8, 98, 106, 119, 120, 146; *Critique of Judgment*, 8, 90, 116 n. 24, 118, 118 n. 31
knowledge, 2, 5, 6, 15, 19, 21, 25, 26, 35, 37, 40, 44, 45, 56, 57, 73, 74 n. 9, 79, 94, 105, 105 n. 14, 144, 164, 180 n. 17, 187, 188. *See also* learning
Knowlson, James, 74 n. 9
Korsmeyer, Carolyn Wilkes, 96 n. 9
Krieger, Murray, 113 n. 21

laconism, 17 n. 14
Lamy, Bernard, 62–64; *De l'Art de parler*, 62
Land, Stephen K., 72–73 n. 7, 144 n. 23, 157, 173 n. 9, 180 n. 18
landscape, 77–78, 82, 83, 86, 103, 165, 193; sublime, 194
language, 2, 3, 4, 5, 6, 7, 9, 12, 14, 18, 22, 24, 25, 25 n. 20, 26, 27, 28, 36, 41, 49–50, 51, 52, 53, 55, 56, 57, 59, 60, 61, 62, 64, 65, 66, 70, 73, 74, 74 n. 9, 75, 77, 79, 86, 86 n. 24, 87, 91, 92, 102, 103, 105 n. 14, 111, 113, 114, 120, 124, 125, 128, 139, 144, 145, 148, 153, 155, 156, 158, 159, 160, 171, 172, 176, 178, 182, 194, 196, 197 n. 30, 201, 203, 204, 205; affective, 104; artistic, 72, 154; as communication, 181; as convention, 80; and emotion, 140; figurative, 55 n. 6, 76, 77, 93, 172, 173, 188; flamboyant, 195; French, compared to others, 192 n. 28; history of, 183; metaphorical, 80 n. 15; natural, 80 n. 17; nonpictorial, 101 n. 11; as object, 84; "of action," 184; order of, 190–91; origin of, 36, 125, 178, 180, 180 n. 18, 183 n. 20, 201; poetic, 77, 196; theatrical, 196; theory of, 110; transparency of, 25, 75; universal, 74 n. 9, 144; and visual image, 177. *See also* rhetoric, words
Laocoon, 173
learning, 15, 16, 19–23, 43, 44, 45, 130
Le Brun, Charles, 163
Le Clerc, J., 63 n. 20, 65
Le Moyne, Pierre, 55 n. 6
Lessing, Gotthold, 8, 91, 100, 104, 106, 110–14, 119, 124, 168, 196; *Laocoon*, 111–14
lies, 33, 34, 63
likeness, 17 n. 14, 130
listener, 5, 9, 15, 19, 21, 23, 26, 28, 30, 31, 32, 41, 43, 61, 81, 184. *See also* audience, spectator, viewer
literature, 3, 42, 58, 59, 70, 77, 79, 91, 92, 98, 111, 113 n. 21, 116 n. 24, 135, 194
liveliness, 7, 19–20, 21, 25, 34, 40, 41, 43,

212 Index

99, 143, 146, 150n. 35, 152, 157. *See also energeia,* vivacity, vividness
Locke, John, 6n. 8, 36, 58n. 10, 59, 62, 70n. 4, 74n. 8, 77; *An Essay concerning Human Understanding,* 49, 72n. 7, 72–75, 78n. 13, 80n. 17, 96–97, 180, 185, 187, 187n. 23; on figurative speech, 73; on language, 74
logic, 28, 29, 56n. 7, 63n. 20, 67, 112, 131, 150, 151, 184; natural, 146n. 30
Longinus, 50, 60, 61, 64, 64n. 22, 65, 76, 76–77n. 12, 77, 85, 87, 172
Lucian, "Heroditus or Aëtioan," 173
Lucretius, 103, 109

McKenzie, Gordon, 121n. 34
Macrobius, 54
Maggi, Vincenzo, and Bartolomeo Lombardi, 133, 134n. 11
magnitude, 131
Malebranche, Nicolas de, 63n. 20
Marin, Louis, 57n. 8
Marinism, 12
Marino, Giambattista, 29
Marshall, David, 124, 162n. 3, 202–3
Martial, 3, 32
marvelous (marvels), 13, 16, 17, 18, 33, 34, 37, 38, 40, 41, 43, 44, 45, 46, 47, 53, 56, 65; *genre merveilleux,* 196
Mazzeo, J. A., 12
Medea, 179
Meier, Georg Friedrich, 110n. 18
melody, 197
memory, 2, 39, 40, 86, 123, 124, 145, 181, 182, 185, 187, 202, 203
Mendelssohn, Moses, 7–8, 70n. 4, 90, 111, 112, 114, 119; *Aesthetische Schriften,* 104–10; *Rhapsody,* 106
metaphor, 1, 3, 5, 6, 13–28, 41, 44, 45, 53, 54, 55, 55nn. 5, 6, 57, 66, 73, 72–73n. 7, 74n. 9, 75, 77, 79, 82, 83, 84, 96, 98, 157, 169, 185; metaphoric form, 27; of proportion 20; as substitution and translation, 74n. 8
metaphysics, 179, 180n. 17
meter (metrics), 44, 134, 183
metonym, 55n. 6
Migliorini, Urbano, 93n. 7
Milton, John, 71, 103, 117, 156
mimesis, 7, 9, 21, 25, 27, 28, 34, 53, 63, 64n. 21, 80, 81, 99, 107n. 17, 108, 134, 143, 168, 179, 185, 189, 203; pleasure from, 124n. 11
mimetic: feeling, 201; representation, 37, 38; theory, 27, 27n. 22
mind, 2, 6, 7, 15, 20, 21, 22, 25, 30, 44, 47, 53, 55, 56, 59, 62, 64, 72, 73n. 7, 78, 78n. 13, 79, 81, 83n. 20, 84, 85, 87, 96, 97, 103, 105, 106, 107, 110, 116, 117, 119n. 32, 121, 123, 134, 147n. 32, 150, 151, 152, 154, 155, 156, 161, 163, 166, 179, 181, 182, 184, 185, 187n. 23, 191, 192, 196

Mirollo, James V., 16n. 12
misery, 142, 143, 144, 145. *See* suffering
Mitchell, W. J. T., 7n. 13, 101–2n. 11, 113n. 21, 172n. 8
Molière, 203
Monk, Samuel H., 86n. 24
Montgomery, Robert L., 7
moral experience, 143
moral sense, 99, 100, 143–44, 153
Morpurgo-Tagliabuie, G., 12n. 2
motions of the soul, 173
moving, 29, 39, 75, 92, 99, 103, 135, 139, 140, 154, 164, 165, 169, 172, 173, 174, 175, 176, 177, 178, 183, 193, 194, 195, 200, 201
music, 36, 81, 97, 115, 183

naming, 3
narration, 149, 150, 168, 169, 172, 193, 194, 195, 196, 205
narrative, 35, 113, 114, 130, 167; dramatic, 5, 20
narrator, 151
nature (natural), 1, 2, 3, 4, 6, 7, 8, 12, 13, 14, 22, 24, 26, 27, 29–30, 33, 34, 44, 46, 47, 50, 51, 52, 53, 54, 56, 59, 60, 61, 61n. 16, 62, 63, 64, 65, 72, 73, 74n. 9, 75, 76, 78, 79, 80nn. 17, 18, 81, 82, 83, 84, 85, 86, 86n. 24, 92, 93, 95, 96, 98, 102, 102n. 11, 107, 109, 113, 114, 115, 116, 119n. 32, 121, 137, 140, 143, 145, 154, 156, 159, 160, 168, 170, 173, 174, 175, 177, 178, 179, 180, 182, 184, 185, 187, 188, 189, 193, 194, 195, 196, 197, 200, 201, 203; and art, 69, 121, 178, 205; natural faculties, 19; natural knowledge, 80; natural objects, 99; natural order of language, 64n. 22; natural perception, 97; natural response, 142; natural scenery, 79; natural world, 166; universal, 179
necessity, 128
neoclassical (neoclassicism), 2, 3, 4, 12, 14, 57, 66, 76, 128, 135, 150; critics, 47, 50, 133; English criticism, 4, 69–87, 194; French, 4, 49–67
Newton, Isaac, 80n. 18
Nicole, Pierre, 63n. 20
Nicolson, Marjorie Hope, 69, 79, 80n. 16; *Mountain Gloom and Mountain Glory,* 69, 70
novelty, 15, 18, 19, 22, 23, 30, 31, 33, 40, 66, 93, 96

object, 2, 6, 7, 8, 14, 15, 18, 21, 22, 24, 25, 26, 28, 29, 32, 33, 34, 35, 36, 39, 41, 42, 44, 45, 53, 55, 56, 57, 59, 66, 72, 74n. 9, 76, 77, 78, 79, 80, 81, 82, 83, 84, 85, 86, 87, 90, 92, 93, 94, 95, 97, 98, 100, 102, 105, 106, 107, 107n. 17, 108, 109, 110, 111, 115, 116, 119, 121, 122, 129, 138, 140, 146, 146n. 30, 147, 151, 154, 155, 157, 158, 161, 162, 167, 171, 174, 175n.

13, 176, 177, 180, 181, 185, 186, 187, 189, 196, 205; aesthetic, 11, 112, 118 n. 30, 142; of language, 64; moral, 143; natural, 99, 163; of representation, 203; sensory, 99, 103
obscurity, 5, 7, 57, 65, 103, 104, 156, 158
Oedipus, 129, 136
order, 139
oration, 20
orator, 24, 25, 41 n. 31, 45, 60
oratory, 17, 62, 191, 195
order (of words, language, etc.), 190–91
ornament, 2, 4, 5, 6, 13 n. 3, 22–24, 27, 27 n. 23, 42, 43, 44, 49, 51, 54, 56, 56 n. 7, 58, 60, 61, 62, 66, 70, 73, 75, 76, 77, 79 n. 15, 84 n. 21, 85, 87, 107, 183
Ogilvy, John, 117

pain, 23, 90, 97, 98, 105, 113, 115, 134 n. 11, 143, 146, 154, 155, 156, 159, 162, 163, 183
painter, 40, 162, 163, 164, 165, 167, 169, 174, 175, 176, 205
painting, 5, 6, 34, 38, 39, 55, 78, 79, 81, 83, 103, 111, 113 n. 21, 123, 154, 156, 164, 167, 168, 169, 170, 170 n. 7, 171, 173, 174, 175 n. 13, 176, 177, 178, 179, 182, 185, 186, 189, 190, 194, 196, 198, 205; genre, 199; history, 165 n. 5; landscape, 166; narrative, 171, 179; portrait, 199; rococo, 198; still life, 166, 199
Pallavicino, Sforza, 4, 5, 11, 12, 13, 30, 34–47; *Considerazioni sopra l'arte dello stile e dialogo*, 35–37, 39–40, 42–47; *Del bene*, 35–42
Pantheon, 71
pantomime, 193, 194, 195, 197 n. 30
Pascal, Blaise, *Esprit de la géométrie*, 59; *De l'Art de persuader*, 59
passions, 1, 2, 3, 25, 26, 38, 39, 41 n. 31, 43, 45, 62, 63, 63 n. 20, 64, 67, 74, 91, 99, 100, 102, 102 n. 11, 103, 114, 115, 119 n. 32, 121, 127, 135–38, 140, 141, 142, 143, 146, 147 n. 32, 148 n. 33, 150, 152–56, 158, 163, 165, 165 n. 5, 166, 167, 168, 171, 178, 181–85, 192 n. 28, 193, 197, 199, 202, 204; artificial, 162, 205; communication of, 147; current of, 149; distinguished from emotion, 122; fictitious, 147; real, 162, 205; transformation of, 141, 152–55
Patey, Douglas Lane, 63 n. 20, 112 n. 20, 144 n. 26, 148 n. 33, 150 n. 35, 168 n. 6
Paulson, Ronald W., 3
Paulson, William R., 188
pellegrina (peregrine), 18, 26
Penelope, 32
perceiving subject, 200
perception, 2, 5, 6, 8, 22, 24, 25, 28, 32, 35, 36, 37, 39, 42, 43, 56 n. 7, 72, 75, 77, 78 n. 13, 80 n. 15, 94, 95, 96–97, 98, 108, 109, 110, 111, 116, 119, 121, 122, 125, 128, 141, 142, 145, 146, 146 n. 30, 149, 155, 156, 159, 166, 203; aesthetic, 8, 37, 105,
106, 114, 120; levels of, 24; natural, 97; sense, 36, 123, 124, 155; structure of, 149; subjective, 101; visual, 113, 169
Peregrini, Matteo, 4, 5, 11, 12, 35, 40, 46; *Delle acutezze*, 29–34
perfection, 107, 109, 114, 117, 119, 120
performance theory, 105, 105 n. 15
peripety, 136
periodic sentence, 24
Perrault, Charles, 62, 66
personification, 33, 41
perspective, 19
perspicacity, 21, 44
perspicuity, 14, 44, 61, 65, 71, 75
persuasion, 25, 29, 32, 61, 84, 91, 143, 152, 177
phantasiai, 41 n. 31
phantasy, 31, 79 n. 14
Piccolomini, Alessandro, 133, 134 n. 11
picture, 7, 8, 16, 21, 53, 74 n. 8, 77, 78 n. 13, 80 n. 18, 81, 85, 86, 155, 164, 169, 170, 174, 175, 176, 185, 199, 200; mental, 156–57
pictorialism, 200; verbal, 76. See *enargeia*
pity, 25 n. 20, 102 n. 11, 131 n. 6, 134, 137, 138, 141, 142 n. 22, 146, 147
pity and fear (terror), 25 n. 20, 128–36, 129 n. 4, 138, 139, 141, 149. See also catharsis, emotion, feelings, passion, purgation
Plato, 31, 165; *Philebus*, 134 n. 11; *Republic*, 38
plausibility, 29
playwright, 9, 203
pleasure, 2, 3, 15, 17, 19, 21, 23, 25, 25 n. 20, 26, 28, 31, 33, 39, 40, 42, 43, 44, 45, 46, 47, 50, 51, 52, 55, 56, 59, 62, 80, 83, 85–86, 87, 90, 92, 92 n. 6, 93, 96–99, 102 n. 11, 105, 106, 107, 107 n. 17, 108, 109, 110, 112, 113, 115, 117, 118 nn. 30, 31, 119, 119 n. 32, 121, 129, 129 n. 4, 134, 134 n. 11, 135, 146, 162, 163, 166, 167, 168, 183, 193; aesthetic, 2, 89, 107, 141; affective, 156; audience, 128; in comparing, 95; imaginative, 64, 73, 80 n. 18; in imitation, 82; of knowing, 166; of learning, 166; sensible, 160, 171; tragic, 4, 60, 127–58, 159; of the understanding, 79, 82 n. 19
Pliny the Elder, 171, 173
plot, 12, 50, 60, 128–29, 136, 137, 149; episodic, 131
Pocock, Gordon, 67, 67 n. 25
poems, types of: acrostics, 70; lipograms, 70; pattern poems, 70; rebuses, 70, 79 n. 15
poet, 3, 3 n. 6, 14, 17, 18, 25 n. 20, 36, 37, 38, 43, 45, 46 n. 35, 47, 50, 51, 53, 60, 62, 71, 82, 83, 87, 90, 93, 94, 96, 100, 104, 113, 127, 143, 145, 151, 159, 163, 164, 167, 176, 190, 192, 197, 198, 202, 203, 204, 205; baroque, 110 n. 18; dramatic, 194; poet as observer, 201; poets as liars, 150
poetry, 1, 6, 7, 11, 12, 13, 19, 21, 34, 35, 36,

37, 38, 41, 47, 53, 59, 61, 62, 66, 67, 70, 91, 93, 96, 98, 99, 103, 111, 113, 113n. 21, 115, 131, 138, 146n. 30, 150, 152, 156, 157, 160, 165, 167, 168, 169, 170, 171, 172, 173, 175, 176, 177, 178, 179, 183, 184, 185, 186, 189, 190, 202; dramatic, 99, 171, 174, 176; epic, 99; French, 165; lyric, 196; Metaphysical, 18; usefulness of, 69
Pope, Alexander, 3, 62, 66, 203; *Essay on Criticism,* 69
Port-Royal, 59
presence, 42, 123, 125; ideal, 124
"present at a distance," 107
prima apprensione. See first apprehension
probability, 38, 50, 54, 60, 63n. 20, 67, 112, 119n. 32, 128, 131, 144, 144n. 26, 148n. 32, 149, 152, 173
proportion, 44, 45, 54, 55n. 5, 65, 101, 138
propriety, 14, 22, 42, 93
prosopopeia, 33, 34
protagonist, 136, 137, 138
prudence, 21
psychology, 7, 97, 98, 99, 105n. 14, 128, 135, 137, 140, 144n. 26, 161, 179; aesthetic, 45, 95; affective, 35, 155; association, 8, 40, 120; audience, 4, 67, 91, 160; faculty, 39; rationalist, 104; Scholastic, 25n. 21
pun, punning, 17n. 14, 28, 51, 52, 71, 85
purgation, 128–40, 142. *See also* catharsis, emotion, feelings, passions, pity and fear

quibbles. See *equivoques,* puns
Quintilian, 41n. 31, 164, 174n. 12, 177

Racine, Jean, 163; *Iphigénie,* 176; *Phèdre,* 189
Raimondi, Ezio, 27, 27n. 22
Raphael, *St. Paul,* 169
Rapin, René, 1, 2, 61–62, 132n. 6, 152; *Reflections on Aristotle's Treatise of Poetry,* 1, 138–40
rapture, 60, 63
rarity, 33
rationality, 202
reader, 5, 8, 9, 15, 18, 19, 26, 37, 38, 39, 42, 44, 45, 46, 50, 54, 57, 58, 75, 77, 79, 81, 83, 84; 85, 86, 87, 111, 169, 173, 186, 192, 204. *See also* audience, beholder, listener, spectator
realism, 66
reality, 34, 37, 38, 49, 58, 59, 67, 116, 117, 149, 150, 150n. 35, 152, 154, 156, 157, 162, 163, 195, 202–4, 204n. 33
reason, 2, 25, 26, 30, 38, 59, 65, 72, 115, 115n. 23, 159, 162
reception, 35, 46, 113
recognition, Aristotle's four types, 136
recreation, 35, 35n. 29, 132n. 9
reflection, 44–45, 182, 184, 187, 201, 202
relation, 121, 121n. 34, 145–46, 149, 150, 151
reminiscence, 181. *See* memory
Renaissance, 2, 4, 7, 21, 24, 25, 32, 39, 47, 58, 76, 128, 131, 133, 134; literary theory, 12, 152n. 37, 153
representation, 9, 15, 22, 25n. 20, 26, 27, 28, 39, 46n. 35, 56, 57, 62, 63, 70n. 4, 79, 96, 99, 100, 102, 106, 107, 107n. 17, 108, 109, 110, 113, 113n. 21, 118n. 31, 130, 131, 142, 142n. 22, 144, 147, 149, 150n. 35, 151, 152, 157, 160, 164, 165, 165n. 5, 166, 177, 181, 184, 185, 186, 193, 194, 195, 196, 198, 199, 204; artistic, 152, 155, 167; authenticity of, 175; dramatic, 193, 194; distinct, 105n. 14; linguistic, 189; mimetic, 37, 38, 175; obscure, 105n. 14; poetic, 203; psychology of, 104; synaesthetic, 179; theatrical, 173, 197n. 30; verbal, 129, 169, 172n. 8, 193; visual, 169, 172n. 8, 193
representational theory, 105
resemblance, 30, 56, 72, 144n. 26, 145, 146, 146n. 31, 147
response, 33, 35, 39, 43, 45, 46, 51, 77, 90, 91, 92, 95, 100, 106, 107, 114, 122, 153, 154, 181, 186, 197, 204; aesthetic, 87, 92, 120, 156; affective, 119, 162, 205; audience, 38–39, 135, 159, 187; emotive, 167, 176, 179; immediate and calculated, 201; reader's, 61; spontaneous, 95, 145; sympathetic, 152
rhetoric, 1, 5, 6, 12, 17, 21, 23, 28, 30, 42, 50, 59, 62, 64n. 21, 73, 74, 77, 84, 86n. 24, 103, 148n. 33, 157, 162, 164, 173n. 9, 189, 190, 200; baroque, 2, 15, 32; classical, 43; figures of, 1, 2, 4, 17, 24, 41; formulas for pleasing, moving, and instructing, 135; rhetorical theory, 35, 100n. 10
rhyme, 44
rhythm, 43
Riccoboni, Antonio, *Poetica Aristotelis,* 133, 134n. 11
Ricouer, Paul, *The Rule of Metaphor,* 14
ridiculous, 46
Roach, Joseph R., Jr., 200n. 31
Robins, R. H., 80n. 17
Robortello, Francesco, *In Librum Aristotelis de Arte Poetica Explicationes,* 132, 135
romance, 36
Ronsard, Pierre de, 5, 50, 51, 58
Rossi, Nicolò, *Discorsi intorno alla tragoedia,* 134
Rothstein, Eric, 142n. 22
Rousseau, Jean-Jacques, 180n. 18; *On the Origin of Language,* 159, 183n. 20
Rousset, Jean, *La Littérature de l'age baroque en France,* 42n. 32, 49

sadness, 183
Saint-Amant, Marc Antoine Girard de, 51
Sarasin, Jean-François, "Discourse on Tragedy," 135
Saunderson, Nicholas, 188
schemes (*scimata*), 23
science, 5, 6, 6n. 8, 26, 28, 42, 43, 74n. 9, 87, 93, 104, 180n. 17

Index   215

sculptor, 203
seeing, 7, 9, 20, 31, 42, 72. *See* sight, visual
self-consciousness, 201
semantics, 157
semiotics, 37, 105, 105n. 13
Seneca the Elder, 54, 142
sensation, 37, 38, 78n. 13, 92, 94, 95, 96, 105, 105n. 14, 106, 133, 145, 146n. 31, 147n. 32, 162, 180, 181, 182, 183, 187, 187n. 23, 189
sense(s), 2, 20, 23, 24, 26, 35, 39, 44, 58n. 10, 78, 96, 102n. 11, 110, 111, 112, 114, 124, 146n. 31, 174, 175, 177, 179, 185, 188, 194, 196; of beauty, 97; internal, 143, 145; and language, 102; pleasures of, 94
sensibility, 79, 164, 182, 201, 202, 204
sensible qualities, 20, 45, 53
sensory, 32, 62, 77, 78n. 13, 93, 146, 187
sentiment, 25, 58n. 10, 62, 75, 92, 100, 115, 115n. 23, 116, 117, 140, 154, 167, 172, 173, 179
sentimentalism, 91, 132n.6, 141
setting, 149
Shaftesbury, Anthony Ashley Cooper, 3rd Earl of, 89–90, 142, 186n. 22
Shakespeare, William, 201
sight, 40, 41, 46, 78, 78n. 13, 79, 79n. 14, 82, 84, 85, 112, 123, 143, 147, 151, 174, 175, 176, 177, 183n. 20, 188, 189, 195. *See* seeing, visual
sign(s), 4, 27n. 23, 77, 80n. 17, 110n. 18, 111, 112, 148n. 33, 164, 171, 181, 182, 183, 184, 185, 187, 187n. 23, 200; accidental, 181; arbitrary, 113n. 21, 144, 170, 175; instituted, 181, 182; language as instituted, 201; natural, 113n. 21, 114, 144, 168, 174, 181; nonverbal, 170; signifiers, 70n. 4; transparent, 114; verbal, 185, 186; visual, 168
simile, similitude, 15, 41, 43, 44, 45, 46n. 35, 55n. 6, 72n. 7, 79n. 15, 83, 84, 96, 98
simplicity, 75, 87; of style, 85
Smith, Adam, 146n. 31
Smith, Barbara Herrnstein, 116n. 24
Socrates, 38
Somers, David, 115n. 23
sophistic, 31, 34
speaker, 24, 29, 31, 32, 62, 135, 157, 192. *See* orator, speech
spectacle, 129, 162, 162n. 3, 163
spectator, 5, 8, 9, 30, 37, 39, 40, 46, 70, 79, 81, 83, 86, 100, 109, 110, 111, 121, 123, 124, 127, 131, 135, 136, 139, 141, 143, 145, 147, 148, 149, 151, 153, 154, 156, 158, 161, 161n. 2, 163, 164, 166, 169–74, 177–79, 186, 192, 194, 195, 197–200, 201, 203, 204. *See also* audience, auditor, reader, viewer
speech, 22, 29, 30, 31, 32, 34, 43, 74n. 9, 81, 119, 123, 148n. 33, 159, 172, 177, 183, 204; order of, 191; "speaking by action," 183, 185

Spenser, Edmund, 71
Sprat, Thomas, 2
stage, 36, 176, 177, 192, 193, 195, 201, 203
statuary (sculpture), 79, 80, 81, 111, 113, 164
Stone, P. W. K., 100n. 10, 147n. 33, 173n. 9
strangeness (in metaphor), 13, 15, 17, 18, 23, 26; and familiarity, 5, 17
style, 3, 4, 5, 6, 11, 12, 16, 17, 20, 23, 29, 30, 34, 40, 43, 45, 46, 47, 50, 52, 56, 57, 60, 61, 63, 64, 65, 67, 75, 77, 85, 172, 197n. 30; barbarism of, 58; figured; 50; metaphoric, 4; Metaphysical, 12, 71; plain and figurative in drama, 196
sublime, 4, 50, 56, 57, 61, 61n. 16, 64, 65, 67, 85, 86, 92, 101, 101–2n. 11, 102, 135, 156, 159, 167, 173, 193, 194
subject, 90, 94, 99, 100, 101, 102, 102n. 11, 105, 108, 109, 110, 122
subjective, 115n. 23, 117
subjectivity, 129, 125; and relation, 146
suffering, 161, 161nn. 2, 3, 175. *See* misery
surprise, 18, 28, 40, 45–46, 49, 60, 65
syllogism, 30, 31, 34
symbol, 21; baroque symbolism, 76; symbolic imagery, 77
sympathy, 2, 24–26, 92, 100, 103, 109, 116, 124, 127, 133, 145, 148, 148n. 33, 149, 156, 157, 199
synchronic, synchrony, 113, 171, 185, 190, 192, 193
synecdoche, 112

tableau, 195, 199
Tartuffe, 203
Tasso, Torquato, 5, 54, 62
taste, 3, 4, 22, 42, 52, 54, 56, 69, 70, 75, 80n. 16, 87, 89–125; 143; standard of, 8, 116, 120; variety of, 117
Taylor, Harold, 146n. 30
teaching, 29
terror, 102n. 11, 154, 156. *See* fear, pity and fear
Tesauro, Emmanuele, 4, 5, 9, 11, 12, 29, 30, 34, 35, 40, 42, 44, 45, 46, 54, 55n. 6, 56, 66; *Il cannocchiale aristotelico*, 16–28, 80n. 15; *La filosofia morale*, 25–26
theater, 5, 9, 18, 41n. 31, 42n. 32, 67, 124, 138, 139, 140, 147, 149, 150, 164, 168, 169, 170, 174, 174n. 12, 177, 179, 185, 188, 193, 195, 196, 197, 204, 204n. 33; French classical, 198; theatrical performance, 178
Thersites, 113–14
Theseus, 179
Thorpe, Clarence D., 73n. 7
thought, 42, 50, 53, 56, 57, 61, 62, 64, 66, 70, 70n. 4, 74n. 8, 78, 84, 121, 142, 144, 146, 161, 169, 181, 182, 184, 187, 187n. 23, 191, 192; order of, 190; thinking and reasoning, 147n. 32
Thyestes, 136
topos, 25n. 20

touch, 43
tragedy, 2, 4, 8, 26, 36, 41 n. 31, 45, 59, 60, 66, 99, 127–58, 147, 160, 163, 165, 176, 178, 179, 195; classical and neoclassical, 203; domestic, 195; English, 142; Racinian, 67
transparency, 70 n. 4, 108, 188; of language, 70, 71, 110; of metaphor, 55
transport, 65
trope, 2, 9, 19, 21, 63, 64, 64 n. 21, 83. *See also* schemes
truth, 11, 12, 24, 28, 30, 34, 35, 37, 38, 39, 41, 42 n. 32, 43, 44, 45, 46, 47, 50, 52–57, 59, 72, 73, 74 n. 8, 76, 84, 87, 115, 150, 151, 188, 196; truth of nature vs. truth of convention, 204
Tuveson, Ernest Lee, 78 n. 13, 83 n. 20, 87

ugliness, 90, 93, 94, 95, 97, 107 n. 17, 113, 114
understanding, 22, 45, 55, 90, 100, 157, 190
unities, 12, 51, 192
unity, 17 n. 14, 44, 55, 199; of faculties, 187; of plot, 149; of setting, 149; or uniformity in variety, 93, 95, 98, 100, 113
universal, 90, 102, 112, 125, 166, 175, 188; language, 74 n. 9; response, 95
urbanity, 17, 28, 31. See also *asteia*, metaphor
usefulness (of poetry), 27, 59
utility (of tragedy), 132–33

Van Loo, Charles André, 199
variety, 25, 28, 43, 44, 60. *See* unity in variety
verisimilitude, verisimilar, 12, 28, 34, 38, 40, 41, 46, 50, 137, 149, 192, 196. *See* probability, *vraisemblance*
Verres, 153
verse, 175, 177, 197
Vettori, Pietro, 133, 134 n. 11
Vickers, Brian, 6 n. 8, 64 n. 21, 22, 173 n. 9
Vien, Joseph-Marie, 199
viewer, 5, 26, 42, 77, 81, 165 n. 5, 174, 186, 194, 198
violence, 143

Virgil, 35, 103, 190; *Aeneid*, 45 nn. 34, 35; *Georgics*, 3
visual, visualization, 8, 14, 19–21, 31, 32, 37, 38, 57, 76–77 n. 12, 83, 86, 87, 98, 99, 101–2 n. 11, 112, 113, 124, 129, 155, 157, 168, 170, 172, 190, 193, 195, 196. *See also* seeing, sight
vivacity, 17, 152
vividness, 20, 38, 41 n. 31, 42, 155, 173
vraisemblance, 50, 53. *See also* probability, verisimilitude

Walker, George, 145, 156
Waller, Edmund, 71
Wasserman, Earl, 144 n. 25
Wellbery, David, 37 n. 30, 70 n. 4, 104 n. 13, 105, 105 nn. 14, 15, 107–8, 107 n. 17, 110
Wellek, René, 91
Wieand, Jeffrey, 116 n. 24
will, 43
Wimsatt, W. K., and Cleanth Brooks, 69–70, 78 n. 13, 91
wit, 4, 9, 11, 16, 17, 18, 21–27, 29, 40, 50, 53, 54, 69, 70, 73, 75, 76; baroque, 5, 15, 161; false, 72; false and mixed, 77; Gothic, 71–72; mixed, 71
Wolff, Christian, 8, 104, 104 n. 13, 105
wordplay, 4. *See also* puns
words, 8, 9, 13, 18, 19, 21, 22, 23, 25, 26, 32, 39, 51, 57, 58, 61, 62, 64, 65, 66, 71, 74, 74 nn. 8, 9, 76, 77, 78 n. 13, 80, 80 n. 17, 82, 104, 123, 144, 146 n. 30, 157, 158, 175, 177, 185, 194, 197, 203, 205; affective power of, 157; and emotion, 103; natural and artificial order of, 190–91; order of, 184; resemblance of, 71; seriality of, 190. *See also* language, speech
Wordsworth, William, 203
writer, 54, 62, 66, 67
writing, 81, 123

Yolton, John, 56 n. 7, 72 n. 6, 146 n. 30, 155

Zeuxis, 173

www.ingramcontent.com/pod-product-compliance
Lightning Source LLC
Chambersburg PA
CBHW031550300426
44111CB00006BA/245